YOUR KNOWLEDGE HAS VALUE

- We will publish your bachelor's and master's thesis, essays and papers

- Your own eBook and book - sold worldwide in all relevant shops

- Earn money with each sale

Upload your text at www.GRIN.com
and publish for free

Bibliographic information published by the German National Library:

The German National Library lists this publication in the National Bibliography; detailed bibliographic data are available on the Internet at http://dnb.dnb.de .

This book is copyright material and must not be copied, reproduced, transferred, distributed, leased, licensed or publicly performed or used in any way except as specifically permitted in writing by the publishers, as allowed under the terms and conditions under which it was purchased or as strictly permitted by applicable copyright law. Any unauthorized distribution or use of this text may be a direct infringement of the author s and publisher s rights and those responsible may be liable in law accordingly.

Imprint:

Copyright © 2016 GRIN Verlag
Print and binding: Books on Demand GmbH, Norderstedt Germany
ISBN: 9783668632233

This book at GRIN:

https://www.grin.com/document/387853

Sabah Noori Abbas Al Mihyawi

Assessment of Investment Attractiveness in Arab Countries

GRIN Verlag

GRIN - Your knowledge has value

Since its foundation in 1998, GRIN has specialized in publishing academic texts by students, college teachers and other academics as e-book and printed book. The website www.grin.com is an ideal platform for presenting term papers, final papers, scientific essays, dissertations and specialist books.

Visit us on the internet:

http://www.grin.com/

http://www.facebook.com/grincom

http://www.twitter.com/grin_com

Uniwersytet Szczeciński
Wydział Nauk Ekonomicznych i Zarządzania

University of Szczecin
Faculty of Economics and Management

Sabah Noori Abbas Al-Mihyawi

Assessment of Investment Attractiveness in Arab Countries

Ocena Atrakcyjności Inwestycyjnej Krajów Arabskich

Rozprawa doktorska napisana pod kierunkiem
dr. hab. prof. US Tomasza Wiśniewskiego

SZCZECIN 2016

Dedication

This dissertation is dedicated to:

The great Messenger Mohammed may Allah grant peace and honour on him and his descendants
My Parents
My Wife and children
My Brothers and Sisters
My Uncles Munassif and Mahdi
The soul of my Uncle Fakhri, and the soul of my Grandmother
My cousin Salah
My best friend Dr Essam

The souls of all Iraqi martyrs

Acknowledgments

All praises are due to Allah, the Lord of the World, and may the peace and blessing of Allah be upon his messenger Mohamed. Without the mercy and aid of Allah, this thesis could not have been started or completed.

I owe special debt of gratitude to prepare this thesis to my supervisor, dr hab. prof. US Tomasz Wiśniewski, whose academic experience, patience, kindness, and encouragement was beyond the call of duty. His continuous support was a driving force behind this thesis.

I am grateful to dr hab. inż. prof. US Kesra Nermend for his advice, discussions and suggestions, which were significantly important to the thesis.

I owe special gratitude to my parents, wife, children, brothers, sisters, cousins, relatives, the closest friends to my heart – Salah and haji Sajid, the best friends - Dr Essam and Dr Ali, friends Ammar, Hassan, and Ayad, and my all other Iraqi and Polish friends. All my success should be attributed to them due to their patience, support, and prayers.

I would like to express my gratitude to all the members of Faculty of Economics and Management that provided me with support and equipment I needed to produce and complete my thesis. Especially to the Dean, prof. zw. dr hab. Waldemar Tarczyński, Vice-Dean dr hab. prof. US Tomasz Bernat, Vice-Dean dr hab. prof. US Małgorzata Łatuszyńska, dr hab. prof. zw. Jerzy Dudziński, dr hab. prof. US Sebastian Majewski and to all the staff of the Faculty.

I would like to express my gratitude to all those who gave me the possibility to complete this thesis.

Finally, I am grateful to the Iraqi government, the Iraqi Cultural Office in Warsaw and the University of Szczecin, who made my scholarship possible.

SABAH Al MIHYAWI,
February 2016

List of Abbreviations

APEC	Asia–Pacific Economic Cooperation
APR	Annual Percentage Rate
BITs	Bilateral Investment Treaties
BOP	Balance Of Payments
CEP	Closer Economic Partnership
CJV	Construction Joint Venture
CPI	Corruption Perceptions Index
EIAs	Economic Integration Agreements
FDI	Foreign Direct Investment
FPI	Foreign Portfolio Investment
FTAs	Free Trade Agreements
FTZ	Free Trade Zone
FZs	Free Zones
GCC	Gulf Cooperation Council
GDP	Gross Domestic Product
HDI	Human Development Index
IATA	International Air Transport Association
I	Inflation
ICT	Information and Communications Technology
IIAs	International Investment Agreements
IMF	International Monetary Fund
IPPAs	Investment Promotion and Protection Agreements
IPR	Intellectual Property Right
IT	Information Technology
ITU	International Telecommunications Union
LDCs	Least Developed Countries
MENA	Middle East and North Africa
MNEs	Multi-National Enterprises
MNC	Multinational Corporation
OAPEC	Organization of Arab Petroleum Exporting Countries
OECD	Organization for Economic Co-operation and Development

OLD	Ownership Location Internalization
OPEC	Organization of the Petroleum Exporting Countries
PTIAs	Preferential Trade and Investment Agreements
QIZ	Qualified Industrial Zones
RTAs	Regional Trade Agreements
TNC	Transnational Corporation
UMA	Union of the Arab Maghreb
UNCTAD	United Nations Conference of Trade and Development
UNDP	United Nations Development Program

Table of Contents

INTRODUCTION

The flow of investments in developing countries varies greatly across countries. In this research, due to the lack of capital markets in some of Arab countries we have been focusing on foreign direct investment as one of types of foreign investment. Foreign investment comprises foreign direct investment (FDI), which inflows have provided the strong impetus on economic development across countries. FDI serves as an important source of supply of funds for domestic investments, promoting capital formation in the host country. Nowadays, more attention is paid to the issues of foreign direct investments at both national and international levels. According to World Investments reports, many developing countries, including the Arab countries, have attracted only small amounts of FDI inflows despite their efforts towards the economic openness.

It means many factors impede the flow of foreign capital to Arab countries. The attractiveness of investment is a set of features and factors that allow the investor to evaluate the potential of any country to be more attractive for investment than the other one. Many factors include economic factors, social factors and political factors, which lead to increase in foreign direct investment. The potential investor considers these factors when choosing a country for investments and evaluating investment attractiveness. The term of investment attractiveness refers to a set of factors that help to provide a suitable investment climate. The term of the investment climate means economic and financial conditions in a country that affect whether individuals and businesses are willing to do an investment there. This climate is usually available through improving the determinants of investment. The problem of policy makers in the Arab countries is to identify the factors that determine the investment attractiveness and to know the factors, which have the greatest influence on it. In this study, we are trying to find out the most important factors having influence on investment in Arab countries. Attracting investment is an important component of competitiveness for any country. It is worth mentioning here that competitiveness means the set of institutions, policies and factors that determine the level of productivity[*] of the country.

The importance of this research to the Arab countries is to provide a composite index that describes factors having an influence on the attractiveness of foreign direct investments. To calculate this composite index we need data that describe factors, which influence the attractiveness of investments. These data have been selected from many sources such as UNCTA

---

[*] Productivity is commonly defined as a ratio of a volume measure of output to a volume measure of input use (OECD, 2001).

9

and Arab Investment and Export Credit Guarantee Corporation. The index shows the rank of selected Arab countries according to their attractiveness for receiving inward FDI and then compare it with Poland as a good basis for comparison (the details are given later in Chapter 1). Also, due to the structure of the index, there is a possibility to conduct and analyse details of attractiveness for each country. Policy makers may use these analyses to draw conclusions about how to improve the country's attractiveness for receiving inward FDI.

Arab countries tried for decades to attract foreign investments. The needs for these countries to attract more funding to meet the growing needs of infrastructure development compel them to look for external sources of funds. There is also the apparent lack of domestic investment in most Arab countries. Arab countries have made many efforts to attract foreign investments, but the volume of foreign investment is lower than they plannned and expected. Therefore, it is necessary to understand the reasons for this situation.

Arab countries share common characteristics such as language, religion, culture or location. However, these common factors do not prevent those countries to be different in other features, such as the structure and size of economy, the population, and the size of natural resources, economic progress and many others. There are different views about what factors are the most important and influential in attracting investment. The theoretical studies indicate that the motives for investment are the most important aspects that determine attractiveness of investment. There are many motives to foreign investments like the search for natural resources, efficiency, markets, low-cost supply of unskilled or semi-skilled workforce, acquisition of technological capabilities, management or marketing experience and organizational skills. In our work, we try to find out what explains the attraction of foreign investment. If the motives to foreign investment in the Arab countries vary from one country to another, the reasons for this situation are differences in the structure and size of their economies. Then, the influencing factors in attracting foreign investment in a particular country are not necessarily the same factors affecting other countries, and this is the **research problem.**

We are doing analyses and test of the most important influencing factors in attracting foreign investment to the Arab countries. As a result, we come up with practical proposals and recommendations to assist decision makers in improving the investment attractiveness. This is done through the knowledge of the most important factors attracting foreign investment to their countries. Also, comparison among Arab countries and Poland as a benchmark has been done.

The main **goal** of the research is to assess the investment attractiveness in Arab countries. This main goal could be decomposed into four detailed sub-goals. **Then the most important issues** in this thesis are as follows:

- identification and analyses of the factors determining the investment attractiveness,
- construction of the measure of investment attractiveness,
- application of the measure for Arab countries,
- proposal of changes that might improve investment attractiveness of Arab countries.
- assessment of investment attractiveness in Arab countries and comparison with Poland as a benchmark.

The main **hypothesis** of the research is the following: Political factors have a major impact on investment attractiveness of Arab countries.

Our **dissertation** comprising of four chapters sets out the below details:

Chapter 1 describes the investment and foreign direct investment attractiveness through three sections. The chapter covers the concept of investment and classification of investments, and theories of foreign direct investment. The chapter demonstrates the history of foreign investment around the world. Determinants of foreign investment as one of the barriers to investment are referred to in this chapter.

Chapter 2 describes the methodology of FDI attractiveness assessment research through three sections. Some indices and studies on foreign direct investment attractiveness are presented in this chapter. The general steps used to build composite indicators are demonstrated. A comparison of the methods used to assess attractiveness investments is also described in this chapter.

Chapter 3 describes the investment specificity in Arab countries through three sections. The overview of selected economic and geographical data of the Arab countries and the subject of our study is presented in section one. The FDI trends in Arab countries are analysed in section two. In section three, we refer to the investment climate in Arab countries through analyses of selected of indicators.

Chapter 4 describes the assessment of investment attractiveness of Arab countries through four sections. In the first section, the analyses of the attractiveness of Arab countries and Poland using vector methods are discussed. We refer to the steps taken to build the composite index by synthetic vector measure and compare our results with other indices. In section two, we analyse the factors that are influencing investment attractiveness in Arab countries, compared to Poland. We discuss the changes in investment attractiveness of Arab countries and Poland in section three. In the last section, we show proposals that may help to increase the flow of FDI into each Arab country separately.

We were limited to data from "only" 13 Arab countries because there were no enough data about the others. For example there were no data on FDI for Sudan, no data about inflation were available for the State of Palestine, there were no data for GDP for Comoros. During the research period, there was a war and unstable political and economic situation in Somalia. In some Arab countries, data were available but unreliable. This study is the first one that compares the investment attractiveness of the Arab countries in the Middle East and North Africa with Poland over the period 2005-2010. We did an investigation both in database of the Iraqi Ministry of Higher Education and Scientific Research and in different databases available on the Internet and there was no study available on the same subject. We selected Poland as a base for comparison and the reasons of that were as follows:

- For comparison, we wanted a country, which was a good benchmark for investment attractiveness. We concentrated on Europe because of the change from a centrally planned economy to a market economy, as this is what happened in some of the Arab countries, which were transformed from a centralised system into a market system, such as Iraq. Poland has become the most attractive country for foreign investment in Central Europe since its transformation from communism more than 20 years ago. There is some instruction of inflows of capital to the country in some Arab countries same like in Poland on communism. Poland has the largest economy in Central Europe and was the only European Union country that recorded economic growth when the other economies declined during the financial crisis in 2009. Poland has one of the strongest stock exchanges, while the financial markets in some Arab countries are characterised by weak or non-existent stock exchanges. Thus, Poland is a good model for countries seeking to develop financial markets. Poland is the largest source of natural resources in Europe, and some Arab countries (such as Saudi Arabia, Iraq, Qatar and others) have huge potential natural resources, such as oil and gas and other minerals (see Chapter 3). Poland may now be at a historical crossroads, in effect becoming one of the leading European countries and a model for Arab economies.

- In some aspects, Arab countries are comparable to Poland. Poland is a religious society in a similar way to Arab countries. To select other countries for comparison - such as China, India, etc. - would have been misleading because of the large difference between the size of their economies and populations and those of each separate Arab country, and therefore it was sensible to choose Poland. Also, Poland has its own independent currency, as is the case with Arab countries.

Our plan was to choose a long period, and it would have been the best if we could choose a long time for a comparison. However, considering the Arab countries, it is difficult to choose any stability period. Many Arab countries are instable because of wars, international sanctions, political unrest and economic crisis. There is also lack of data. Some Arab countries still refrain from publishing economic data for many reasons. Thus we selected the period 2005-2010 because:

- in the years before 2005, the region experienced a long period of instability. That was because of the wars in Iraq, and imposing economic sanctions on Iraq. Therefore, the Arab region has suffered from a state of political and economic instability. As well as the FDI inflows, percentage of world total FDI inflows before 2005 was insignificant and did not exceed 3.4 percent. While this percentage increased to 4.8 percent in 2005 and reached a maximum of 7 percent in 2009.

- since the beginning of 2011, the Arab world has witnessed a lack of political and economic stability, which lasted until now. It was caused by the Arab Spring or the Arab revolutions. There were not enough or reliable data for many of the Arab countries for the period that followed the events of the Arab Spring.

Many factors influence FDI attractiveness, and in our work for the **methods;** we decided to use the factors recognized in three groups: economic factors, social factors and political factors. These three groups can give a clear view about the impact of factors on attracting investments. In our study we selected 16 possible factors and 13 Arab countries, according to a literature review that we refer to in details in Table 1-9.

We used these factors as input data in synthetic vector measure in two ways. The first approach called vector measure method we have used all the data, and we get 16 input factors. In the second approach called composite vector measure, we used the data in three groups (economic factors; social factors; and political factors). After the colocation of each group we have only three input factors to make the comparison much easier. These comparisons make easy to improve the country in FDI influence. The quality of index was measured using the correlation between actual inflows of FDI and proposal FDI attractiveness index.

Since we aim to work dynamic analyses (during consideration of the year 2005 as a reference to the other years), we had to use synthetic vector measure instead of other approaches'. In the other approaches,' the possibility to conduct such a dynamic analyses is not available.

Our input data are chosen from various sources such as World Bank, United Nations Conference on Trade and Development, World Bank, Arab Monetary Fund, Arab Central Banks, Arab Trade Financing Program, Arab League, Arab Industrial Development and Mining Organization, Union of Arab Banks, Council of Arab Economic Unity, as well some other sources.

CHAPTER ONE: Investments and Foreign Direct Investments Attractiveness

The foreign direct investment (FDI) importance has increased in the past decade. There is a discussion about the negative and positive effects of FDI inflows around the world. FDI can help in development and in creating a better economic environment. Foreign direct investment can support the growth of per capita income in the host country. It works to expand the methods of use of modern management and local raw materials. Moreover, this, it can help in developing and training of human resources (Hassan, 2003, p. 4). However, it does not preclude the existence of a negative impact of foreign direct investment on the balance of payments and competition in local markets. Foreign direct investments (FDI) around the world have grown significantly in recent years. Between 2005 and 2010, FDI inflows around the world increased by 42 percent. However, most of the FDI transactions were among the developed countries. There are difficulties in attracting foreign direct investment in developing countries; there are also variations in distributing foreign direct investment. FDI inflows have provided a strong impetus for economic development in various countries (Yan, 2008) and issues relating to foreign direct investment were subject of research in many studies. FDI is increasingly important to developing countries, as the attractive investments can help countries to attract capital, knowledge, and competitiveness (Ballotta, 2004). Despite this fact over the past few years, the share of the developing countries in global FDI inflows has been declining.

Foreign direct investment is based on many factors such as the openness of the economy, the quality of the workforce, the national economy growth potential, financial and technological, quality of physical infrastructure, natural resources, and the size of the economy. Each year more FDI is flowing from not only developed economies into developing economies but also between developing and transition economies.

1.1. Investments and Classification of Investment

Economies of both developed and developing countries are affected by the investment, as one of the important economic variables. There is an important role, which it plays in creating production capacities, as well as expands and supports the production potential. First, we must distinguish between different definitions of investment. In finance, investment means the purchase of a financial product or another asset with the expectation of the future positive returns. Also, in general terms, investment means the use of funds or other resources in expecting of making future benefits (Bodie, Kane, & Marcu, 2008). According to UNCTAD, the investment means every kind of asset invested directly or indirectly by investors in the territory (UNCTAD, 2008a). The concept of investment has changed over time as the nature of international economic relations has changed. Thus many types of investment appeared.

The types of investment distinguish by contrast and differences in the relative importance and characteristics of each form. They also differ by forms and preferences of each of the host countries, likewise the multinational corporations* in adoption a form or forms of investment. For example various levels of economic progress in the host countries pay to follow the forms of foreign investments in them. The size and shape of the investments (Multinational Corporations) affect the choice of form of investments. If investors who expect to increase their profits, costs, or technical factors, they have to execute the foreign direct investments in different forms. Therefore, it could be said there is no common definition of the foreign investment (OECD, 2008, p. 9). However, US - Rwanda bilateral investment treaties (BITS) in 2008, showed that the "investment" means all the indirect or direct assets owned by the investor, such as a capital, profits, or other resources (Malik, 2008, pp. 3-4).

We may perceive investments from different points of view:
- investments from the viewpoint of the exporting countries,
- investments related to the property,
- foreign portfolio investment.

Investments from the viewpoint of the exporting countries. This group includes horizontal investments, which refers to all foreign products and services manufactured almost similar to those the company produces in its domestic market. It duplicates the same activities in various countries. Horizontal FDI arises because it is too expensive to serve foreign markets through export due to transport costs or trade barriers (Protsenko, 2003).

Second group are vertical investments, which comprise investments where the fragmentation of the production process is done vertically across the border. The companies are located in one country and the other ones - producing parts in another country. It means the production of

---

* The terms "corporation", "firm", and "company", are generally used interchangeably, the term "enterprise" is sometimes preferred as clearly including a network of corporate and non-corporate entities in different countries joined together by ties of ownership. The term "multinational" refers to the activities of the corporation or enterprise involving more than one nation. Certain minimum qualifying criteria are often used in respect of the type of activity or the importance of the foreign component in the total activity. A transnational corporation (TNC) regarded as an enterprise comprising entities in more than one country. (Department of Economic and Social Affairs, 1973)

intermediate goods is abroad and companies introduce them to the home country to use them in the final product (Alfaro & Charlton, 2007).

The investments related to property, include:

1. **Bilateral foreign direct investments**. There are two major types of international investment agreement (IIAs): first are the bilateral investment treaties (BITs, known as investment protection and promotion agreements or IPPAs). Bilateral agreements between the countries aim at protecting and promoting the interests of investors of one country in the country where the investment is made (Fulton & Richard, 2011). Second are the preferential trade and investment agreements (PTIAs). PTIAs include provisions to invest in bilateral and multilateral agreements on economic integration (EIAs), such as regional trade agreements (RTAs), free trade agreements (FTAs), and closer economic partnership (CEP) agreements. Increasing the drafting of the investment as part of the agreements, those are covering a wide range of issues, including trade in goods and services. That has led to increased variety of international investment treaty law and a new set of issues, especially concerning the relationship between investment and services in PTIAs. While BITs are still by far, the most number of PTIAs and the latter occupies a more important place in the international investment regime than it was a decade ago. Some countries more and more prefer to address traditional investment protection and liberalization, and the latest issues in the context of these broader agreements, where the investments are only part of a broader economic integration framework (UNCTAD, 2008a).

The first ratification of the bilateral direct foreign investments between Germany and Pakistan took place in 1959 (Yackee, 2010). The bilateral investment treaties grew up during the eighties of the last century. In 1990, there were 470 treaties, which increased to 1513 in 1997, involving 169 countries and territories (Walter, 2000). By the year 2000 of the last century there were about 2000 bilateral investment treaties (BITS). At the beginnings of the early years of this decade, the overall international investment agreements (IIAs) comprised 3164 agreements, which included 331 other IIAs and 2833 BITs. The purpose of developing countries to sign bilateral investment treaties is to attract more foreign direct investments. These agreements offer to all foreign investors in the host country ways to protect their investments and give them advantages over local investors. There are many rights guaranteed by the BIT agreements. Some of them guarantee investors to protect private property rights. Also, bilateral investments treaties give the investor the right to sue the host government if the government would take over the company (Yannaca-Small, 2008, p. 8). That is through the ICSID Convention, which is the main tool for the settlement of disputes of the investor countries, limits the jurisdiction of its centre to disputes between investors from different countries (Mann, 2008, p. 4). Investments treaties have been developed by capital-exporting countries to promote investments and protect their investors in capital-importing countries. With capital flowing from more developed countries to less developed ones, the bulk of these investments treaties traditionally were concluded between developed and developing countries.

2. **Wholly owned direct foreign investments** are when a single investor, either a legal or natural person acquires a productive asset in a foreign country and controls and operates that asset to make a profit. To buy that asset, the investor must make a series of contracts with other persons and may have to contract with a host country for permission to operate the investment or to obtain desired incentives, such as tax exemptions (Salacuse, 2013). The investor keeps the right to ownership of the investment project. Besides that, investors can manage and control all the operations, and through investment establish branches of the company in the host country. The multinational corporations (MNC)* are one of the common and popular kinds that have increased their investments in developing countries. These investments can make links to the developing economies from developed countries. One of the advantages of these investments is that the increase in amount of foreign investments inflows to the host countries leads to increase in the goods and services inflows to the domestic market. Moreover, reduced import and the surplus of export is observed, which leads to improve the Balance of Payments (BOP). The large size of these projects leads to a transfer of technology. While, the cons of this type of investment is that the host countries are afraid of the danger of monopoly (Hallward Driemeier, 2003).

---

* There is no single agreed-upon definition of the multinational (or transnational) companies because in fact that these companies has many dimensions and may be viewed from any of several different perspectives – economic, political, legal, managerial, and others. Some observers regard ownership as the key criterion in their view the companies becomes multinational only when the headquarters or parent company is effectively owned by nationals of at least two countries. Second definitions see that an international company is seen as multinational only when the managers of the parent company are nationals of several different countries. Another definition see that an international company is seen as multinational only when the parent company that controls a large cluster of corporations of various nationalities. For more details see (Franklin R, 1990)

3. **Investments in the free zone. Free zone is** a region of a country where the customs and taxes are exempt or lower than in the rest area of a country. These exemptions allow the freedom of trade and therefore, may contribute to attracting investment (ḥṣawna, 2010, p. 13). Free trade zones (FTZ) are usually located near international airports and ports. It is one of the economic tools that contribute to economic development through attracting modern technology; establishment of export-oriented industries; providing jobs, and maximizes foreign currency. There were over 1735 free zones in 133 countries in 2010 (Bost, 2011, p. 3).

The Foreign Portfolio Investment (FPI) and foreign direct investment (FDI) are considered as long as distinct and separate forms of international capital inflows exist. However, in today's world there are reasons for treating them as if they were interconnected phenomena (Humanicki, Kelm, & Olszewski, 2013). FPI means foreign investment and direct ownership of some securities from stocks and bonds of national institutions by non-resident individuals and institution without any control or participation from the person in the organization and management of the project. This is called a short-term investment, hot money. The parent company provides management branch and foreign ownership requirements, and this distinguishes FDI from the indirect foreign investment. This investment sometimes is called the portfolios of investment securities. Another issue are forms of foreign investment overlapping between direct or indirect investments. This can be treated as a form of foreign direct investment because of its process of transforming technological resources, material, and human resources, and such forms can refer to the following (UNCTAD, 1998, p. 351; Ming, 2010; Salacuse, 2013):

A. Licensing Contract: it is an agreement or a contract between a multinational company and a domestic investor, sometimes referred to as a "concession agreement" (UNCTAD, 2004a). Through this agreement, the foreign investor gives the right to the investor to use the national technology or brand. That helps a foreign investor in transferring production methods and products to new markets.

B. Product-In-Hand Project; it is an agreement between the foreign investor and the domestic investor. It is provided that the local investor must pay the value of the project to the foreign investor. The foreign investor submits a design of the project and methods of operation, maintenance, and administration (especially in the start phase). The host country will pay the cost of obtaining machinery, plus transport costs (Robinson, 1967, p. 166).

C. Managerial Contract; It is an agreement between the foreign investor and the host country. Under this agreement, foreign investor is running a part of the operations of a specific project in the host country to participate in profits (L.S.Walsh, 1983, p. 77).

D. Contract for the Agency; the model that appears in the field of trade, it is an agreement between a foreign investor and the host country. Under the contract, one of the parties employs another party called the agent to facilitate the sale of goods and products of the foreign investor to the final consumer (L.S.Walsh, 1983, p. 64).

E. Subcontracting Business Arrangement; The purpose of this type of contract is to hold an agreement between one company (the contractor or "principal"), and another company (the "subcontractor") to export, supply or produce basic components of goods. The second party (subcontractor) uses a brand obtained from the first party in the production of final products (EIM Business & Policy Research, 2009, p. 12).

F. Construction Joint Venture (CJV: exists when two or more enterprises (design units, equipment suppliers, construction contractors) sign a consortium contract to form a joint bidding consortium to undertake a project through various forms (financial, human resources, etc.) (Ming, 2010). This investment (CJV) can be in one of three forms: legal shapes, partnership consortium/contractual, or corporation (Šryf, 2003).

There are other types of investments, which are called foreign direct investment in land by a foreign company or a country (Kamal). These investments give rights to land-use or land ownership; these rights can be valid for a limited period and can extend (Görgen, Rudloff, Simons, Üllenberg, Väth, & Wimmer, 2009).

In this research, the focus will be on the foreign direct investment due to the lack of another kind of investments in the Arab countries.

1.2. Concept, Theories, and Practice of Foreign Direct Investments

There is a belief about the benefits of foreign direct investments (FDI) to economies of both the host and investor's countries. Therefore, foreign direct investments have more attention, at each of the international and national level.

It is believed that FDI originated within American companies, and some of its forms, as we know today were developed mainly in American companies. However, Lipsey said that the East India Company, which chartered in London in 1600, established branches abroad. According to Lipsey the first foreign direct investment in Virginia State took place through the company that was chartered by King James I in 1606 with the purpose to establish the first permanent English settlement in Jamestown (Lipsey, 2001). Before the mid-nineteenth century, the capital inflows across borders were mainly in the form of lending by European investors to borrowers in other European countries (Kindleberger, 2006). For the first time the concept of foreign direct investments emerged in the writings of Herbert before the First World War. At this period, the people of Western Europe used a large part of their savings and income to finance foreign governments and enterprises in other regions of the world (Kamga Wafo, 1998). By the mid-twentieth century, the largest share of FDI was in the natural resources. Therefore, the concession agreements for natural resource extraction became an issue of importance in international law (UNCTAD, 2005a). At the end of the last century, after the spread of technological innovations in all parts of the world forms of foreign investment have become more diverse.

The definition of foreign direct investment is the transmission of foreign capital to invest abroad directly in working in industrial units, financing constructions, agriculture, or service. The motive of this foreign direct investment is the profit (Alasrag, 2005). FDI means that investor exercises a powerful influence on the management institution established in the host country (Kehal, 2004, p. 14). The parent company is allowed to control foreign assets of much larger, including those funded through retained earnings and by borrowing from domestic or foreign creditors (Feldstein, 1995, p. 46). According to the United Nations Conference on Trade and Development (UNCTAD) a growing group of owned assets is owned by foreigners with economic value, and can, therefore, be a foreign direct investment (UNCTAD, 2011a).

FDI is the total funds held outside the local economic system by the investor (Alzhrany, 2004, p. 26). Foreign direct investment is also the goal of making a permanent interest that the company is seeking to achieve in the foreign economy (Duce, 2004). Foreign direct investment is the flow of investment capital into the host countries to achieve the benefits and maximize profits. It can also be shared with local capital in those countries (Msaadawi, 2008, pp. 163-164). The foreign direct investment has three components, which are equity investment, reinvested earnings, and intra-company loans (UNCTAD, 2004b, p. 345; 'bd Alǧfar, 2002, p. 15). The measurements and definitions of FDI still differ among countries, despite efforts of international agencies to push for the agreement.

1.2.1. Theories of Foreign Direct Investment

Various FDI theories provide the motivations and determinants of FDI. The theories try to answer the questions why the firms prefer to invest abroad and how they enter into the foreign countries, etc. All the new marks in the new theories are to add some new elements and criticism to the earlier ones. Economists classified the FDI theories into micro-level and macro-level FDI theories. The micro-level theories (such as the theory of monopolistic advantage, the theory of internalization, and eclectic FDI theory) discuss the motivation of FDI associated with the firm level. The macro-level FDI theories (such as capital market theory, FDI theories based on exchange rates, and FDI theories based on economic geography) give the macroeconomic factors that determine the FDI. Besides these two categories, the development theories of FDI (which combine both the micro level and macro level FDI theories (such as Life-cycle theory) also discussed the motivation of FDI inflows (Denisia, 2010, p. 53).

We list the most important theories of FDI in below theories ('bd Alğfar, 2002; Denisia, 2010);

- the theory of monopolistic advantage,
- the theory of internalization,
- the eclectic theory,
- product life-cycle model,
- the theory of exchange rates in imperfect capital markets,
- theory based on economic geography.

Stephen Hymer (1976) developed **the theory of monopolistic advantage**. According to this theory, firms invest abroad because of certain firm-specific advantages such as access to raw materials, economies of scale, trade names, patents, low transaction costs, etc. Also, these features are limited to the company enabling it to get the monopoly profit. Hymer stated that local firms will always be better informed about the local economic environment, and to have FDI taken place there must be certain conditions. The theory assumes investments to be viable, and the markets of these benefits must be imperfect ('bd Alğfar, 2002).

Casson and Buckley developed **the theory of internalization** in 1976 (Rugman & Verbeke, 2007, p. 156). According to this theory and due to imperfect market* firms try to make use of their monopolistic advantage themselves. Buckley and Casson (1976) suggest incorporation a vertical union in bringing new operations and activities under the governance of the firm. Earlier

---

*Imperfect market means a market where information is not quickly distributed to all its participants and where pairing of buyers and sellers is not immediate. Forms of imperfect competition include oligopoly, in which there are few sellers of a product.

the intermediate firms carried out these activities. In the same year Hymer added two major determinants of FDI to this theory; first is advantages that some firms possess in a special activity and the second is the removal of competition (Denisia, 2010).

The eclectic theory; in 1980, John H. Dunning developed a comprehensive theory of foreign direct investment. Dunning believes there are three factors or three advantages called Ownership Location Internalization (OLI) paradigm (Zhu, 2008, p. 16), which must be existing to make decision of foreign direct investments (Dunning, 2001):

1. Ownership (O) - Ownership advantages refer to the assets (such as natural resources, patents, trademarks, etc.) which are possessed by the firm and may be transferred within MNCs at lower costs, and lead to reduction of costs or increase of incomes. The ownership advantage helps the company to compete with local companies in the foreign economy (Johnson, 2005, p. 19).

2. Location (L) - when the first condition is achieved, then location advantages decide who will become the host country for the activities of MNCs. Choose of the host country will accord to specific location advantages. Such as distance from the home country, lower costs of transportation, natural resources availability, telecommunications, government policies, market size, taxes, tariffs or lower labour cost , etc. (Root, 1998; Brouthers, Brouthers, & Werner, 1996).

3. Internalization (I) - advantages, will be achieved when the first two conditions are achieved, it must be useful for the firm to use these advantages in collaboration of some factors outside the home country.

According to Liu Wenke and others, these advantages are complementary and not substitute for each other in explaining the activities of FDI (Wenke & Jingfeng, 2005, p. 14).

The theory of exchange rates in imperfect capital markets; In 1985, "Cushman pointed to some cases of uncertainty, which could theoretically contribute to the increase of foreign direct investment" (Cushman, 1988). He believes that the stability of the currency and the economic stability are a motivation for foreign direct investment. Cushman concludes that rise in the value of dollar has led to decrease in the value of foreign direct investment in the United States by 25 percent. However, this theory cannot explain simultaneous foreign direct investment between countries with different currencies (Denisia, 2010, p. 56).

Theory based on economic geography. One of the macroeconomic FDI theories is based on economic geography. It focuses on countries and explains why internationally successful industries develop in particular countries. These explanations were based on the differences among countries regarding the availability of natural resources, nature of labour and local demand, infrastructure, etc. The FDI theories based on economic geography present also how governments can affect the resources within the control by different policy actions (Krugman, 1998).

Raymond Vernon proposed the **product life cycle theory** in the mid 1960 s (Hill, 1997, p. 136). The theory analyses the relationship between product lifecycle and possible FDI inflows. The concept includes four consecutive stages: product introduction, product growth, product maturity, and product decline. The life cycle starts when a company introduces a product that is wholly or partly differentiated from old products. At the first stage, the product is a specialty and, nowadays the manufacturer has a monopoly.

The theory mentions a cycle where a domestic company produces a product, and then to capture the world market, the firm's foreign assistant produces the product and finally the product is produced in any parts of the world where the cost of production of the product is the lowest. However, as more companies enter the market the different brands become more and more alike to each other in the consumers' viewpoint. The product may slip into the third stage as a mature product. Brand competition now gives way to price competition (Franklin R, 1990, pp. 125-126). The last stage demand for the product will go down, and it will become obsolete.

From the FDI theories discussed above, we found some determinants of FDI, such as exchange rate, interest rate, labour force, taxes, tariffs, political stability,economies of scale, natural resources, good infrastructure, labour costs, government policies, etc.

1.2.2. Practice of Foreign Investment Over Multiple Historical Periods

Since the inception of foreign direct investment it has passed through different stages of time, as presented below:

- before the First World War (1800-1913),
- between the two Worlds Wars (1919-1945),
- a recovery period of foreign investments after the Second World War (1946-1969),
- modern trends of foreign investments (1970-2010).

During the period **before the First World War (1800-1913)**, the great depression had a negative impact on the global economy, through a relatively simple direct investments and international movements of capital and their effects on trade of goods and services across the borders (Winder, 2006, p. 789). In this period, the international business developed from intermediate forms, such as the foreign agencies and licensing arrangements, to multinational corporations (Harvey & Jon, 1990). Before the first war and between 1897 and 1908 the value and number of investments in European manufacturing were about three times higher compared to the years 1881-1897 (Bova, 1995). In the literature before this period, it was considered that the majority of international investments were indirect investments. This belief was based on a study published in 1938 by Chon Lewis, and accepted as fact for over 40 years. In reality, the majority of international investment is a direct investment (Trends, p. 24).

From the mid-seventies, some economists checked the accounts of the United Kingdom, as the largest international investor at that time. The conclusion was that the investments were almost direct investments. Before the First World War, the United States was the largest importer of foreign capital in the world (Chang, 2004). Table 1-1 shows the share of direct investment in foreign private investment in the United States and US private investment abroad for the years 1897-1914. In this period most the foreign investments in the United States were portfolio investments. About 80 percent of the stock of long-term investments in the United States was portfolio investments (Lipsey, C, H, & N, 1999). Also over 50 percent of the world investments were in the primary sector (agriculture and raw materials) 20 percent were in railroads, 15 percent in manufacturing, and 10 percent in services (Akrami, 2008, p. 137).

Table 1-1. Share of Direct Investment in Foreign Private Investment in the United States and US Private Investment Abroad: Selected Years, 1897 to 1919(Percent)

Year	U.S. Private Investment Abroad (Percent)	Foreign Private Investment in the US (Percent)
1897	93	-
1908	65	-
1914	75	18

Source: Author's elaboration according to (Lipsey, 1993).

In the period **between the two Worlds Wars (1919-1945)**, there were a few different estimates of total foreign investment. A significant reduction in foreign direct investments (FDI) inflows on the list of biggest investors changed the positions of countries. The United States had emerged creditor from the war. Also, the European investment in the United States, Latin America, and Britain liquidated about US $ 4 billion from their investments abroad.

Robert E. Lipsey and others argue that the period after the First World War witnessed the first U.S. portfolio investment abroad, including the large loans to foreign governments. By the end of 1919, direct investments reduced to slightly more than half of private investments in the United States abroad. However, this represented less than a quarter of the total foreign investments including government loans (Lipsey, C, H, & N, 1999, pp. 313-314).

The 1920s are characterized by rapid growth in both direct and portfolio private investments abroad. The direct investments amounted to more than twice the value of the past decade. By 1929, the value of U.S. private portfolio investments exceeded that of direct investments for the first time. The international investments in the twenties took the form of foreign direct investments. There has been a regular increase in the share of FDI from the main oil companies. In 1929, the international investments reached US $ 55 billion, the share of the United States was about US $ 15.7 billion (Akrami, 2008). The share of the United Kingdom in the international investments was about US $ 19 billion while the share of the Latin America was about US $ 13 billion (Twomey, 1998).

The foreign investments have slowed a lot after the great depression of 1929 until the period before the Second World War. This decline was due to the collapse of international trade, increased unemployment, lower commodity prices, worsening political unrest and imposing restrictions on foreign exchange, especially during the great depression 1929-1932. Table1-2 shows the yearly British and U.S. investments in the period 1919-1938. After the crisis, both the United States and Britain sought re-stream the capital through an established many investment projects in the first sector and the services sector (Taylor & Wilson, 2011, p. 273). By 1940, direct investments were about 60 percent of U.S. private outward investments

Table 1-2. Average Yearly British and U.S. Investments 1919-1938(US $ Million)

Countries/Years	1919-1923	1924-1928	1929-1931	1932-1938
U.S.	531	1 142	595	28
UK	516	578	399	143

Source: Author's elaboration according to (Akrami, 2008, p. 137).

At Recovery Period of Foreign Investments, after the Second World War (1946-1969), economists around the world expected that the great recession could be followed by inflationary boom after the war. The recession appeared after few years in 1949, and it was both mild and short-lived (Blyth, 2013). The United States controlled the global foreign direct investment inflows after the end of World War II. The United States got about three-quarters of foreign direct investments (including profit reinvested) in the period 1945-1960. The net flow of foreign direct investments in the period 1951-1955 were about US $ 3.3 billion, mostly in developed countries. Since that time, the FDI has become a global phenomenon (Anand, 2006, p. 43).

The U.S. companies dominated foreign direct investments through the Marshall Plan, the wars and crises in the period 1950 to 1965. The value of foreign direct investments abroad in the United States increased from 62 percent in 1950 to 65 percent in 1960. The total foreign direct investment in the world was US $ 67 billion in 1960. The United State had the biggest share of that with about US $ 33 billion, and United Kingdom US $ 11 billion (Twomey, 1998).

Over the period "between" 1961-1964 the European countries got from the U.S. investments about 50 percent of the total American investments abroad. In 1964, the foreign investments in the United States had increased by 8.9 percent, and most were from Britain.

After the mid-sixties, Japan and Germany had become the largest exporter of the volume of FDI investment instead of U.S. When the European investors' started investing in the U.S., the Japanese industry competed with U.S. industry as well. The direct investment inflow to the U.S was less than 10 percent of the total inflow to developed countries in 1960 and 17 percent in 1967-1969 (Lipsey, 1993, p. 116).

The **Modern Trends of Foreign Investments** as a phenomenon started at the beginning of the seventies of the last century. Here, we can divide this stage into the following periods;

- the seventies of the twentieth century,
- the eighties of the last century,
- the beginning of the nineties until 2010.

The seventies of the twentieth century is a stage characterized by the operations' development of multinational companies in product, volume of sales, with an increase in the integration of market economies. As well as the crisis transmission of the U.S. dollar to the rest of the world, has led to a crisis of global recession. Also, there was the process of correction in oil prices in 1973, and the second correction in 1979. This led to large financial surpluses and had an active role in feeding the international financial market. The funds of about US $ 590 billion in 1979 including US $ 64 surpluses to OPEC (Bergendahl, 1984, p. 37), were employed mostly as deposits with international banks and international financial institutions.

The bulk of geographical distribution of foreign investments during this period was among the developed countries. The share of the Organization for Economic Cooperation and Development countries[*] in the total global investment inflows was about 95 percent (Qasm, 1987, p. 116). The share of the developed economies in the global total foreign direct investment was more than 75 percent in the period 1970-1979 (Sundaram, Schwank, & Arnim, 2011, p. 10). The FDI inflows in Arab countries were about US $ 0.5 billion in 1970, to US $ 1.4 billion in 1975, and decreased in 1979 amounting to US $ -0.1 billion[**]. FDI inflows in Eastern and South- Eastern Asia excluding China were about US $ 0.6 billion in 1970, increased in 1975 to reaching US $ 2.5 billion, and increased to US $ 2.6 billion in 1979 (see Table 1-3).

The second period covers the eighties of the last century. The inflows of global foreign direct investments increased by 28 percent- from US $ 42.2 billion in 1979, amounting to US $ 54.1 billion in 1980. In 1985, the inflows of global FDI increased to US $ 56.1 billion. However, the United Nation in the first world investment report noted that the worldwide outflows of foreign direct investment rose by 20 percent in both 1988 and 1989, amounting to US $ 198.3 billion (UNCTAD, 1991, p. 3).

Moreover "according to International Monetary Fund data, during the second half of the eighty's world FDI increased by average yearly rates of 41 percent" (Bajo-Rubio & Muñoz, 2000, p. 3). The FDI inflows in developed countries increased from US $ 33.7 billion in 1979, amounting to US $ 46.5 billion in 1980. In 1985, the FDI inflows in developed countries decreased to US $ 41.8 billion and to US $ 166.9 billion in 1989. However, the share of the developed economies of the world's total foreign direct investment was 75 percent for the period 1980-1989 (Sundaram, Schwank, & Arnim, 2011).

The FDI inflows in Arab countries have significantly decreased by 3000 % in 1980, from US $ -0.1 billion in 1979, to record US $ -3.1 billion in 1980. In 1985, the FDI inflows in Arab

---

*In 1970 the Organization for Economic Cooperation and Development including: Austria, Belgium, Canada, Denmark, Finland, France, West Germany, Greece, Iceland, Ireland, Italy, Japan, Luxembourg, Netherlands, Norway, Portugal, Spain, Sweden, Switzerland, Turkey, United Kingdom, and United States (OECD).
**Data on FDI flows presented on net bases (capital transactions' credits less debits between direct investors and their foreign affiliates). Net decreases in assets or net increases in liabilities recorded as credits (with a positive sign); while net increases in assets or net decreases in liabilities are recorded as debits (with a negative sign). Hence, FDI flows with a negative sign called reverse investment or disinvestment, in another meaning the registration of foreign direct investment on a net basis: where are recording direct investment flows during the period usually years. Flows such creditor or contained; buy tools from the original equity capital minus debit flows like pulling an investor who has already pumped in periods previous, which explains the emergence of a statement contained direct investment flows to state what is negative during some years (UNCTAD, a).

countries increased to US $ 2 billion and reduced to US $ 1.6 billion in 1989. Table 1-3 shows the Regional Distribution of FDI Inflows over the period 1970–1989 (US $ Billion).

Table 1-3. Regional Distribution of FDI Inflows, 1970–1989 (US $ Billion)

Area	1970	1975	1979	1980	1985	1989
Developed Countries	9.4	16.8	33.7	46.5	41.8	166.9
European Union	5.1	9.8	17.2	21.2	16.2	81.1
Japan	0.1	0.2	0.2	0.3	0.6	-1
USA	1.2	2.5	8.7	16.9	20.4	69
Developing Countries excluding China	3.8	9.7	8.5	7.4	12.3	27.9
Eastern and South- Eastern Asia excluding China	0.6	2.5	2.6	3.5	2.7	13.3
Latin America	1.1	2.8	4	5.8	5.7	8.1
Arab Countries	0.5	1.4	-0.1	-3.1	2	1.6
Africa	0.9	0.7	1.9	0.4	2.8	4.9
China	0	0	0	0	1.9	3.3
World	13.3	26.5	42.2	54.1	56.1	198.3

Source: Author's elaboration according to (UNCTAD, a).

The final period was from the beginning of the nineties until 2010. At the beginning of 1990s global foreign direct investment inflows growth was at much higher rates than global economic growth or trade (Carson, 2003). In 1990, the total inflows of foreign direct investment in the world amounting to US $ 208 billion by average growth 5 percent of the previous year. Developed countries attract over four-fifths of global foreign direct investment inflows in 1990. The Japan, United States, and the European Community accounted for 70 percent of global inflows (United Nations, 1992, pp. 1-3).

The FDI inflows in Arab countries decreased by 25 percent to the amount of US $ 1.2 billion in 1990, from US $ 1.6 billion in 1989. The FDI inflows in Arab countries significantly increased by 83 percent in 1991, to reach US $ 2.2 billion (see Table1-4).

In 1992, the global inflows of foreign direct investment to US $ 167.4 billion with average growth 8 percent of the previous year. In this year, the FDI inflows in Arab countries significantly increased, compared to the second year with 73 percent, to reach US $ 3.8 billion.

In 1993, after a two-year slowdown in global inflows of foreign direct investment, it recovered to reaching US $ 222.7 billion, by average growth 33 percent. The FDI inflows in Arab countries increased slightly with 3 percent, to reach US $ 3.9 billion, comparing with US $ 3.8 billion in the previous year.

In 1994, the Mexican financial crisis[*] has started. According to the World Investment report 1995, the devaluation of the Mexican peso had a mixed effect on foreign direct investment. On the one hand, the devaluation has created a new possibility for export-oriented investment and lowered the cost in exchange. On the other hand, the domestic market-seeking investment was suffering from the recession (UNCTAD, 1994; UNCTAD, 1995). The annual average of foreign direct investments was US $ 200 billion during the period 1989-1994 (UNCTAD, a). Table1-4 shows the regional distribution of FDI inflow for the period, 1990–1994.

In 1994, the global inflows of foreign direct investment reached US $ 255.9 billion, by average growth 15 percent. The FDI inflows in Arab countries decreased by 10 percent, to reach US $ 3.5 billion, compared to US $ 3.9 billion in 1993.

Table 1-4. Regional Distribution of FDI Inflows, 1990–1994 (US $ Billion)

Area	1990	1991	1992	1993	1994
Developed Countries	173	115.3	112.2	142.6	150.3
European Union	97.8	81	79.4	78.1	82.4
Transition Economies	0	0	0.1	1.4	0.9
Japan	1.8	1.2	2.7	0.2	0.9
USA	48.4	22.7	19.2	50.6	45
Developing Countries excluding China	31.5	35.4	42.4	49.5	69.9
Eastern and South- Eastern Asia excluding China	18.4	17.5	18.4	25.2	30.8
Latin America	7.8	10.2	14.9	12.5	26.2
Arab Countries	1.2	2.2	3.8	3.9	3.5
Africa	2.9	3.2	3.7	5.4	5.7
China	3.4	4.3	11	27.5	33.7
World	208.1	155.3	167.4	222.7	255.9

Source: Author's elaboration according to (UNCTAD, a).

In 1995, the global inflows of foreign direct investment reached US $ 331.1 billion, by average growth 29 percent compared to the previous year. Table1-5 shows the regional distribution of FDI inflows for the period 1995–2000. The FDI inflows in Arab countries were reduced by 20 percent to the second year, to reach US $ 2.8 billion, comparing with US $ 3.5 billion in 1994.

---

[*] There is no precise definition of "financial crisis," but a common vision is that the turmoil in the financial markets rises to the level of crisis when credit inflow to households and businesses it restricted, and the real economy of goods and services adversely affected. The financial crises have common elements and multi-dimensional and it is difficult to distinguish using a single index. It comes in many forms. Often the financial crisis is associated with one or more of the following cases (the budget deficit, government support, change in asset prices, the change in the volume of credit, and a collapse in the financial markets) (Claessens & Kose, 2013; Jickling, 2008)

According to the United Nations, China has been the largest developing-country recipient of FDI since 1992 (UNCTAD, 1995). In 1996, the global inflows of foreign direct investment reaching US $ 384.9 billion, by average growth 16 percent of 1995. The foreign direct investments inflows in Arab countries were increased by 75 percent, to reaching US $ 4.9 billion, comparing with US $ 2.8 billion in 1995.

In 1997, the Asian crisis originated in South East Asia, with two periods: the first from July 1997 to December 1997, when the first international aid was provided. While the second from the middle of 1998, when crisis expanded outside the region such as, China, Brazil, and Russia. Also, many Southeast Asian countries had a breakdown in economic growth rates and decreased in foreign direct investment's projects because of the crisis. (Karunatilleka, 1999, pp. 3-36). The South East Asian companies got a competitive trade advantage from the depreciating currencies. The Asian economies started investing abroad to keep the exchange rates of their currencies low. As a result, capital flowed from Asia to internet stocks in the United States, which led to rising stock prices (McKibbin, Warwick J; Stoeckel, Andrew, 2009, p. 4). The Global foreign direct investments inflows were about US $ 478 billion in 1997, with annual growth 24 percent of 1996. The FDI inflows in Arab countries are increased by 24 percent, reaching US $ 6.1 billion, comparing with US $ 4.9 billion in 1996.

Table 1-5. Regional Distribution of FDI Inflows, 1995–2000 (US $ Billion)

Area	1995	1996	1997	1998	1999	2000
Developed Countries	221.6	235.3	286	510.3	853	1 142.3
European Union	113.5	109.6	127.6	261.1	467.2	617.3
Transition Economies	3.9	5.3	9.8	7.1	7.1	5.9
Japan	0	0.2	3.2	3.3	12.7	8.2
USA	58.5	84.5	103.4	174.4	295.0	281.1
Developing Countries excluding China	113.3	152.5	187.4	188.4	222.0	240.2
Eastern and South- Eastern Asia excluding China	38.9	48	53.1	41.1	70	109.6
Latin America	32.3	51.3	71.2	83.2	110.3	86.2
Arab Countries	2.8	4.9	6.1	5.1	4.3	5.8
Africa	4.7	5.6	7.2	7.7	9.0	8.2
China	37.5	41.7	45.2	45.4	40.3	40.7
World	331.1	384.9	477.9	692.5	1 075.0	1 270.8

Source: Author's elaboration according to (UNCTAD, a).

In 1998, the global FDI inflows growth increased by 45 percent to reach US $ 692.5 billion. The FDI inflows in Arab countries were reduced by -16 percent, to reaching US $ 5.1 billion in 1998, comparing with US $ 6.1 billion in 1997. In 1999, the global FDI inflows growth increased by 55 percent to reach US $ 1075 billion. Developed countries increased by 67 percent and reach US $ 853 billion in 1999.

The FDI inflows in Arab countries dropped by the same percentage achieved in 1998 by -16 percent, to reach US $ 4.3 billion in 1999, compared with US $ 5.1 billion in 1998.

In 2000, the global FDI inflows growth increased by 18 percent to reach US $ 1270.8 billion. The FDI inflows in Arab countries in 2000 were increased by 35 percent, to reaching US $ 5.8 billion, comparing with US $ 4.3 billion in 1999 (see Table1-5) (UNCTAD, 2001).

In 2001, the global FDI inflows declined sharply by -34 percent from about US $ 1270 billion in 2000 to US $ 837.7 billion (see Table1-6). That decrease due to the microeconomic and macroeconomic factors such as the sharp decrease in cross-border mergers, weak economic growth, and low corporate profits (UNCTAD,b). The FDI inflows in Arab countries in 2001 were increased by 62 percent, to reaching US $ 9.4 billion, comparing with US $ 5.8 billion in 2000. In 2002, the inflows of global FDI in the world declined by -25 percent of the previous year to reaching US $ 628.7 billion. The FDI inflows in Arab countries in 2002 reduced by -23 percent, to reaching US $ 7.2 billion, comparing with US $ 9.4 billion in 2001.

Table1-6.Regional Distribution of FDI Inflows, 2001–2005 (US $ Billion)

Area	2001	2002	2003	2004	2005
Developed Countries	603.3	446.2	388.8	423.9	622.8
European Union	386.8	315.7	287	228.3	503.5
Transition Economies	8.1	10.1	18	29.1	32.4
Japan	6.2	9.2	6.2	7.8	2.7
USA	159.4	74.4	53.1	135.8	104.7
Developing Countries excluding China	226.1	172.3	197.4	284.6	341.4
Eastern and South- Eastern Asia excluding China	64.1	31.2	56.5	77.8	100.8
Latin America	68.1	52	42.4	62.9	69.5
Arab Countries	9.4	7.2	16	25.2	47.4
Africa	13.1	13	17.4	16.4	24.3
China	46.8	52.7	53.5	60.6	72.4
World	837.7	628.7	604.3	737.6	996.7

Source: Author's elaboration according to (UNCTAD, a).

In 2003, for the third year the total FDI inflows in the world reduced by -4 percent from US $ 628.7 billion in 2002, to US $ 604.3 billion in 2003. That was the lowest level since 1998. Several factors, such as landing the pace of privatization in some countries were behind the slowdown in economic growth in many countries (UNCTAD, 2003, p. 13).

The FDI inflows in Arab countries have a significant growth in 2003 with 122 percent, to reaching US $ 16 billion, comparing with US $ 7.2 billion in 2002.

In 2004, the global FDI inflows rose first time after three years of declining inflows with average annual 22 percent and reaching US $ 737.6 billion. According to the UNCTAD, foreign direct investment rose especially in developing countries and Transition Economies due to the growth of competition between many companies, and the high prices of many goods industries. This stimulated the inflows of FDI to countries with many natural resources such as minerals, gas, and oil (UNCTAD, 2005a, p. 7). The FDI inflows in Arab countries in 2004 increased by 58 percent, to reaching US $ 25.2 billion, comparing with US $ 16 billion in 2003.

In 2005, for the second year after the events of September 11 in 2001, the total FDI inflows in the world rose by 35 percent from US $ 737.6 billion in 2004, to US $ 996.7 billion in 2005. According to the UNCTAD, the merger of cross-border companies in 2004 stimulated the increases in FDI (UNCTAD, 2006, p. 17). The FDI inflows in Arab countries in 2005 increased by 88 percent, to reaching US $ 47.4 billion, comparing with US $ 25.2 billion in 2004. Table1-6 shows the Regional Distribution of FDI Inflows, 2001–2005 (US $ Billion).

The global FDI inflows rose in 2006 to reach US $ 1461.8 billion with average growth of 47 percent from the previous year (see Table1-7). This reflects the strong economic performance in many parts of the world (UNCTAD, 2008b). The FDI inflows in Arab countries in 2006 increased by 48 percent, to reaching US $ 70.1 billion, comparing with US $ 47.4 billion in 2005. The rise in global FDI inflows in part because the corporate profits all over the world and resulted in rising stock prices that raised the value of merger of cross-border companies (UNCTAD, 2007, p. 16).

In 2007, the global FDI inflows growth and rose by 35 percent to reach US $ 1970.9 billion, exceeding the record level achieved in 2000 by about US $ 700 billion. The inflows of FDI continued growth in some economic groups, despite the start of the financial crisis in 2007. The FDI inflows in Arab countries in 2007 increased by 17 percent, to reaching US $ 82 billion, comparing with US $ 70.1 billion in 2006.

At September 15, 2008, Lehman Brothers filed for bankruptcy, the global financial crisis has sent a wave of risk on financial markets around the world; banks stopped lending to each other. Cross-border bank lending decreased a lot and lending fell by 58 percent on average between countries (Haas & Horen, 2012). At this time, Losses in securities based on debt in the housing sector amounted to about US $ 500 billion (Mishkin F. S., 2010).

At this time, the international banks played a significant role in transferring the crisis to the economies of other countries (Contessi & Pace, 2011, p. 2). As a result, in 2009, the global financial crisis has been largest, and, many of developed economies faced a deep recession. Warwick J McKibbin and Andrew Stoeckel, study, showed that the financial crisis that started in the United States was not limited only to the United States but had an impact on the global economy (McKibbin & Stoeckel, 2009).

How can that affect the economic crisis on the size of foreign investments flowing to developing countries? Three main channels accord to study for United Nations University 2009 in Finland (Naudé, 2009, pp. 4-7):

- reductions in domestic lending, and banking failures,
- reductions in export revenues,
- reductions in financial inflows to developing countries.

Table 1-7. Regional Distribution of FDI Inflows, 2006-2010 (US $ Billion)

Area	2006	2007	2008	2009	2010
Developed Countries	988.2	1 322.7	1 032.3	618.5	703.4
European Union	635.8	895.7	514.9	387.8	313.1
Transition Economies	60.4	88	117.6	70.6	70.5
Japan	- 6.5	22.5	24.4	11.9	- 1.2
USA	237.1	215.9	306.3	152.8	228.2
Developing Countries excluding China	429.4	573	658	510.5	573.5
Eastern and South- Eastern Asia excluding China	127.2	168.1	137.4	114.3	198.3
Latin America	98.4	169.5	206.7	140.9	159.1
Arab Countries	70.1	82	97.6	82.4	68.6
Africa	46.2	63.1	73.4	60.1	55
China	72.7	83.5	108.3	95	105.7
World	1 461.8	1 970.9	1 744.1	1 185	1 243.6

Source: Author's elaboration according to (UNCTAD, 2011b, p. 187; UNCTAD, a).

In 2008, the global FDI inflows growth reduced by -12 percent to reach US $ 1744.1 billion. In 2008, developing countries FDI inflows grew by 15 percent from the previous year, to reach US $ 658 billion. Developed countries reduced by 22 percent and reached US $ 1032.3 billion. This reduction in investments in developed countries led to increasing the share in global FDI inflows to developing economies, and Transition Economies (UNCTAD, 2009b). The FDI inflows in Arab countries in 2008 increased by 19 percent, to reaching US $ 97.6 billion, comparing with US $ 82 billion in 2007.

Global FDI inflows reduced in 2009 by -32 percent of 2008, to reach US $ 1185 billion. The FDI inflows in Arab countries in 2009 reduced by -16 percent, to reaching US $ 82.4 billion, comparing with US $ 97.6 billion in 2008. Global FDI inflows increased in 2010 by 5 percent of 2009, to reach US $ 1243.6 billion. This growth was mainly the result of higher inflows to developed countries and the USA. According to United Nations, the FDI inflows in 2010 were about 37 percent below their peak in 2007, and about 15 percent below their pre-crisis average (UNCTAD, 2011b, p. 2). The FDI inflows in Arab countries in 2010 reduced by -17 percent, to reaching US $ 86.6 billion, comparing with US $ 82.4 billion in 2005. Table1-7 shows the Regional Distribution of FDI inflows for the period 2006-2010 (US $ Billion).

1.3. Determinants of Investments Attractiveness

The process of making decision relating to foreign direct investment by multinational corporations, is the most powerful force in the investment activity in the world, from the most complex processes. These issues are discussed thoroughly in the economic literature and by applied research specialist. According to the literature there are many factors which determine investment decisions of multinational corporations. To assess the investment attractiveness we need to refer to determinants of investments and they are different. Determinants of investment are the factors that stand in the way of the inflow of investments into the country. It might be different views of investment attractiveness. If you are looking for the regional definition it is described as a set of incentives for investment i.e. offering wide-ranging benefits that may be gained when managing business activities in given areas (Nizielska, 2012, p. 55). But when we are looking for more objective definition of investment attractiveness it is defined as a set of factors that help to provide a suitable investment climate.

The term of the investment climate refers to the economic and financial conditions in a country that affect whether individuals and businesses are willing to do investment there. International attractiveness for investment is the ability of the country in a given period of time to attract investment projects in a various fields, and attract production companies and components of capital, expertise and creativity in various fields (The Arab Investment & Export Credit Guarantee Corporation, 2013).

There are several types of motives for foreign investment, including search for natural resources, search for efficiency, and the search for markets (Mottaleb & Kalirajan, 2010, p. 2). The first studies tried to find the factors that affect foreign direct investment decision in developed countries (Barclay, 2002, p. 3). Perhaps the determinants of investments depend on the sector, type and motivation of foreign direct investments. If a country is going to attract foreign direct investments, which depends on the knowledge, this is difficult without enough human resources and local technology. Moreover, it is difficult to attract foreign direct investments for efficiency-seeking business if the conditions of the investments are not proper. To know the factors of FDI attractiveness it is necessary to know the determinant factors that attract FDI (Kokkinou & Psycharis, 2004). The main factors affecting FDI inflow are the determinant factors of FDI (Collier & Gunning, 1999). Taylor pointed out that local and global factors are important in determining the quantity and quality of investment inflows to developing countries (Taylor & Sarno, 1997, pp. 451-470). Within these factors there are various categories such as regulatory framework, resourcefactors, infrastructure, the stability of political and macroeconomic situation and the capacity for economic management (The World Bank, 1997, pp. 49-50).

These categories can overlap, and sometimes it is difficult to differentiate between them. Numerous studies have addressed the attractiveness of foreign direct investment, and many studies have focused on the motives of investment. Most empirical studies have looked at different keys of these factors, and their results were different not only regarding the importance or statistical significance of these factors but the direction of the effect. Therefore, the literature review shows there are several categories of these factors; some economists divide them into (Kawash, 2010; Soumia & Abderrezzak, 2013; Alavinasab, 2013; Hasen & Gianluigi, 2007; Hailu, 2010; David & Ashoka, 1992):

- market size, or the economies of scale (GDP per capita), which is one of the most important determinants of FDI it is usually measured as the total GDP (Population x GDP per capita) produced (Heshmati & Davis, 2007, p. 11),
- the quality and developing basic infrastructures, such as road transport, railway transport, telecommunications, information, and energy is a major determinant of the FDI in the host countries. The good infrastructure is necessary to keep country's economic growth,

because its make the operating cost low, which can increase the return on investment and, therefore, improve FDI (Soumia & Abderrezzak, 2013, p. 303),

- the level of trade openness, the Trade-to-GDP ratio often used to measure the openness of trade,
- human capital and technology considered as a determinant of economic growth. Human capital also effects on growth through its dealing with FDI. Some studies suggest the secondary school enrollment as a factor refers to the skills,
- macroeconomic and political stability, and developing the financial system of the host country are an important factor to attract FDI,
- the rate of return on investment, the profitability of investments is of key importance to foreign investors. For this, the decision to invest in the host economy depends on the risk and return on investment in the economy.

Table 1-8. The Determinants of the Host Country for FDI

Economic conditions	Markets	Size; income levels; urbanization; stability and growth prospects; access to regional markets; distribution and demand patterns
	Resources	Natural resources; location
	Competitiveness	Labour availability, cost, skills, trainability; managerial technical skills; access to Inputs; physical infrastructure; supplier base; technology support
Host country policies	Macro policies	Management of crucial macro variables; ease of remittance; access to foreign exchange
	Private sector	Promotion of private ownership; clear and stable policies; easy entry/exit policies; efficient financial markets; other support
	Trade and industry	Trade strategy; regional integration and access to markets;ownership controls; competition policies; support for SMEs
	FDI policies	Ease of entry; ownership, incentives; access to inputs; transparent and stable policies
MNEs strategies	Risk perception	Perceptions of country risk, based on political factors, macro management, labour markets, policy stability
	Location, sourcing, integration transfer	Company strategies on location, sourcing of products/inputs, Integration of affiliates, strategic alliances, training, technology

Source: (UNCTAD, 2009a, p. 8).

Agarwal survey in 1980, on the determinants of economic attractiveness of the country, suggested three main factors (Sekkat & Ange, 2004, p. 4):

- the difference in the rate of return on capital between countries,
- diversify investors' portfolio,

- the size of the market in the host country.

The difference in the rate of return depends on the incentives for foreign investors and the supply of cheap labour. However, the study showed that the incentives offered by the host country have only a small effect on FDI. Table1-8 displays the Determinants of the Host Country for FDI.

Study to J.H.Dunning, shows the same three main key factors in Table 1-8 but in different names. He refers to three groups of factors: policy framework for FDI, business facilitation, and economic determinants (Pilarska & Wałęga, 2014, p. 1169).

According to the World Investment Reports (2002, 2003, ,2007 and 2009) and some studies, the main determinants of inward FDI can divide into several categories. We show them as follows (UNCTAD, 2002; UNCTAD, 2003; UNCTAD, 2007; UNCTAD, 2009b; Ḥšad, 2008; Mndwr, 2010; ʿbd Almqṣwd, 2008; Lintunen, 2011; Çeviis & Çamurdan, 2007; Piteli, 2009):

- general policy factors, e.g. political stability, privatization policy, trade policy,
- FDI policies that include; incentives, performance requirements, investment promotion, international trade, and investment treaties,
- macroeconomic factors, such as; human resources, infrastructure, market size and growth,
- firm-specific factors for instance; technology, ICT[*] developments, raw materials, labour cost.

Other studies classified the determinants of FDI to some or all of the three groups below. Here we should refer to the existence of an overlap between the factors among the group classification (Hailu Z. A., 2010). Some may affect one type of FDI, and not affect the others (Lim, 2001). The main key factors are identified as (Gareib, 2012; Glese, Kahley, & Riefier, 1990):

- economic factors,
- social factors (in some studies referred to as quality factors),
- political factors.

Economic Factors, including such as:
1. Tariffs
2. Labour
3. Natural resources
4. Economies of scale (GDP per capita)

---

[*] Information and communications technology (ICT) is often used as an extended synonym for information technology (IT)

5. Exchange rate
6. Economic stability
7. Openness of Trade
8. Interest Rates
9. Wage Rates
10. GDP, and GDP growth
11. External debt
12. Import/GDP
13. Inflation/ GDP deflator
14. Urban population
15. Tax

Tariffs are taxes levied on imported goods and services. The tariff is levied as a fixed fee based on the type of commodity. The sources of data are the UNCTAD data, World Bank, the Arab Economic Report, and Arab Labour Organization.

Labour is a primary factor of production. The size of a countries labour force is determined by the size of its adult, and the extent to which the adults are either working or are ready to offer their labour for wages. The sources of data are the UNCTAD data, World Bank, the Arab Economic Report, and Arab Labour Organization.

Natural resources are available naturally; they offer the benefits through the provision of raw materials and energy used in the economic activity,

Economies of scale (GDP per capita), or market size; many studies have shown, there is a relationship between the increases in GDP per capita, with increased FDI inflows in the host countries. Leonard K. Cheng and Yum K. Kwan (2000) found that the size of a region's market has a positive effect on all roads which attract FDI to Chinese (Cheng & Kwan, 2000). The GDP per capita is available in, UNCTAD data, World Bank data, and the Arab Economic Report. Local or foreign currency measures it.

Exchange rate is the price for which the currency of a country can exchange for another country's currency. Factors that influence exchange rate include: interest rates, inflation rate, trade balance, political stability, internal harmony, transparency, general state of the economy, and quality of governance.

Economic stability is a term used to describe the financial system of a country. An economy with constant output growth and low and stable inflation will be considered economically stable.

The openness of trade is an indicator calculated for each country as the simple average of total trade to GDP (Rodriguez, 2000). Attracting FDI depends on integration into the global economy. This indicator is popular as a measure of trade openness and policy (David, 2007).

An econometric analysis for 29 Africa countries over the period 1990 -1997 indicates that GDP growth rate and trade openness can be used to attract the interest of foreign investors (Moreira, 2009). A decrease in the level of restrictions imposed on trade exchanges leads to increase in horizontal FDI in host countries. Data relating to the openness of trade is available in, UNCTAD data, World Bank data, and the Arab Economic Report.

Interest rates in economic theory, interest is the price paid for the money saved, not spent. It can be expressed as a percentage of interest rates usually paid annually or as the present value of the amount due in sometime in the future (Patterson & Lygnerud, 1999).

Wage rates can be calculated based on the wage rate of pay for the completion of certain work, or based on hourly wage rate or a day. It is measured in local currency.

GDP, and GDP growth measures the monetary value of final goods and services, and those that are purchased by the end user in a particular country in a period (for example, a quarter or a year) (Callen, 2008). GDP includes all outputs generated within a country's borders. It includes some non-market production, such as defence or education services provided by the government. GDP comprises the total goods and services produced for sale in the market. The sources of data are the UNCTAD data, World Bank, and the Arab Economic Reports.

External debt is money borrowed by a country from foreign lenders. Some research has focused on external debt for reasons related to the problem of funding and external borrowing may lead to debt crisis (Panizza, 2008, p. 1).

Import/GDP is the value of import of goods and services divided by GDP value; it is measured as a percent. It can be a causality relationship between FDI and imports. According to studies of Liu, Wang and Wei (2001), and Alguacil (2003), the FDI increases the import of goods and services and intermediates for use in production, and there may be a negative impact on investment aimed to import substitution. In our study, we are assuming that the value of import/GDP is destimulant. Both factors data are from the UNCTAD data, World Bank, and the Arab Economic Reports.

Inflation/ GDP deflator[*] is a percent of inflation divided by GDP deflator value; it is measured as a percent. The factor data is from the UNCTAD data, World Bank, and the Arab Economic Reports.

---

[*] GDP deflator: Is the implicit price deflator for GDP, is a measure of the level of prices of all new, domestically produced, final goods and services in an economy. GDP stands for gross domestic product, the total value of all final goods and services produced within that economy during a specified period (OECD).

Urban population is a term used to refer to the number of people living in an urban area in a particular country. The sources of data are the UNCTAD data, World Bank, and the Arab Economic Reports

Tax is a fee levied by a government on a product, income, or activity. According to OECD, the term "tax" means obligatory, unrequited payments provided to the general government. Unrequited means that the benefits provided by the government for taxpayers are not usually equal to their payments (OECD, 1996). The taxes may affect or not the attraction of foreign investment. There are many studies about that and many views if the taxes have a positive, negative or no impact on investment. For example, studies of Kemsley (1998), and Billington (1999) demonstrated that the tax has a significant impact on FDI. Study of Wheeler and Mody's (1992) found that it has insignificant impact on FDI. In our study, we used the number of tax payments, in this case of Poland as a country for comparison. Generally, we noticed that it was a high number of payments in case of Poland comparing to the Arab countries. Therefore, we decided to deal with the number of taxes as a stimulant factor. The sources of data are the UNCTAD data, World Bank, and the Arab Economic Reports

Social Factors includes:

- human capital and technology,
- type of FDI,
- economic policy,
- energy,
- marketing, communication, and transportation.

Human capital and technology are considered as a determinant of economic growth. Study of the Organization for Economic Cooperation and Development in 2002 concluded that the multinational companies can positively influence human capital in developing countries through, for example, training policies that are necessary for the competitive ability of all companies (Blomström & Kokko, 2002, p. 7). People may want to attain a higher level of education to access better job provided by the foreign investor (Checchi, De Simone, & Faini, 2007, p. 2). The labour force characteristics of efficiency, achievement, skill, and techniques, as well dealing with technology lead to increasing the economic competitiveness. Some studies suggest the secondary school enrolment as a factor referring to the skills (Fugazza & Trentinin, 2014, p. 8). It can be measured in person, and the sources of data are the UNCTAD data, World Bank, and the Arab Economic Reports.

Type of FDI has already been noted in this chapter as the types of investments. The types of investment are highly important in determining the value and direction of investment.

Economic policy (such as fiscal policy, tax policy, trade policy), can be measured through the Global Competitiveness Index (GCI), which published annually by the World Economic Forum.

Energy is sometimes referred to the electricity tariff or the price of electricity that differs from country to another. It also means the production, transmission, and consumption of energy. In our search, we will refer to the production of electricity because the data are available to the simple search. The sources of data are the World Bank data.

Marketing, communication, and transportation providing good infrastructure increase and stimulate FDI inflows (Asiedu, 2002, p. 111). Regarding the Arab countries, we could not get enough statistical data for these variables concerning all countries in the sample and the term of the search.

Political Factors means an activity related to government policy and its administrative practices that can affect businesses, including:

- economic freedom; it is measured through the Wall Street Journal and the Heritage Foundation that created the index of economic freedom (Heritage Foundation). We should note here we will refer to the index in details in the third chapter,
- corruption (transparency); it is measured through transparency index, which was found by Johann Graf Lambsdorff,
- Bureaucratic quality; include many factors related to the time required to complete the process, such as export, import, and the time required to start a business. Can be measured by the ease to do business index of the World Bank, or Global Governance Indicators of the World Bank,
- law of investment, legal stability, stable government, and effort of states to attract FDI, are important to attract all kinds of investment to any country. It can be measured through the World Bank Worldwide Governance Indicators,
- political stability, it can be measured through the World Bank Worldwide Governance Indicators.

The latter category is showing four classifications. According to this category, the determinants of FDI are (Groh & Wich, 2009):

1. Importance of Economic Activity: The state of the economy in a country affects the size and direction of FDI. Elements such as the size of the market, GDP, industrial growth and trade openness has a significant positive impact on FDI inflows. Besides the

country's level of development measured by real per capita Gross National Product (GNP), the balance of payment is one of the most important economic parameters.

2. Importance of the Legal and Political System: The legal and political system also affects a country's attractiveness for FDI investors. The regulatory and country risk factors affect FDI inflows. Legal stability is important to increase transparency regarding the legal framework of the country, which reflected a positive impact on FDI decisions, and thus stimulate investment inflows. The transparent, governance systems that support the rules of law are important and Political instability regarding civil wars, financial market instability and political corruption has significant effects on FDI.

3. Importance of the Business Environment: The business environment in any country is another key driving force, and the labour costs are a key determinant for FDI inflows. The difference between the productivity of labour and its cost play a key role. The Bureaucratic procedures and time requirements are affecting investment decisions. Moreover, corruption limits the foreign direct investment inflows.

4. Importance of Infrastructure: The infrastructure of the country such as communications and transport is one of the important factors for investors. Developing countries suffer from the problem of infrastructure.

There is a difficulty of identifying the appropriate factors for our composite measure. There is neither agreement about the most important factors for FDI activity nor any ranking.
Some factors are more generally discussed and of high significance. It remains unclear how these connect.

For our index calculation, it would be ideal to include all the presented factors. However, some of the cited papers focus on particular economies or regions, depending on the data available, and their datasets are neither available nor comparable to the datasets that exist for all Arab countries we aim to cover. However, our attempts to cover all Arab countries faced below difficulties:

- the lack of data for each period of the study for certain countries,
- the availability of data for certain countries but not available for other countries,
- some of the data were estimated from the source , which cannot be trusted,
- some of the data were from not reliable sources , cannot be relied upon,
- some Arab countries for many reasons, still obscure many data.

Hence, we try to find the best possible substitute for the key drivers of FDI. From the foregoing review of prior research, we identified three main key determinants that ultimately determine inward FDI: economic factors, social factors and political factors. These three key determinants include listed below indicators (see Table 1-9).

Table 1-9. The chosen of Groups Input Data

Group Factors	Factors	Study
Economic factors	GDP growth (annual %)	Gaurav Agrawal (2011), Groh & Wich, (2009),Torrisi (2008), Benassy (2007),
	GDP per capita or Market size (constant 2005 US$)	Vogiatzoglou (2007), Al Nasser (2007),), Janicki and Wunnava (2004), Fung (2002), Shatz and Venables (2000), Groenewold and Tcha (2000), UNCTAD Report (1999), Billington(1999), Katrakilidis (1997), Barreell and Pain (1996), Milner and Pentecost
	GDP per capita (Market size) growth (annual %)	(1996), Yang Rubio and Rivero (1994), Nigh (1986), Kravis and Lipsey (1982), Root and Ahmed (1979), Kobrin(1976), Scaperlanda and Mauer (1969)
	Trade (% of GDP) or Open trade	Groh & Wich, (2009), Torrisi (2008), Al Nasser (2007), Kandiero,Tonia, and Chitiga, Margaret(2006), Nonnenberg and Cardoso (2004), Janicki and Wunnava (2004), Addison and Heshmati (2003), Asiedu (2002), Bouklia and Zatla (2001), Yang Groenewold and Tcha (2000), Resmini (2000), Singh and Jun (1995), Loree and Guisinger (1995) Akhter (1993), Wheeler and Mody (1992), Kravis and Lipsey, (1982),
	Tax payments (number)	Billington (1999), Kemsley (1998), Wheeler and Mody's (1992), Lim (1983), Shah Toye(1978)
	Inflation, GDP deflator (annual %)	Onyeiwu and Shrestha (2004), Yang Groenewold and Tcha (2000), Katrakilidis(1997)
	Imports of goods and services (% of GDP)	Bhag Wati (1978)
Social factors	Urban population (% of total)	Abdul Aziz, Bilal Makkawi (2012)
	Labour force, total	Groh & Wich, (2009),Noorbakhsh, Paloni and Youssef (2001)
	Secondary education, general pupils	Seetanah Boopen and others (2009), Rubio and Rivero (1994), Rojid Sawkut,
	Electricity production	Khondoker Abdul Mottaleb and Kaliappa Kalirajan (2010)
Political factors	Political Stability	Groh & Wich, (2009), Naude and Krugell (2007), Presley and Malik (2004), Aseidu (2002), Jaspersen et al. (2000), Ramcharren (1999), Hanson (1996), Singh and Jun (1995), Loree and Guisinger (1995), Akhter (1993), Edwards (1990), Nigh (1985), Schneider and Frey (1985), Schneider and Frey (1985), Root and Ahmed (1979), Root and Ahmed (1979)
	Rule of Law	Choi and Samy (2008), Naude and Krugell (2007), Busse and Hefeker (2007), Jakobsen and de Soysa (2006), Baniak (2005), Busse (2004), Li and Resnick (2003); Oneal (1994)
	Transparency	Wei (2000) Groh & Wich, (2009)
	Time to export(days)	Lorena Škuflić, Petra Rkman, and Sandra Šokčević (2013)
	Time to import(days)	

Source: Author's elaboration.

It should be kept in mind we have chosen these factors, not others. First, choosing other factors could be possible if we chose only a few countries from our 13 sample countries. Nevertheless, we decided to take all the 13 Arab countries in our study with the possible factors. The problem faced by the researcher is the difficulty of obtaining sufficient data for all indicators referred to above as the most important influence on attracting investment indicators, despite numerous attempts to get this data from various sources. Sources such as (World Bank, United Nations

Conference on Trade and Development, World Bank, Arab Monetary Fund, Arab Central Banks, Arab Trade Financing Program, Arab League, Arab Industrial Development and Mining Organization, Union of Arab Banks, Council of Arab Economic Unity, as well some other sources).

Despite these difficulties, the data selected as described above based on many studies proved its importance in describing the factors attracting foreign investment. This chapter refers to some of these studies; others are shown in Table 1-9. We use several databases with annual data for the period 2005 to 2010. To guarantee comparability we deflate some data series either by GDP or by population.

CHAPTER TWO: Methodology of Foreign Direct Investments Attractiveness Research

Initially of the 1990s, the pace of economic and financial globalisation accelerated with closer economic and financial relations between different countries. This situation contributed to the wider use of criteria and indicators to help countries and investors make appropriate decisions to invest at the international level. These indicators allow us to look closely at several important things (Karanikas & Theodoulidis, 2002, p. 7).

In this chapter, we address theoretically, how to build composite indicators (or simply an index) to reach a single number that allows for the classification of the economies of individual countries regarding foreign investment attraction. This index represents a wide range of measurements on the multiple aspects of 'conceptual entity' such as the cost of living, the status of social wellbeing or FDI attractiveness. An indicator's (index) main role is quantification and simplification of information in a manner that promotes understanding of investigated complex problems for both decision-makers and the public. The method for index formation follows the approach of constructing composite indicators (Freudenberg, 2003; Michela, Giovannini, Hoffman, Tarantola, Saltelli, & Saisana, 2005; Castaings, Stefano, & Ari, 2008; Dalsgaard, 2013). The formulation of an indicator involves several computation methods, and their theoretical grounds and related options are described. Some methods used to assess the explanatory power of the indicator are proposed. The final FDI attractiveness index, which embraces the economies of 13 Arab economies, and Poland* as a reference country, allows their ranking and supports the decision-maker process of firms regarding the location of FDI.

Many composite indicators focus on different areas such as governance, investment climate, economic factors, and corruption. To understanding the importance of such indicators, in general, below are their main pros and cons of the composite indicators (Hub-European, 2008, pp. 13-14; Saltelli, Nardo, Saisana, & Tarantola, 2005, p. 361; Michalos, Andrew, & Nazeem ; Mishra, 2007):

Pros

- the maker's policy decision can use the composite indicators for summaries of complex or multi-dimensional issues to assist in decision-making,

---

* Selection of countries of the index and Poland as a reference country is described in chapter 4.

- instead of relying on many separate indicators, composite indicators minimise the time and effort to reach a certain goal. Therefore, they help in the task of ranking countries according to complex issues and assess the progress of countries over time,
- composite indicators can help attract public interest by providing a summary figure that helps to compare the performance of different countries and this progress over time,
- they reduce the size of a set of indicators that use the same information base.

Cons

- composite indicators may send misleading, non-robust policy messages if they are constructed poorly or misunderstand,
- the formulation of composite indicators should be transparent and based on reliable statistical principles,
- they may lead to unsuitable policies if some variables that are difficult to measure are ignored.

2.1. Review of Foreign Direct Investments Attractiveness Assessment Methods

Single level indicators produce an indicator (index, measure) based on a set of individual indices, measuring important attributes (determinants, characteristics) of inward FDI attractiveness. Their weights define the contribution of individual indices to resultant index. Multilevel (hierarchical) indicators divide the set of indices into some number of levels. They are organized in a tree structure: individual FDI determinants describing different aspects of FDI attractiveness are the leaf nodes of the tree, which are grouped into key indices, forming the second level of the hierarchy, and the root level, in the form of one composite measure of FDI attractiveness. Another classification of composite indicator depends on the determination of an ideal 'object" and ranking all object at hand according to their "distance" from this ideal, called pattern (sometimes as development pattern). One of such approach was introduced by (Hellwig, 1968), where the pattern was defined based on standardized object's attributes (characteristics), classified as "stimulants" (attributes values increase for objects treated as better ones), "destimulants" (attributes values increase for objects treated as worse). Such classified attributes are used to determine the "ideal" object, making up a coordinates of pattern in the space of objects' attributes. All objects are the points in this space, and their ranking is evaluated as a function of their distance from the "ideal". Another approach defines the "ideal" direction in the space of attributes (Nermend, 2006; Nermend , 2007). The method of ranking using "ideal" direction is called the synthetic vector method. This approach is the main method for object's ranking in this dissertation. This dissertation is the first work presenting synthetic vector measure in application to assessment of FDI attractiveness between Arab countries and Poland.

The literature presenting the composite indicators in different applications is ample. Underneath we describe different FDI attractiveness measures, published in the relevant literature. Their main differences among them are of key indicators (second level of the hierarchy), and methods used for weighting and agglomeration of FDI determinant; Examples of such indicators are described below.

UNCTAD's Investment Compass, (UNCTAD, 2005b) is an interactive software tool designed to policy analyses and it compares the investment environment. Compass investment is allows comparison between the countries and is specially designed for developing countries. Compass includes 60 indexes based on national surveys conducted by UNCTAD specifically and to international statistics. Among other information, it contains a table - the FDI Scoreboard - showing latest data for FDI inflows, FDI stocks, FDI inflows as a percentage of gross fixed capital formation (GFCF)*, and FDI Stock as a percentage of GDP.

UNCTAD's Inward FDI Potential Index, (UNCTAD, 2012) assesses the ability of the host country to attract foreign direct investment inflows compared to other countries. According to the authors of the index, some factors related to foreign direct investment such as social, political and institutional factors are difficult to be quantified (Sulstarova).

The Inward FDI Potential Index deals with several factors expected to affect investment attractiveness. The index covers 140 countries around the world. The index is the average values scoring (normalized to yield the result between 0 for the lowest scoring country, and 1, on top of the 12 variables. The list of variables composing index is:

- GDP per capita,
- the rate of GDP growth over the previous ten years,
- the share of exports in GDP,
- the average number of telephone lines per 1000 citizen and mobile telephones per 1000 citizen,
- commercial energy use per capita, to measure the availability of traditional infrastructure,
- the share of R&D spending in GDP captures local technological capabilities,

---

* Is a macroeconomic concept which is a part of the expenditure on gross domestic product (GDP), refers to net additions of capital stock such equipment, buildings and other intermediate goods added in the economy as investment.

- tertiary students, and the high-level skills workforce,
- country risk,
- exports of natural resources as a percentage of the world production,
- imports of parts and components of automotive and electronic products as a share of the global market,
- services exports as a share of the global market,
- FDI stock, in the country as a share of the world.

In 2002, the Analytic Hierarchy Process (AHP)** approach is uses to the assessment of FDI attractiveness. To resolve the problem in the presence of multiple criteria in the 12 variables, those are used by UNCTAD to calculate the "potential index UNCTAD Inward foreign direct investment". The AHP was used to deal with "UNCTAD Inward FDI Potential Index" variables as independent variables, to make the regression on the dependent variable called "Inward FDI Performance Index" (Şahin & Şener, 2006).

Instead of the importance of AHP but it has several cons described below (Kabir & Hasin, 2011);
- the AHP method is chiefly used in nearly poor decision applications,
- the AHP method creates and deals with a very unbalanced scale of judgment,
- ranking of the AHP method is rather incorrect,
- the individual judgment, selection and preference of decision-makers have a big influence on the AHP results.

UNCTAD Inward FDI Performance Index, (UNCTAD, 2012) ranks countries based on the volume of FDI relative to the size of their economies. In other words, the percentage shares of certain countries of the global FDI inflows to its share in global GDP. If the indicator value is greater than one, this means that a country receives greater foreign direct investment than the size of its economy. If the index value is less than one, it means that the amount of foreign investment has been less than the size of their economy. If the index is negative, it means that foreign investors do not invest in that period.

DHAMAN FDI Attractiveness Index, (Jelili, 2013) is an index for the Arab agency joint investment. Headquartered in Kuwait, was established in 1974, and includes all the Arab countries suggest a composite measure of the attractiveness of the foreign direct investment in

---

** (AHP) is one of Multi Criteria decision-making method that was originally developed by Prof. Thomas L. Saaty. In short, it is a method to derive ratio scales from double comparisons. The input can be obtained from real measurement such as price, weight etc., or from subjective opinion

the host country. The index ranks a set of 111 countries, representing 92 percent and 95 percent of the world inward FDI inflows and stocks respectively, according to their attractiveness for receiving inward FDI. The index covers 114 different indicators (index) are detected as sufficient substitute for the FDI key drivers categorized according to three major axes:

- prerequisites or initial conditions,
- underlying factors or factors motivating Multinational Enterprises' FDI,
- differentiation and Agglomeration economies.

A.T. Kearney FDI Confidence Index, (A.T.Kearney Leading Global Management, 2014) is index issued by AT Kearney Inc. in 1998, which is one of the largest consulting firms in management in the world. The index has been prepared using the data from the property survey administered to senior manager of the leading companies in the world. The sample includes 300 companies in 26 countries and covers all sectors of the industry. The index is calculated as a weighted average of the number of answers depending on the degree of low, medium, and high, for several questions about the possibility of direct investment in the market over the next three years. If the index values are high, it indicates that the investment objectives are more attractive for investment. FDI Confidence Index is not designed to identify the classification of different countries, but it shows investors' opinion about the future.

Besides indicators, there are surveys' and studies attempted to analyses the investment attractiveness and their determinants. Examples of such of them are described below.

EY's Attractiveness Survey Europe 2014, (Ernst & Young Global Limited, 2014) consider as a major source of insight on foreign direct investment. Through two-step analyses, it is the future vision for foreign direct investment in a particular country. Survey results are based on the views of the local and international opinion leaders and policy comprising political and economic decisions.

Evaluation of the FDI Attractiveness of the European Countries using PROMETHEE Method (Škuflić, Rkman, & Šokčević, 2013; S.C.Deshmukh, 2013) is a survey covers 27 countries in the European Union and six South Eastern Europe (SEE-6). Which includes (Albania, Bosnia and Herzegovina, Kosovo, FYR Macedonia, Montenegro, and Serbia) to assess investment attractiveness. Using PROMETHEE (Preference Ranking Organization Method for Enrichment Evaluations), it is an outranking method, typical of the European (or French) MCA school. According to this method identify the advantages and disadvantages of each country to creation and redefinition of macroeconomic policies to address them. Through the difference between the assessments according to a certain standard obtained by the comparison between the two countries, and convert it to preference ranging from zero to one. This paper used these determinants organized in the hierarchical structure:

1. Macroeconomic determinants:
   - inflation,
   - unemployment,
   - government gross debt as a percent of GDP,
   - export as a percent of GDP.
2. Market seeking:
   - GDP per capita,
   - GDP growth rate,
   - export growth rate,
   - population.
3. Resource seeking:
   - labour,
     - labour force,
     - total enrolment percent (primary school).
   - natural resources,
     - agricultural land %,
     - forest area %.
   - capital.
     - interest rate,
     - lending interest rate.
4. Efficiency-seeking:
   - infrastructure.
     - rail lines and roads,
     - electric power consumption,
     - mobile phone subscriptions.
   - time for doing business:
     - time to export,
     - time to import.

The PROMETHEE method has several cons described below (Macharis , Springael , Brucker , & Verbeke , 2004);

- PROMETHEE suffers from the rank repeal problem when a new choice is introduced,
- PROMETHEE does not provide the possibility to structure a decision problem. It is provided many options may become difficult for the decision maker to obtain a clear view of the problem and to judge the results,
- PROMETHEE provides no formal guidelines for weighing but assumes that the decision maker can weigh the measure properly.

A study of **Groh and Wich** used a different method to construct a composite measure that describes a country's attractiveness for receiving FDI. The study cover 127 countries include 12 Arab countries (UAE, Qatar, Bahrain, Oman, Saudi Arabia, Kuwait, Tunisia, Morocco, Egypt, Algeria, Libya, and Syria) for the period 2000-2008. In this study the FDI determinants and identify 20 factors that affect a host country's attraction for FDI. Divided into four categories that we are referred to them in chapter one as key drivers: Economic Activity, the Legal and Political System, the Business Environment, and Infrastructure. The results show that Singapore is the most attractive country for FD investors while Chad was at the end of list country. The study shows that both market size and openness are the high factors attractive for FDI in developed countries while the economic growth has the high rank in developing countries (Groh & Wich, 2009). In chapter 4, we will try to make a compare between our index and the index of this study.

From the above mentioned it can be concluded that they are different methods are used by different authors' some of methodology are based on survey some of the measures' and some of opinion. Analyses of multi-dimension assessment methodology should be made on the equipment of the aim of analyses. So we should take in mind the goal of the study. Synthetic vector measure of FDI attractiveness is the basic approach used in our dissertation because only in this approach we can make dynamic analyses (Nermend, 2009, p. 36).

As we aim to work dynamic analyses (during consideration of the year 2005 as a reference to the other years), we had to use this method instead of other approaches. Like the other approaches in which the possibility to conduct same analyses is not available. We want to see if the method synthetic vector measure is a valuable tool to measure the FDI attractiveness to analyses countries. We classified the factors of our input data as stimulant and destimulant according to their impact on the investment (see Appendices 1-14). The Table 2-1 shows these factors with specification and sources of information.

Table 2-1. Factors Specification and Sources of Information

Group Factors	Factors	Source of indicators
Economic factors	GDP growth (annual %)	The world Data Bank
	GDP per capita (constant 2005 US$)	
	GDP per capita growth (annual %)	
	Trade (% of GDP)	
	Tax payments (number)	
	Inflation, GDP deflator (annual %)	
	Imports of goods and services (% of	
	Urban population (% of total)	
	Labour force, total	Joint Arab Economic Reports
	FDI	UNCTAD (United Nations Conference on Trade and Development)
	FDI/WORLD	
Social factors	Secondary education, general pupils	The world Data Bank
	Electricity production (kWh)	
Political factors	Political Stability (-2.5 to 2.5)	Worldwide Governance Indicators
	Rule of Law (-2.5 to 2.5)	
	Transparency	Transparency Index created by the
	Time to export(days)	Worldwide Governance Indicators
	Time to import(days)	Worldwide Governance Indicators

Source: Author's elaboration.

2.2. Composite Measure of Foreign Direct Investments Attractiveness

In the following, we describe the most important points for creation of composite measure (indicator) of FDI attractiveness. These points are described in work of Andrea Saltelli, and others and application of those general recommendations to a specific task, i.e. construction of FDI attractiveness measures is presented in (Elavarasi, Akilandeswari, & Sathiyabhama, 2011). Findings presented in it are used as reference data and compared to the results of synthetic vector measure of FDI attractiveness (Saltelli, Andrea; Annoni, Paola ; Tarantola, Stefano, 2008). They recommend a 10-step procedure to construct composite indicators, presenting different options and methods to be used in each step. Based their work we shortly describe each step involved. It is stressed that the process of construction the measure is iterative.

Step 1-Theoretical/Conceptual Framework

This step provides the basis for selecting a set of variables to build a composite index, considering the opinion of experts and those who have interest. This step requires clear understanding and definition of the multidimensional phenomenon to be measured, discussion of the benefit of the composite indicator. Considering the nested structure of the sub-groups of the phenomenon, and determining the list of selection criteria for the underlying variables, e.g., input, output, process.

Step 2-Data Selection

Data should be selected by their country coverage, scientific soundness, connection to the phenomenon being measured and relationship to each other, and measurability. Using substitute variables should be considered when data are rare, considering the opinion of experts and those who have an interest in the matter. The method of quality assessment of the available indicators is required and critical assessment of strengths and weaknesses of each selected indicator. Data used should be described using the statistical tools of descriptive statistics (e.g. mean, median, skewness, kurtosis, min, max, variance, and histogram).

Step 3-Data Treatment

This step comprises imputing missing data, (eventually) treating outliers and/or making scale adjustments. Outliers should be treated by applying Box-Cox transformations such as square roots, logarithms, and other, as necessary by, e.g., taking logarithms of some indicators so that differences at the lower levels matter more.

Step 4-Multivariate Analyses

At this stage, exploratory analyses should review the overall structure of the indicators, assess the suitability of the dataset and explain the methodological choices, such as weighting, aggregation. Statistical and conceptual coherence in the structure of the dataset should be assessed e.g. cluster analyses are used to identify groups of similar countries, through the main component analyses.

Step 5-Normalisation

It should be carried out to make the variables comparable. Variables should be identified as stimulators or destimulators. A suitable normalisation method (e.g., min-max, z-scores, and distance to the best performer) should consider respects the conceptual framework and the data properties.

Step 6-Weighting and Aggregation

It is one of the most important steps in the construction of composite indicators. Indicators should be aggregated and weighted according to the underlying theoretical structure. Compensability that are among indicators needs to consider and either be corrected for or treated as a need to retain in the analyses.

Step 7-Uncertainty and Sensitivity

Analyses should assess the robustness of the composite indicator and identify assumptions that are more important in determining the final rating regarding, e.g., the aggregation method, the mechanism for including or excluding single indicators, the normalisation plan, the choice of weights and the imputation of missing data. It is important to note that a trade-off between robustness and multi-dimensional in the composite indicator, given that a mono-dimensional index could be more powerful than a multi-dimensional one. This does not imply that the first index is better than the second one. Robustness analyses should not be treated as an attribute of the composite indicator but of the inference, which the composite indicator has been called upon to support. Besides that, it should be considered the different methodological ways to build the index are possible, identify the sources of uncertainty underlying the development of the composite indicator, and provide the composite scores (ranks). Moreover, explain the causes of the certain countries improve or not their relative position given the assumptions, and show the sources of uncertainty that are the most influential in determining the scores (ranks), through a sensitivity analyses.

Step 8-Relation to Other Indicators

In this step, links are selected through regressions and making the correlate of the composite indicator (or its dimensions) with existing (simple or composite) indicators.

Step 9-Decomposition into the Underlying Indicators

Should be carried out to reveal drivers for good/bad performance and profile country performance at the indicator level to reveal strengths and limitations.

Step 10-Visualisation of the Results

In this step, it is important to enhance interpretability. Proper presentational tools for the targeted audience should be suggested. In this step, we select the visualisation technique, which communicates the results without hiding vital information. Present the results in a clear, easy to grasp and accurate manner.

This general procedure is differently applied in specific measures and it is usually comprises the majority of above steps. In our work, we will rely on the procedure of the Synthetic Vector Measure in section 2.3.1.

2.3. Aggregate Methods in the Study of Attractiveness of Investment

To make any comparison possible, we need a common measure of items to be compared. The main feature of many of the economic realities it is sometimes we use quantitative or qualitative terms to describe them. Quantitative attributes require some "standard" units of measurements or definition of "pattern" to assess the quantitative relationship between such variable and its unit. Qualitative attributes require a set of names of its possible categories, like kind of fruits (oranges, apples, etc.) – so-called nominal variables, or ordered categories, like good, better, etc. – so-called ordinal variables. A measure obtained by aggregation of individual variables (features, attributes) of considered compound facts will be called compound measures (index) or synthetic measures (index). Section 2.3 is devoted to the detailed presentation of proposed methods of FDI attractiveness measured using several methods.

2.3.1. Synthetic Vector Measure

Procedure to construct synthetic vector measure encompasses five steps: selection, elimination, and Normalisation of variables, determining the pattern and anti-pattern and a synthetic vector measure (see Figure2-1). These steps are described below:

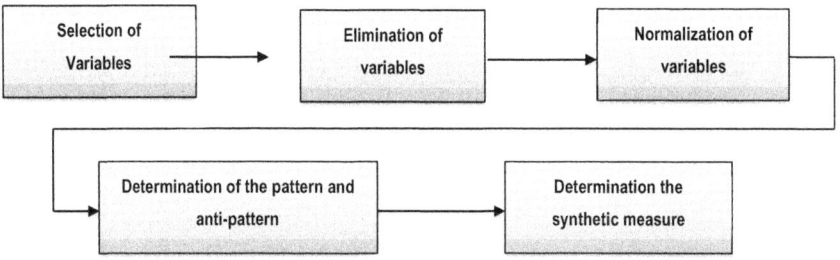

Figure 2-1. Steps of synthetic vector measure construction

Source: (Nermend, 2009).

1. Selection of variables

This step is crucial to the success of synthetic vector measure application, and at the same time is the less formalized than the other steps involved in measure construction. Which variables are potentially most useful in representation (or discrimination) of analysed phenomenon depends on the subject matter at hand, and should be decided by an expert in this domain.

Phenomenon/objects are characterized by a set of n attributes (variables, features), and results of their measurements (observations) on all m objects are organized as $m \times n$ data matrix X, (Nermend, 2009):

$$X = \begin{bmatrix} x_1 & x_2 & \cdots & x_k & \cdots & x_n \\ 1 & 1 & & 1 & & 1 \\ x_1 & x_2 & \cdots & x_k & \cdots & x_n \\ 2 & 2 & & 2 & & 2 \\ \cdots & \cdots & \cdots & \cdots & \cdots & \cdots \\ x_1 & x_2 & \cdots & x_k & \cdots & x_n \\ i & i & & i & & i \\ \cdots & \cdots & \cdots & \cdots & \cdots & \cdots \\ x_1 & x_2 & \cdots & x_k & \cdots & x_n \\ m & m & & m & & m \end{bmatrix}$$

where:

m - number of objects

n - number of variables

xij – value of i-th variable for the j-th object

2. Elimination of variables

Step comprises assessment of individual variable usefulness based on its variability. Elimination of variables is usually performed by using significance coefficient characteristics, (Nermend, 2009):

$$v_{x_i} = \frac{\sigma_i}{\bar{x}_i}$$

where:

x_i = the i-th variable

σ_i – standard deviation of the i-th variable

$\bar{x}_i$ – mean value of the i-th variable

Nermend was specified that the variables whose significance factors values are within the <-1, 1> range constitute the quasi-constant variables (Nermend, 2009). Such variables should be eliminated from the set of variables under consideration.

3. Normalisation of variables

Variables used in the studies are heterogeneous; in fact they describe different properties of objects. For this reason, the step to be performed in constructing the synthetic measure is to normalize the variables. This process not only leads to the elimination of units of measurement but also to the Normalisation of variable values. They can be illustrated in various units of measure, which additionally hinders any arithmetical calculations that are necessary for individual procedures. The next necessary stage of constructing the development measure is variable Normalisation. This process leads not only to the elimination of the measurement units but also to the equalization of the variable values. The process ends when the statistical mean (μ) (here it is, and it is the first step) of all values in one column is made equal to zero, and the standard deviation (σ) equals one x.

Several techniques can be used to or normalize or standardize variables (Freudenberg, 2003):

a) *Standardization (or z-scores), Standard deviation from the mean*, which is imposes a standard normal distribution (i.e. a mean of 0 and a standard deviation of 1). Thus, positive (negative) values of a given indicator indicate above (below)-average performance:

$$y_{ij} = \frac{x_{ij} - \bar{x}_j}{\sigma_j}$$

where:

y_{ij} – standardized j variable for i-th object (so called z-score)

x_{ij} – original j-th variable value for object i-th

$\bar{x}_j$ – mean value of variable j

σ_j – standard deviation of variable j

b) *Distance from the group leader*, which assigns 100 to the leading (maximum) variable and other variables are ranked as percentage points away from the leader:

$$\gamma_{ij} = \frac{x_{ij}}{\max (x_{ij})} \times 100$$

max *(xj)* maximum value of variable j-th,

c) *Distance from the mean*, where the (weighted or unweight) mean value is given 100, and variables receive scores depending on their distance from the mean. Values higher than 100 indicate above-average performance:

$$y_{ij} = \frac{x_{ij}}{\bar{x}_j} \times 100$$

d) *Re-scaling (distance from the best and worst performers),* where positioning is in relation to the global maximum and minimum, and the index takes values between 0 (laggard) and 100 (leader):

$$y_{ij} = \frac{x_{ij} - \min(x_j)}{\max(x_j) - \min(x_j)} \times 100$$

where:

x_{ij} = each indicator for variable i *(i= 1,2,...,n)* and country j *(j = 1,2,...,m)*

$\min_j (x_j)$ = minimum value of x_{ij} across all countries j *(j = 1,2,...,m)*

$\max_j (x_j)$ = maximum value of x_{ij} across all countries j *(j = 1,2,...,m)*

n= number of variables

m= number of countries

Here standardization is based on the range rather than the standard deviation, and these extreme values (the minimum and maximum) may be unreliable outliers.

e) *Categorical scale,* where each variable is assigned a score (either numerical such as between $[1...k]$, $k>1$, or qualitative - high, medium, low) depending on whether its value is above or below a threshold.

f) *Ranking,* this simply ranks each object on each of the variables:

$$y_{ij} = rank(x_{ij})$$

where: *yij* is the transformed variable of *xij* for variable *j-th* for object *i-th*

The ranking is based on ordinal levels so the main disadvantage is the loss of absolute level information. It does not allow conclusions to be drawn about the difference in performance between the objects being evaluated, as there is no measure of the distance between the values of the ranking indicator.

g) *Number of variables above the mean minus number below the mean;* this method defines an arbitrary threshold around the mean and takes the difference between the number of indicators above and below the mean. The main drawback is the loss of interval level information, as units will be assigned as being above/below average regardless of how much better/worse they are. This may be applied as follows:

$$y_{ij} = \frac{x_{ij}}{\bar{x}_j} - (1 + p)$$

where: p is an arbitrary threshold above and below the mean.

h) *Percentage of annual differences over time;* The approach taken in this method is to use the values of the indicators of the preceding year are taken and standardized

$$y_{ij}^t = \frac{x_{ij}^t - x_{ij}^{t-1}}{x_{ij}^t}$$

where: t indexes time. The value assigned to each variable is the difference in the value between the current year and the previous year, divided by the value at the previous year.

The standard deviation approach (z-score) is the most common because of the presence of many of the desirable characteristics when it comes to collect variables, note that each method has its advantages and disadvantages. It converts all variables to a common scale and assumes a "normal" distribution; it has an average of zero, meaning it avoids introducing aggregation distortions stemming from differences in variable means. In the other approaches, the scaling factor is the range of the distribution, rather than the standard deviation so that extreme values can have a large effect on the composite index. Categorical scales have high subjectivity as the scale, and the thresholds are by and large determined arbitrarily. Such ranking also approaches omit a great deal of information on the amount of variance between variables.

4. Determination of the pattern and anti-pattern

After normalizing of the variables, the next step is the design of the pattern of development. Collected variables are divided into stimulants and destimulants (Hellwig, 1968). The criterion of the division is the impact of each of the selected variables on the level of development of the units. Variables, with a positive, stimulating effect on the level of units, are called stimulants, as opposed to inhibitory variables, or so-called destimulants. Sometimes the optimal level of development for a given variable is achieved, which is then called the nominate. In the Hellwig's measure, a pattern is defined on the basis of the values of variables. The coordinates of the pattern in Hellwig's measure are defined as the maximum value of stimulants and a minimum value of destimulants. The nominate are usually transformed into stimulants or destimulants. In vector measures, the position of the pattern is not important but the direction (vector) indicating positions of the best objects. The direction is determined based on the pattern that is characterized by high values of both stimulants and destimulants. Anti-pattern and pattern can be selected as real objects. It is also possible to automatically determine both the pattern and the anti-pattern based on the first and the third quartile of input data (Nermend, 2009). At the same time, variables for stimulants in the third quartile and variables for destimulants in the first quartile are considered to be the coordinates of the pattern:

$$y_{w,j} = \begin{cases} q_{3,j} & \text{for stimulants} \\ q_{1,j} & \text{for destimulants} \end{cases}$$

where:

$y_{w,j}$ – coordinate j of pattern vector,

$q_{3,j}$ - coordinate j of the 3th quartile,

$q_{1,j}$ - coordinate j of the 1st quartile.

In the case of an anti-pattern, the procedure is reversed. To achieve more accurate, the values of the stimulants from the first quartile and the values of destimulants from the third quartile should constitute the coordinates of the anti-pattern:

$$y_{aw,j} = \begin{cases} q_{1,j} & \text{for stimulants} \\ q_{3,j} & \text{for destimulants} \end{cases}$$

$y_{aw,j}$ – coordinate j of anti-pattern

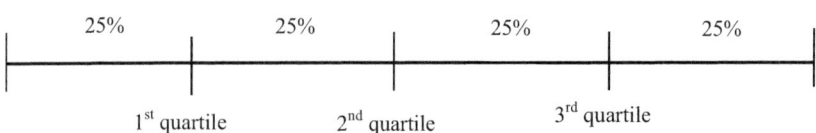

Figure 2-2. Location of quartiles in the set of all observations

Source: Dodge, Y.; The concise encyclopaedia of statistics, Springer Science & Business Media (2008)

Quartiles are location measures of a distribution of observations. Quartiles separate a distribution into four parts. There are three quartiles for a given distribution. Between each quartile, we find 25 percent of the total observations (see Figure 2-2).

Note that the second quartile equals the median. When we have all the observations, quartiles are calculated:

- the n observations must be arranged in the form of a frequency distribution;
- quartiles correspond to observations for which the relative cumulated frequency exceeds 25 percent, 50 percent, and 75 percent.

Computation of jth quartile:

Let i be the integer part of $j \cdot (n+1)$ 4 and k the fraction part of $j \cdot (n+1)$ 4,

Let xi and $xi+1$ be the values of the observations respectively in the ith and $(i + 1)$ th position (when the observations are arranged in increasing order). The jth quartile is:

$$Qj = xi + k \cdot (xi+1 - xi)$$

The patterns specified in this way are insensitive to the values of variables in irregular objects. As opposed to the measure submitted by Zdzisław Hellwig (1968), they are not ideal objects to which other items should drift. They only provide direction in which all the objects should evolve. Another way of determining this direction could also adopt a real object as both the pattern and anti-pattern. Importantly enough, those need not be the best, and the worst objects – suitable proportions of the variables should simply characterize them.

5. Determining the synthetic measure

In the vector space, the values of the variables in the examined objects are interpreted as coordinates of the vectors. Each object represents a specific direction in space. The difference in pattern and anti-pattern is also a vector designating the direction in space. Along this direction, the value of the synthetic measure is calculated for each object. This measure could be seen as a one-dimensional coordinate system. Given this, the process of determining the measure becomes the process of determining the coordinate in the coordinates system, which can be shown through the formula (Nermend, 2006; Nermend , 2007):

$$m_i = \frac{\sum_{j=1}^{n}(y_{ij} - y_{aw,j})(y_{w,j} - y_{aw,j})}{\sum_{i=1}^{n}(y_{w,j} - y_{aw,j})^2}$$

where:

m_i – synthetic measure of object i,

y_{ij} – coordinate j of object i

$y_{w,j}$ – coordinate j of pattern vector,

$y_{aw,j}$ – coordinate j of anti - pattern.

For the measure constructed in such a way, all objects, which are better than the anti-pattern and worse than the pattern, will be characterized by the value of measure ranging from zero to 100. Hence, the pattern will have the value of a measure equal 100 while the anti-pattern equal zero. It is feasible to determine the values of measurement in objects, which are better than the pattern. They will have a value of measure greater than 100. Objects that are worse than the anti-pattern will have a negative value. One can easily determine the object's position in the ranking, referring to the pattern and the anti-pattern.

2.3.2. Synthetic Measure Using PCA Method

Karl Pearson is the first who introduce the Principal component analyses (PCA analyses) in early 1900 (Hardy & Magnello, 2002). Formal treatment of the method is due to Hotelling (1933) and Rao (1964). The principal component is called a linear combination of original variables; the goal of using it is to describe the objects of investigation. Principal component looks several linear combinations that can summarize the data, and losing little information as possible. A detailed description of PCA analyses contains e.g. (Mardia, T, & Bibby, 1979; Chen, Chong, & She, 2014). The Principal Components Analyses (PCA) is one of the most popular statistical tools available to reduce the dimensions of a set of data because it is relatively simple regarding computation and to understand. The main objective of principal components analyses is to reveal hidden structure in a data set. It is done through identify how different variables work together, decrease the dimensionality and the redundancy in the data, and compress and filter the data, prepare the data for further analyses using other techniques.

The transformation means that the new variables are uncorrelated. The first principal component PC1 is the normalized linear combination of the x variables with maximum variance; while the second principal component PC2 is the normalized linear combination having maximum variance out of all linear combinations uncorrelated with $v1$; and so on. It is better to be the first few components account for a large proportion of the variance of the original variables. From the practical side, principle components can be found by computing the singular value decomposition of the data matrix.

There is a geometrical interpretation of PCA. PCA is performed in two steps. In the first step the data matrix is centered, it is the origin of the coordinate system is moved to the centroid (mean value) of the data matrix. In the second step, the coordinate system turns around its origin. That mean value of the sum of squares of all data points projections on the first axis will be maximized (projections are maximally spread along the first coordinate axis) – the second axis is orthogonal to the first one, and also has the maximal spread of projected data point, etc. Figure 2-3 illustrated that.

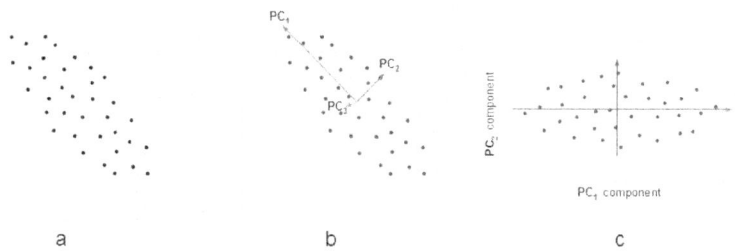

a   b   c

Figure 2-3. Illustration of the geometrical meaning of principal component analyses

a) Scatterplot of original 3D data, b) orthogonal coordinate system moved to the centroid of data and then rotated to have first axis along maximal spread of data, second axis orthogonal to first and having maximal spread of data, etc. c) Spread of data along first two principal component axes.

Source: author's elaboration.

The Figure 2-3 illustrates the derivation of first principal component axis geometrically. After moving the origin of the coordinate system to data centroid, we seek such axis emanating from this origin. The mean value of sum of squares of data points projections on this axis is maximal (average of sum of squares of length of segment *OP1, OP2*, etc. is maximal, or, the mean value of sum of squares of orthogonal distance from data points *P1, P2*, etc. -red segments *V1, V2*, etc.- is minimal). For *m* points in *n*-dimensional space (data matrix *X* of size *m x n*) these two steps can be expressed algebraically:

Centred data matrix: $Xc = X - 1c$, where 1 is a column vector of *n* ones, *c* is a vector of data mean value.

First axis direction: let first axis be determined by unit vector *a*,

Figure 2-4, illustrate that, directed so that mean value of the sum of squares of all data points projections on axis a be a maximum: $(Xca)T(Xca)/m \rightarrow$ max, under the constraint $aTa = 1$ (vector a of unit length). These leads to classical Eigen problem: $(1/m)\ XcTXca = \lambda a$, where λ is eigenvalue. Next unit vectors defining the other coordinate system axes are derived analogously: mean value of the sum of squared projections on these axes should be maximal, under the constraint these vectors are of unit length and orthogonal to all previously determined vectors.

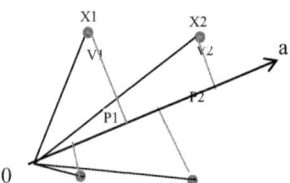

Figure 2-4.Geometrical interpretation of derivation of the first axis of principal component

Source: Author's elaboration.

These procedures have some important consequences: the first axis is the most important, as running along the direction of biggest spread of the data, and this importance equals the biggest eigenvalue of matrix $(1/m)XcTXc$. The second axis is along the biggest data spread in a direction orthogonal to the first axis, etc. It means that data can be represented with little loss of information about their relative position, in a coordinate system built from a few first principal component axes. Because "importance" of these axes is measured by the values of their corresponding eigenvalues, we have the control of how much information about the spread of data will be retained in chosen number of axes – for reduction of data dimensionality.

In some applications, the principal components are an end of the applications and may be open to interpretation. Note, that elements of loading vector are the coefficients of linear combination used to determine the principal components:

$$pc = w_1 x_1 + w_2 x_2 + ... + w_n x_n$$

where:
pc is a principal component,

w_i is *i-th* element of loading vector[*]

x_i is *i-th* variable

Also, their value *wi* is a measure of *xi* variable "importance" in determining the principal component. In this way, we can assess which variable have the biggest influence on the principal component, and with negligible influence.

2.3.3. TOPSIS Method

The technique for order preference by similarity to an ideal solution (TOPSIS) system is a numerous criteria technique to recognize arrangements from a limited arrangement of choices. The essential guideline is that the chosen alternative should have the farthest distance from the negative ideal solution and the shortest distance from the positive ideal solution. The system of TOPSIS can be communicated in an arrangement of steps (Jahanshahloo, F, & Izadikhah, 2006):

(1)   Calculate the normalized choice matrix. The normalized quality n_{ij} is given as:

$$n_{ij} = x_{ij} / \sqrt{\sum_{i=1}^{m} x_{ij}^2}, \quad i=1,......,m, \quad j=1,.....n.$$

(2) Calculate the weighted normalized choice matrix. The weighted normalized quality *vij* is given as:

$$vij = wjnij; \quad i = 1; ... ; m; \quad j = 1; ... ; n;$$

where: *wj* is the weight of the *ith* attribute or criterion, and $\sum_{j=1}^{n} w_j = 1$

(3) Determine the negative and positive perfect arrangement

$$A^+ = \{v_1^+, ..., v_n^+\} = \{(max_j \ v_{ij} | i \in i), (min_j \ v_{ij} | i \in j)\}$$
$$A^- = \{v_1^-, ..., v_n^-\} = \{(min_j \ v_{ij} | i \in i), (max_j \ v_{ij} | i \in j)\}$$

where: i is associated with benefit criteria, and j is associated with cost criteria.

(4) Calculate the separation measures, using the n-dimensional Euclidean distance. The separation of every option from the perfect solution is computed as

---

[*] Loading vector: coordinates of the new axis showing the relations between original coordinate and new ones. How important and original data in a creation of new data.

$$d_i^+ = \left\{ \textstyle\sum_{j=1}^{n}(v_{ij} - v_j^+)^2 \right\}^{\frac{1}{2}} \quad i=1\ .....,m$$

Similarly, the separation from the negative ideal solution is calculated as

$$d_i^- = \left\{ \textstyle\sum_{j=1}^{n}(v_{ij} - v_j^-)^2 \right\}^{\frac{1}{2}} \quad i=1\ .....,m$$

(5) Calculate the relative closeness to the perfect arrangement. The relative closeness of the option Ai as for $A+$ is defined as:

$$R_i = d_i^- /(d_i^+ + d_i^-), \quad i = 1 .....,m$$

since $d_i^- \geq 0$ and $d_i^+ \geq 0$ then, clearly, $Ri \in [0, 1]$.

(6) Rank the preference order. For ranking alternatives using this index, we can rank alternatives in decreasing order.

The essential rule of the TOPSIS technique is that the picked option ought to have the "briefest separation" from the positive perfect arrangement and the "most remote separation" from the negative perfect arrangement. The TOPSIS strategy presents two "reference" focuses, yet it does not consider the relative significance of the distances from these focuses.

There are two primary disadvantages to TOPSIS system (Mohammed, Hazem A, & Ayman M, 2013, p. 6467). The main con of this system is the operation of the normalized choice matrix. The normalized scale for each criterion is usually derived a narrow gap among the performed measures. A limited gap in the TOPSIS method is not good for ranking and cannot reflect the true dominance of alternatives. The second con is that we never considered the danger evaluation for a decision maker in the TOPSIS method. As per danger propensity, it has been regularly watched that decision makers differ in that willingness to overestimate the probability of a gain or loss, the danger attitudes for a decision maker is typically categorized as risk seeking, risk-neutral, and risk-averse. Without considering risk propensity, the subjective propensity associated with different decision maker preference cannot be resolved

CHAPTER THREE: Investment Specificity in Arab Countries

The terms *Arab countries, homeland Arab, Arab nation, Arab region*, and *Arab world* * all refer to the 22 countries where Arabic is spoken and which comprise the Arab League (Elbadawi, 2004). The Arab countries are bordered by Morocco and the Mediterranean Sea in the north, Mauritania and the Atlantic Ocean to the west, the Arabian Sea in the east, and the Indian Ocean and Horn of Africa in the south (Alzahrani, et al., 2013).

Most Arab countries confront several economic problems; the most important of which are low development and domestic savings rate, which lead to limited investment. That is due to the low-income level that limits both individual and national savings. Other factors, like wealth and interest rates, have also led to low savings rates. The determinants of non-savings income, like the tax revenues, inflation, export earnings, external financing, and political, and social factors, have also worked to reduce savings. Despite the multiplicity of channels for amassing domestic savings, the overall investments that can be funded from those savings remain low. This fact has forced many of these countries to seek external sources of alternative funding, including external borrowing, international aid, and foreign direct investment.

3.1. Culture and Economic Geography in Arab Countries

The Arab Region is linking three continents of Asia, Europe and Africa (Mirkin, 2010, p. 7). Throughout history, Arab countries have been united by several common factors, including (Alfra', 2003):

- the continuity of Arab land, which has virtually no natural barriers to mobility and communication among Arab populations,
- a range of climatic zones within the tropical context which led to a diversity of plants and crops,
- a common culture,
- religious similarities, with Islam as the majority religion and Christianity occupying second place in the number of followers,
- the Arabic language.

However, these similarities do not prevent Arab countries from differing widely in other ways, such as the nature and size of economies, populations, natural resources, economic progress, and

---

* The Arab world is; the term used by the World Bank.

other important factors. The Arab world has become the major urban zone in developing countries (Smith, 2011).

In March 1945, a group of six countries (Saudi Arabia, Lebanon, Iraq, Jordan, Syria, and Egypt) agreed to establish the Arab League with the ultimate goal of creating a single Arab country (Pinfari, 2009). The Arab League now includes 22 Arab countries (Palestinian Territory, Iraq, Egypt, Libya, Oman, Syria, Morocco, Tunisia, Mauritania, Lebanon, United Arab Emirates (UAE), Sudan, Jordan, Comoros, Djibouti, Algeria, Yemen, Qatar, Somalia, Bahrain, Kuwait, and Saudi Arabia) (Al'tby, 2010).

The total area of the Arab countries is about 14.2 million square kilometers or just 10 percent of the Earth's area. The Arab world features several religion and ethnicities like Coptic Christians, Shiites, Kurds, Africans, Jews, Berbers, etc. (Puschmann & Matthijs, 2012, p. 5).
The phrase "Arab" more often referrs to the phrase the Middle East. It includes; Kuwait, Bahrain, Iran, Cyprus, Iraq, Lebanon, Palestinian, Sudan, Qatar, Syria, Oman, Saudi Arabia, Turkey, Jordan, Algeria, Egypt, United Arab Emirates, Morocco, Libya, Mauritania Tunisia and Yemen (Özalp, 2011, p. 10). Lebanon is the smallest Arab country with area 10,452 square kilometers while Bahrain with the area 665 square km is the smallest island in the Arab country. The area of Algeria is the largest geographic area of the Arab League and the African continent with 2.4 million square kilometers (Arab Monetary Fund, 2010, p. 3).

Arab countries have a combined population of around 355 million people, according to 2010 data, with a density of up to 27 people per square kilometers. In the Arab world, about 55 percent is below age 25 (Dubai Press Club, 2010, p. 15). In 1996, the population was only 261 million people. This indicates a high mean growth rate estimated at 2.4 percent annually and higher than the global growth rate, which is estimated at 1.7 percent. Distribution of population in Arab homeland is as follows (Arab Monetary Fund, 2011);

- Egypt is the most populated Arab country, with 22 percent of the population of the Arab world at 76 million people, according to 2010 data,
- four countries range in population between 28 and 43 million people (Saudi Arabia, Algeria, Sudan, and Iraq),
- three countries have a population between 10 and 20 million people (Tunisia, Somalia, and Syria),
- Jordan, the UAE, and Libya have between 5 and 10 million people,

- several countries have one to five million people (Bahrain, Oman, Kuwait, Mauritania, Lebanon, and Palestine),
- two countries have less than one million people (Qatar, Djibouti).

The geographical distribution of Arab labor in 2010 revealed that about 57.4 percent of the total Arab workforce surplus is centered in five countries. The Arab total workforce was about 135 million workers in 2009, with half-concentrated in Lebanon, Egypt, Syria, Jordan, Morocco, and Tunisia (Chaaban, Jad, 2010). The agricultural sector is the major employer in poor Arab countries with about 25.4 percent of labour force work in agriculture (The Arab Fund for Economic and Social Development, 2010). There are about 10 million jobs in this sector in the Arab world (Abaza, Saab, & Zeitoon, 2011). The main rivers of the Arab are the Tigris, Euphrates, and the Nile. Which supplies water to Iraq, Syria, Sudan and Egypt, The Arab region is considered arid, but rainfall varies widely from an average annual rainfall of only 51 mm in Egypt to 660 mm in Lebanon (Moore, Galli, & Wackernagel, 2012, p. 24).

Arab countries suffer from high rates of unemployment, reaching about 14.5 percent in 2008, which is the latest year for which data is available to all the Arab countries (Arab Labor Organization, 2014). The rate was less than 12 percent during the 1990s (United Nations, 2011, p. 40). The reasons for the increase are population growth and the weakness of economic efficiency in Arab countries on the one hand (Economic Research Department, 2013, p. 12), and an imbalance between demand and supply in the labor market on the other (Arab Labor Organization, 2012, p. 7).

In the Arab world, there are many economic and political organizations beyond the Arab League, such as the Gulf Cooperation Council (GCC), comprising the countries of the Arab Gulf*, and the Union of the Arab Maghreb (UMA) (Safi, 2012). There are several establishments and economic unions such as Arab Economic Unity Council, the Arab Organization for Agricultural Development, the Organization of Arab Petroleum Exporting Countries (OAPEC), the Arab Labor Organization, and the Arab Organization for Industrial Development and Mining. In addition, there are many Arab finance institutions like Arab Authority for Agricultural Investment and Development, Arab Bank for Economic Development in Africa, Establishment Arab Investment Guarantee Corporation and Export Credit, the Arab Fund for Economic and

---

* In many sources, it is the Persian Gulf; it is located in Western Asia between Iran to the northeast and the Arabian Peninsula to the southwest. The Persian Gulf is an extension of the Indian Ocean (Gulf of Oman) through the Strait of Hormuz.

Social Development, and Arab Monetary Fund (Arab Organizations and Unions Administration - Economic Affairs, 2013).

All Arab countries are considered developing countries according to the World Bank's classification of GNI of each Arab country. Below are the classifications of Arab countries by different organizations:

1. The Human Development Index (HDI), published by the United Nations Development Program (UNDP) ranks countries into three categories according to the indicators of education, income, and life expectancy. Countries with an index equal to or above 0.8 are classified as *High Human Development* countries. The group of *Medium-Human Development* countries has HDI score between 0.5 and 0.799. If HDI is below 0.5, that country is classified as a *Low Human Development* country. The 1994 and 1997 reports classified Arab countries as follows (United Nations, 1997; United Nations, 1994; Limam, 1998; Nielsen, 2011):

   - the UAE, Qatar, Libya, and Bahrain have high human development,
   - Egypt, Oman, Tunisia, Syria, Morocco, Iraq, Algeria, Jordan, Saudi Arabia, and Lebanon have medium human development,
   - Yemen, Mauritania, Sudan, Comoros, and Djibouti have low human development.

2. The Arab-Joint Report 2011 on poverty in Arab countries classified them into three groups based on the share of the poor citizens in the total population, according to the available surveys on household income. The first group, with poverty levels of over 40 percent, comprises Yemen, Mauritania, Palestine, Somalia, Sudan, Djibouti, and the Comoros. The second group with poverty levels ranging from 10-25 percent comprises Bahrain, Syria, Jordan, Egypt, and Iraq. The final group, with poverty levels below 10 percent, is Tunisia, Algeria, Lebanon, and Morocco, as well to the GCC countries, for which no comparable data are available (Arab Monetary Fund, 2011, p. 7).

3. The United Nations classified the Arab countries into three groups, GCC Gulf Cooperation Council Countries namely Kuwait, Qatar, Oman, United Arab Emirates, Saudi Arabia, and Bahrain. Another group is the least developed countries, which includes Mauritania, Comoros, Djibouti, Somalia, Sudan, and Yemen. A third group includes the most diversified economies, i.e.: Palestinian Territory, Algeria, Egypt, Jordan, Libyan, Tunisia, Morocco, Iraq, Lebanon, Syria (UNCTAD, 2011b).

4. The Arab Investment and Export Credit Guarantee Corporation Establishment classified the Arab countries into four groups; First group is the GCC countries. A second group is the Levant or Arab Mashreq countries: which comprises Iraq, Egypt, Lebanon, and Jordan. The third group is the Maghreb countries grouping Libya, Morocco, Algeria, and Tunisia. The last group is the Low FDI performance countries: this is the only non-geographic category, which groups together Mauritania, Sudan, Syria, and Yemen (Arab Investment and Export Credit Guarantee Corporation, 2012-2013).

5. The World Bank defines Sudan, Iraq, Algeria, Somalia, and Yemen as middle-income countries; Bahrain, Kuwait, Oman, United Arab Emirates, Qatar, and Saudi Arabia as high-income countries; and the other are classified as low-income level countries (Maystadt, Trinh Tan, & Breisinger, 2012).

6. Some policy-makers and scholars often divide Arab countries into four sub-groups based largely on trade policy and location. These categories include first the Maghreb countries (Morocco, Algeria, Mauritania, Libya, and Tunisia). Second the Mashreq countries (Iraq, Egypt, Lebanon, Jordan, and Syria). Third the GCC countries (Qatar, Bahrain, Saudi Arabia, Oman, Kuwait, and the United Arab Emirates (UAE)). Fourth the "other" countries (Sudan, Somalia, Djibouti, and Yemen) (Gendrano, 2007, p. 7).

7. Some economic research are classifying Arab countries into four groups: mixed oil producers including Algeria, Libya, and Iraq; diversified economies including Egypt, Syria, Jordan, Lebanon, Morocco, and Tunisia; Gulf Cooperation Council (GCC) and, primary producers[**] (PP) including Comoros, Mauritania, Sudan, Djibouti and Yemen (Ali, 2001, pp. 2-3).

Many mineral resources are available in the Arab world, and the most important are oil and gas. Global production of crude oil is about 72.1 million barrels per day in 2010, while the production of Arab countries was 21.2 million barrels per day during the same year, which about 29.4 percent of total production in the world in 2010. The reserves of Arab countries constitute about 57.5 percent of all the world reserves according to 2010 data (OPEC, 2011). The most important economy activities and industries in the Arab countries are the fertilizer, cement, iron, zinc, lead, copper, and coal. These industries have contributed to the increase in the value-added sector of the extractive industries in GDP from US $ 439 million in 2005 to US $ 719 million in 2010.

[**]Primary producing countries are usually classified into two subgroups a group of mineral economies and group composed of agricultural, fishing, forestry, and hunting countries.

The added value of manufacturing sector rose "either " from US $ 110 million in 2005, to US $ 188 million in 2010 (Arab Monetary Fund, 2010, p. 323; Arab Monetary Fund, 2006, p. 62).

Also, the industry is based on the agricultural sector output, as the sugar industry, vegetable oils industry, textile industry, etc. Arab countries have a large share in the International trade of certain crops, like long-staple cotton, dates, Arabic gum, grapes, and olives. Agriculture contributes significantly to the national income in some Arab countries, and the agricultural cultivable land area is about 68.8 million hectares[*] in all Arab countries. The contribution of the agricultural sector in GDP rose to 6.2 percent in 2010 compared with 6.1 percent in 2005 (Arab Monetary Fund, 2011). The share of the agricultural export in the all agricultural intra-trade reached about 21.7 percent of 2010. The share of agricultural import within the trade of agricultural products was up to 20.6 percent in 2010 (Said & Shelaby, 2014, p. 134).

The production of cereals in Arab countries rose from 37606 thousand ton in 2005 to 49702 thousand ton in 2010. The Arab Joint Report 2011 refers that the production of pulses increases from 1255 thousand ton in 2005 to 1353 thousand ton in 2010. The production of vegetables in Arab countries as well rose from 39164 thousand ton in 2005 to 56789 thousand ton in 2010. The fruit production in the Arab countries was 31516 thousand tons in 2010compared to 27367 thousand tons in 2005. As well, the production of sugar cane increased from 22897 thousand ton in 2005 to 23346 thousand ton in 2010. Also, sugar beets production increased from 7325 thousand ton in 2005 to 9080 thousand ton in 2010 (Arab Monetary Fund, 2011, p. 67).

Fisheries and Livestock are important sources of national income for many of the Arab countries. The production of red meat was 4.9 million tons in 2010. The Arab world has a long seacoast and many of fresh and salt lakes, which are all suitable for breeding fish, where the production of fish was 4.0 million tons in 2010 (Arab Monetary Fund, 2011, p. 69).

---

[*]The hectare is a metric unit of area defined as 10,000 square meters (100 m by 100 m, 0.01 square kilometres), and primarily used in the measurement of land.

Table 3-1. Summary Indicators in the Arab Countries 2005-2010

Year/ Indicator	2005	2006	2007	2008	2009	2010
GDP at Current Market Prices(US $Million)	1 099 541	1 307 356	1 504 657	1 898 619	1 743 251	2 027 293
Population (Thousand Person)	311 595	318 945	326 731	334 500	346 241	355 167
Public Revenues and Grants (US $ Million)	421 015	526 857	580 374	854 873	596 178	707 054
Official Foreign Reserves (US $ Million)	250 315	328 455	752 399	918 437	924 519	1 008 261
Agricultural Production (US $ Million)	70 479	81 212	90 526	103 385	113 158	124 493
Total Export(US $ Million)	559 611	680 960	792 287	1 049 816	722 331	904 497
Total Import(US $ Million)	348 871	400 559	530 733	701 616	594 336	655 213
Agricultural Export (US $ Million)	11 184	11 840	13 602	11 019	16 903	17 781
Agricultural Import (US $ Million)	39 258	41 959	50 578	60 172	66 664	76 343
Oil Reserves (Billion barrels)	664.49	668.43	669.70	672.08	683.66	683.66
Crude Oil Price (US $)	50.6	61.1	69.1	94.4	61.0	77.4
Crude Oil Production (Thousand b/d)	22 734	23 073	22 340	23 719	21 121	21 217
Natural Gas Reserves (Billion cubic meters)	53 334	53 574	53 594	53 717	54 526	54 806
Marketed Natural Gas (Billion cubic meters)	364	393	404	433	435	435

Source: Author's elaboration according to the (Arab Monetary Fund, 2006; Arab Monetary Fund, 2010; Arab Monetary Fund, 2011; Arab Monetary Fund, 2012; Arab Monetary Fund, 2013).

In 2010, the total reserve of the crude oil in the Arab world was about 43.2 percent of world reserves. In the Arab world, a large natural gas reserves amounted to about 26.3 percent of the total world reserves (Fattouh & El-Katiri, 2012, p. 10). The production of the crude steel in the Arab countries amounted to 19 million tons in 2010 (Lachgar, 2011, p. 2). The Table 3-1 shows summary indicators in the Arab countries for the period 2005-2010.

There are common factors among the Arab countries, and there is the advantage of the characteristics of each country on the other. We were planning to include in our study all the twenty-two Arab countries. However, due to the lack of sufficient data or some data were provided from unreliable sources we focused on the 13 following countries only: Algeria, Bahrain, Egypt, Iraq, Jordan, Kuwait, Lebanon, Morocco, Oman, Qatar, Saudi Arabia, Tunisia, and United Arab Emirates (UAE). Below we will refer to the characteristics of each country briefly:

- *Algeria*

Algeria is the second-largest country in Africa and the 10th largest in the world. Its population of approximately 37 million is made up primarily of Arab-Berbers according to the 2010 census (Economic and Social Commission for Western Asia). The borders of Algeria, Niger, and Mali are from the south, Mauritania and Morocco to the west, Libya, and Tunisia to the east; the north overlooks the Mediterranean Sea. Its capital is Algiers. Algeria has large oil and natural gas reserves. Algeria is the fourth-largest gas producer in the world, and the eighth in the world in natural gas reserves amounting to 159 trillion cubic feet (Tcf is a volume measurement used by the oil and gas industry, a trillion cubic feet (1,000,000,000,000 cubic feet)) (Layachi, 2013). The budget of Algeria revenues depends on oil and gas revenues, which contributes for two-thirds of the budget revenues in 2010, and about 98 percent of total exports in 2010 (Alonso-Gamo & Marston, 2010). The total oil reserves in Algeria were about 12.2 billion barrels in 2010, while crude oil production was 1.19 million b/d (OPEC, 2011). By attracting more foreign direct investments, Algeria is trying to increase the production capacity of crude oil (Business Monitor International, 2010). The contribution of the agricultural sector, with only - 8 percent of the gross domestic product (GDP) cannot meet the food needs of the country's population (Federal Research Division, 2008).

- **Bahrain**

The Kingdom of Bahrain is a small country on the Arabian Gulf, and one of the Gulf Cooperation Council countries. Its capital is Bahrain. Bahrain has a population of 1.26 million people, according to the 2010 census (Economic and Social Commission for Western Asia). Bahrain depends largely on oil. In 2010 GDP at current prices was 8245.6 million Bahrain dinars (one US $= 0.376 Bahrain Dinar) (Central Bank of Bahrain, 2010, pp. 79-80). The gas amounted about 44 percent of GDP in 2010 (Bahrain Economic Development Board, 2013, p. 9). In 2010, GDP grew by 4.5 percent, due to the construction expansion by 3.2 percent, finance by 5.2 percent, and manufacturing by 7.5 percent (Bahrain Economic Development Board, 2010). Industries like aluminum production, financing, and construction their contribution are less in GDP.

- *Egypt*

Egypt's geographical location between Asia and Africa plays a big role in the trade exchange between Arab countries that are located in the two continents. Egypt population in 2000 was almost 70 million. In 2010, the population of Egypt was 82 million people. United Nations Projections suggest that the population will exceed 127 million by 2050 (R.Weeks, Getis, Hill, Gadalla, & Rashed, 2004). Its capital is Cairo. Egypt is bordered by Sudan, the Gulf of Aqaba, Palestine, the Mediterranean Sea, Libya, and the Red Sea. In Egypt Nile River, begins near the equator in Africa, inflows north to the Mediterranean Sea. Egypt is unique among developing countries; it is completely dependent on irrigation systems. Egypt depends on the limited water capacity of the Nile River to expand the land used for agriculture (Robinson & Gehlhar, 1995, p. 1). Agricultural is the mainstay of the national economy of Egypt, where the total area of agricultural land is now 8.6 million hectares, about 3.5 percent of the total area of Egypt (El-Gindy, 2011). In Egypt, work in the agricultural sector represents about 35 percent of the labour force (Karimi, Molden, Notenbaert, & Peden, 2012, p. 143). GDP in 2010 amounted to about 1206640, billion Egyptian pounds (Egyptian pound was 5.95 US $ in 2010) (International Monetary Fund).

Livestock is important to agriculture. Also livestock and complementary products are essential part of agricultural production. The livestock share of total agricultural output is about 20 percent. Fisheries considered in Egypt are one of the most important sources of national income. Egypt has also mineral wealth like metallic minerals, metallic salts, and energy sources such as coal, oil, and stones valuable in building engineering and construction. The most important minerals in Egypt are iron, manganese, phosphate, lead, zinc, copper, gold, tin, tungsten, titanium, chromium, kaolin, coal, oil, and natural gas (Central Intelligence Agency, 2014).

OAPEC statistical refers that Egypt's proven reserves of crude oil are about 4.4 billion barrels at the end of 2010 while the volume of oil production was 554000 barrels per day in 2010. The reserves of natural gas amounted to 2.4 billion/cubic meters at the end of 2010, and gas distribution globally amounted to about 62 million/cubic meters per the same year (OAPEC). The industry also has an important contribution to the Egyptian economy, and can be classified as the food industry, textile industry, mining, petroleum, chemical industry, build materials industry, and mechanical engineering industries, electrical industries, wood, and other industries. Egypt is ranked at 11th place in the world in the production of cement (Taib, The Mineral Industry of Egypt, 2012a, p. 13.1). Tourism activity also is a part in the Egyptian economy; Egypt attracts tourists from around the world since ancient times. The tourism in Egypt is a part of economy, where cultural tourism impacts attract tourists, especially in winter in Upper Egypt, where there are most of the Pharaonic monuments scattered along Nile Valley and Upper, and recreation and tourism.

- *Iraq*

Iraq is located in the northeastern edge of the Arab world. Iraq area is 437 thousand square kilometers. Its capital is Baghdad. Iraq population was about 30.8 million people in 2010 with a growth rate of residential 2.9 percent (Central Department of Statistics and Information). Iraq has, mostly in the provinces of Basra and Kirkuk, an oil-rich area; where crude oil reserves proven 143.1 billion barrels in 2010, as it is Iraq's oil reserves from the top countries in the world (OPEC, 2011). Iraqi Oil Ministry confirms that about 100 billion barrels are still unexplored. The oil industry dominates the Iraqi economy. Oil contributes 60 percent of GDP, 99 percent of exports and over 90 percent of government revenue (Inter-Agency Information and Analysis Unit, 2011). Iraq used to produce about 2.46 million barrels per day of crude oil by the year 2010 (OpenOil). Iraq is ranked with this quantity as the thirteen countries in the world in oil production. It also produced natural gas, by the year 2010 about 15 billion cubic meters. This quantity makes Iraq the second among the thirty countries in the world in natural gas production. Iraq has large reserves of natural gas what makes it one of the world's top ten, with 112 trillion cubic feet (Japan the Institute of Energy Economics, 2011). Approximately 70 percent of these reserves are in the province of Basra (Energy Information Administration, 2011).

The area of agricultural land in Iraq is about 13.4 million hectares; 9 million hectares are cultivated naturally (rainfall) and the rest with irrigation systems. The agricultural sector's contribution to GDP in Iraq decreased from 9 percent in 2002 to 3.6 percent in 2009 because of the war. (Lucani & Saade, 2012, p. 8). Grain crops contribute about 75 percent of the total agricultural. Wheat is an important crop, which is growing in the north; 1 million tons with natural irrigation (rainfall) and the center and south with irrigation systems, and consumed locally. The production of corn was 267000 metric tons (Schnittker & Ahmed, 2012). Rice production was over 110 thousand tons and it was concentrated in the center and south of Iraq (United States Commercial Service, 2012, p. 50). There is also growing crops like agricultural raw materials, cotton agriculture, which is used in the cloth industry. Iraq is one of the largest producers of dates but because of the wars the quantities produced and exported decreased (El-Juhany, 2010). In the period between the 1980s and mid-1990s, Iraq was the world's largest producers of dates in the world (Walsborn, 2008). Livestock in Iraq occupies third place, after Sudan and Morocco, in the production of livestock. The most important are goats, sheep, camels, and cows. Fishery is limited in Iraq; in 2010 the production was about 22.8 thousand tons (Young, 2011, p. 11).

- **Jordan**

It is officially the Kingdom of Jordan. In 2010 Jordan's population was about 6.5 million people, and about 78 percent of Jordan's population lives in the urban region (United Nations Population Division). Its capital is Amman. In Jordan, there is a best education indicator at the level of the area. Jordan is classified in the range of lower to middle-income countries, where the average per capita gross national income in 2010 was US $ 4350, and ranked 117 in the world according to the World Bank (The World Bank, 2011). In Jordan, the economy suffers from the non-availability of sufficient resources of water, oil, gas, etc., and the government's heavy reliance on foreign aid (Central Intelligence Agency). Jordan's economy is an open economy after the structural reforms undertaken by the government to trade liberalization over 15 years (Bekhet & Al-Smadi, 2015). Services sector plays an important role in the Jordanian economy, and represents about 64 percent of GDP. Jordan's economy depends mainly on trade, tourism, the pharmaceutical industry, mining, and foreign aid (Jaradat, 2010, p. 2). There are phosphate mines in the south of the kingdom, making Jordan the major producer in the Middle East, and the second-largest source of this metal in the world (Alrawashdeh, 2013, p. 191). The arable land and water resources are limited and mostly rare. Only 5 percent of lands receive sufficient rainfall to support agriculture (Elaine Denny, Donnelly, McKay, Ponte, & Uetake, 2008, p. 4).

- *Kuwait*

Kuwait is a member of the (GCC), located on the continent of Asia. In 2010 Kuwait population was 3.05 million people (Economic and Social Commission for Western Asia). Its capital is Kuwait. Kuwait is a small area but has large reserves of crude oil is estimated at 102 billion barrels (OPEC, 2011). These reserves are about 7.3 percent of world reserves. Oil sector represents about half of GDP and 93 percent of government revenue (Mobbs, 2012). Kuwait is characterized by a set of non-oil industries such as shipping and cement industry, as well as financial services. In Kuwait, there are several other financial institutions such as the Gulf Bank and Kuwait Finance House. Kuwait has the fifth-largest sovereign fund in the world, which the General Authority manages for investment (Kuwait Investment Authority).

- *Lebanon*

The Republic of Lebanon is an Arab country in the Middle East, in the southwest of the Asian continent. According to 2010 census the population of Lebanon was 4.3 million people (United Nations Population Division). Its capital is Beirut. The private sector contributes 75 percent of total demand in the economy of Lebanon with a large banking sector to support this demand. The telecommunications, banking and trade in services sectors are the main contributor to GDP in Lebanon (Mottu & Nakhle, 2010, p. 2). The GDP in Lebanon was 55965 billion Lebanese Pound (one US $ = 1500 Lebanese Pound), and the growth of GDP at prices of 2009 was 7 percent in 2010 (Kasparian, 2011, p. 11). The industrial sector contributes about 20 percent of GDP, and the most famous services and products are: banking, tourism, food processing, wine, jewelry, cement, wood and furniture products textiles, mineral and chemical products, oil refining, and metal products. The agricultural sector contributes about 4 percent of GDP, and the labour force in this sector is about 3 percent of the total workforce (European Commission, 2011, p. 25). The major agricultural products in Lebanon are olives, tomatoes, grapes, apples, vegetables, potatoes, tobacco, and citrus.

- **Morocco**

It is officially the Kingdom of Morocco. The capital is Casablanca. Morocco is on the country of Africa, borders Algeria to the east, the Mediterranean Sea to the north, Algeria, and Mauritania to the south, and the Atlantic Ocean to the west. Morocco has an area of 477 thousand square kilometers and a population of about 32 million people, according to statistics of 2010 (United Nations Population Division). Morocco's economy depends on tourism and agricultural sectors, with an estimated area of arable land in Morocco of about 95000 square kilometers. The share of the agriculture sector in the GDP decreased from 16 percent in 1998 to 12 percent in 2010 and this share differs from year to year, depending on weather, and climatic conditions (AfDB Group's Governance Strategic Framework, 2012, p. 2). The most important crops and activities are; grain (wheat, barley, maize and pulses, lentils, beans), citrus plantations marketing, growing of fruit trees, and olive trees. Morocco was the second largest exporter of citrus in the world, with production 1.4 million MT* in 2010, and export 476529 MT in the same year (Ahmed, 2010). Also, Morocco is the seventh producer of olive oil. Morocco is one of the largest producers of fish in the world, produced about 1098 thousand tons in 2010 (Arab Monetary Fund, 2010). Morocco also has some industries such as industries of sugar, canning, and fish preservation. Also, the mineral industries play a key role in Moroccan economy. Morocco phosphate production was about 27 percent of world demand in 2010. Morocco produces 14 percent of the world's production of phosphate rock, 2 percent of the world's production of cobalt, 7 percent of the world's production of barite, and 1 percent of the world's production of fluorspar (Newman, 2012, p. 30.1).

- **Oman**

Officially, it is the Sultanate of Oman. The capital is Muscat. Oman has the border with Saudi Arabia to the west and Yemen on the southwest, the United Arab Emirates in the northwest of the country. Oman is one of the Gulf Cooperation Council countries (GCC) which is the second largest country of the Council. (Bayliss Associates Pty Limited). The country has an area of

---

* MT is the symbol of tonne, a measurement of mass equal to one thousand kilograms

309.5 thousand square kilometers and a population of 2.9 million (United Nations Population Division). Oman's currency is Omani Rial.

In 2010 GDP growth in the Sultanate of Oman was 5.6 percent, which is a middle-income country and it is highly dependent on oil resources (The World Bank). The share of the oil and gas sector in nominal GDP recorded a strong growth of up to 41.2 percent in 2010, and the share of non-oil sectors grew by 11.1 percent in the same year (Central Bank of Oman, 2011). Production of oil and gas started in 1967. The oil and gas in Oman are contributed by about 85 percent of government revenues and nearly 35 percent of GDP in 2010. The Oil exports to the total exports were about 68.9 percent in 2010 (Hasan, 2012, p. 3). According to Annual report of Ministry of Oil and Gas 18 domestic and international oil companies, operated in Oman in 2010. Oman's oil reserves amounted to about 5.5 billion barrels in 2010 (Italian Multinational Oil and Gas Company, 2010, p. 8). There are many mineral resources in the Sultanate, such as dolomite, zinc, chromite, iron, limestone, gypsum, cobalt, silicon, copper, and gold. The gas reserves in Oman in 2010 were 27.97 billion cubic meters (Italian Multinational Oil and Gas Company, 2010, p. 42).

The arable land in Oman is about 15 percent of the territory of the Sultanate, only half of them are cultivated, that is over 2.3 million hectares of arable land in the Sultanate (General of Agriculture& Livestock Research, 2011). In 2010 the share of the agriculture sector in Oman was 1.2 percent of GDP. (Ministry Of Agriculture And Fisheries, 2012, p. 15). Also, Oman agriculture contributed 37 percent of all non-oil exports and employed 60 percent of the population in 2009. Oman in 2010, supplies about half of its vegetables, 71 percent of its fruits, 24 percent of its poultry, and 52 percent of its eggs (Technology Integration Division, 2012).
Oman is the leading livestock producer among the Gulf countries with a livestock such as camels and horses (Ministry Of Agriculture And Fisheries, 2012, p. 22). Other live animals are imported for consumption of their meat. In the Sultanate of Oman, there is over 94 thousand head of cattle, and three-quarters of a million goats and 148 thousand sheep and 94 thousand camels. Oman can produce half a million tons of fish per year.

- *Qatar*

Qatar is overlooking the Arabian Gulf, and is in southwest Asia in the Arabian Peninsula, and is one of the Gulf Cooperation Council (GCC) countries. Qatar has the border with the Kingdom of Saudi Arabia, the United Arab Emirates, and Bahrain. According to the 2010 census, Qatar has a population of 1.76 million people (Economic and Social Commission for Western Asia). Its capital is Doha.

Qatar is the largest exporter of natural gas in the world. The revenues of Oil and gas sector increased from 55.4 billion Qatari Riyal (QR) in 2006, to reach 96.9 QR billion in 2010 (1 QR= 0.27 US $) (Ibrahim & Harrigan, 2012, p. 16). Therefore, the GDP per capita was US $ 74621 in 2010 (Qatar Investment Fund, 2011). The natural gas sector of Qatar contributes over 58 percent of the country's gross domestic (Administration; Department, 2012, p. 4). The proven natural gas reserve in Qatar was 25.370 billion cubic meters in 2010 (European Gas Advocacy Forum, 2011). The contribution of non-mining sectors (such as petrochemicals, financial services) in real GDP rose from 53.6 percent in 2006 to 55.7 percent in 2010. Qatar produced ammonia of about 1.4 percent of the total production in the world in 2010 (Taib, The Mineral Industry of Qatar, 2011). Qatar produces some a metal included aluminum, crude steel, concrete reinforcing bar (rebar), continuous, and cast billet. Moreover, it produces industrial minerals such as urea, ammonia, lime, gypsum, sulfur, limestone, cement, and washed sand. Also, Qatar produces methanol, helium, and refined petroleum products (Taib, The Mineral Industry of Qatar, 2012b).

- *Saudi Arabia*

Officially, the Kingdom of Saudi Arabia, it is the biggest country among the Gulf Cooperation Council countries. Its capital is Riyadh. The population in Saudi Arabia is 28 million people (UNCTAD), 4.1 percent of them work in agriculture (Hartmann, Khalil, Bernet, Ruhland, & Al Ghamdi, 2012, p. 13). The Saudi Arabia area is about 2.25 million square kilometers. The Kingdom area is about 80 percent of the Arabian Peninsula area. It borders the Persian Gulf, Bahrain, the United Arab Emirates, and Qatar in the Middle; Yemen and Oman in the south and the Red Sea in the west, and with Kuwait, Jordan, and Iraq to the north. The climate in the Kingdom is desert, which is not suitable for agriculture (Baig & Al-Zaharani, 2012). For that, Saudi Arabia established investments in agricultural sectors in Sudan, Pakistan, and the Philippines, due to lack of arable area in the Saudi Arabia (House, 2013, p. 7).

Saudi Arabia has large reserves of oil, and occupies the second place in the world in this regard and occupies the sixth place in the natural gas reserves in the world. Oil exports contribute for nearly 90 percent of the total exports of Kingdom (OpenOil). The oil sector contribution to GDP in Saudi Arabia at current prices in 2010 was close to 60 percent (Fayad, Raissi, Rasmussen, & Westelius, 2012, p. 5). According to the report "Doing Business" in 2010 from the International

Finance Corporation, Saudi Arabia occupies the 13th position as the most competitive country in the world economically. (Saudi British Bank, 2010, p. 8). Saudi Arabia is also one of the largest producers and exporters of chemicals and polymers in the world. The proportion of the manufacturing sector amounted to 17 percent of GDP in 2010 (Arab Monetary Fund, 2011).

- *Tunisia*

The capital city of Tunisia is Tunis. Tunisia borders are Libya to the southeast and the north and east, and west of Algeria. Tunisia has a population of 10.6 million people, according to the 2010 census (Economic and Social Commission for Western Asia). In 2010, total national income (GNP) per capita current US $ was 4070 in Tunisia (Chemingui & Sánchez, 2011). Tunisia's economy depends on the agricultural, industrial and tourism sectors. These products have a great importance in the agricultural sector, citrus, grains, olive oil, tomatoes, sugar beets, dates, almonds, dairy, and beef products. The agriculture sector contribution to GDP in Tunisia at current prices in 2010 was about 8.1 percent; overall, the contribution of agriculture sector annually between 12-1 percent of GDP depending on the size of the produce (Verner & Breisinger, 2013, p. 48). While the manufacturing sector contribution to GDP in Tunisia at current prices in 2010 was close to 18.7 percent (African Development Bank Group, 2012, p. 4). According to the Joint Arab Economic report 2011 the added value of manufacturing industries, at current prices in Tunisia was US $ 6,602 million in 2010 (Arab Monetary Fund, 2011, p. 78). The most important industries are the mining industry such as iron ore, phosphates, and the oil industry, beverages, tourism, footwear, textiles, agro-industries (Almokhtar, 2010).

- *United Arab Emirate(UAE)*

The United Arab Emirates is a federation (abbreviation is UAE). It is on the southern coast of the Arabian Gulf and is one of the Gulf Cooperation Council (GCC) countries. It is one of the few petroleum countries n, where the number of citizens was about 930 thousand, according to the 2010 census, and the total population is 8.3 million in the same year (United Nations Population Division). Its capital is Abu Dhabi. The United Arab Emirates is a federation of seven emirates, which are Abu Dhabi, Ajman, Dubai, Fujairah, Ras al-Khaimah, Sharjah, and Umm al- Quwain. Abu Dhabi contains about 90 percent of oil reserves and annual production to the UAE (Nyarko, 2010, p. 6).

The oil sector contribution to GDP declined by 25 percent in 2010 (Planning and Decision Support Department, 2012, p. 20). The UAE production of crude oil in 2010 was 2.320 million barrel per day (Moukahal, 2011, p. 17). UAE had large reserves of crude oil, of about 97.8

billion barrels, holding in 2010 the seventh position in the world. It also owns a proven natural gas up to 6 trillion cubic meters. It is equivalent to about 3.2 percent of total global reserves, ranked at seventh place, globally (OAPEC). The UAE is one of the world leading suppliers of aluminum metal to over 45 countries in Asia, Europe, North America, and Africa. The UAE produce about 3.4 percent of the aluminum smelter in the world. Also, the UAE produces nitrogen fertilizers, cement, gypsum, refined petroleum products, sand, steel, and sulfur (Mowafa, 2012c, p. 57.1).

3.2. Analyses of FDI Trends for Arab Countries

The government in developing countries seeks to activate the total investment in both the public and private sectors. Foreign investment is a key goal for economies. Therefore, the government plans to develop different investment and capital inflows of different types and divisions. FDI in the Arab world has grown rapidly in the late twentieth century, although the region is full of risk and suffers from political instability, which does not encourage investors to invest (Safi, 2012). Foreign direct investments are concentrated in the Arab world in a few countries and sectors. About 80 percent of foreign direct investments in 2010 are concentrated in five countries: Saudi Arabia 47 percent, Egypt 10 percent, Qatar 8 percent, Lebanon 8 percent, and United Arab Emirates 6 percent (The Arab Investment and Export Credit Guarantee Corporation, 2011).

In this section, we will try to focus on the trends in the growth of foreign direct investments in selected Arab countries. We have selected Algeria, Bahrain, Egypt, Iraq, Jordan, Kuwait, Lebanon, Morocco, Oman, Qatar, Saudi Arabia, Tunisia, and the United Arab Emirates to our dissertation.

3.2.1. FDI in Arab Countries

The FDI inflows to the Arab countries at the period 2005- 2010 are fluctuating from one year to the other. Table 3-2 shows that. The inflow of foreign direct investments coming in the Arab countries in 2005 witnessed a considerable increase. Below we will review the evolution of inflows of foreign direct investments for the selected Arab countries for the period 2005-2010. The total inflow of foreign direct investments to the Arab countries 22 countries during the year 2005 was US $ 47.4 billion against US $ 25.2 billion in the year 2004. That was an increase of 88 percent forming about 4.7 percent of the total inflows of foreign direct investment in the world, reaching US $ 996.7 billion. These inflows formed about 13.8 percent of the total inflow of foreign direct investment in the developing countries that reached US $ 341.4 billion in 2005.

It was due to a significant increase in the flow of foreign direct investment to 13 Arab countries. This increase in the value of foreign investments to the Arab countries is attributed to increasing investment in the service sector such as telecommunications, transportation, power generation and oil and gas sectors and the increase of the industrial and tourism and real estate projects. Also, many Arab countries working to simplifying and improve the systems and procedures relating to investment, and promotion of investment (The Arab Investment and Export Credit Guarantee Corporation, 2005).

Table 3-2. FDI Inflows in Arab Countries, 2005-2010 (US $ Million)

Region/Economy	2005	2006	2007	2008	2009	2010
Algeria	1 081	1 795	1 662	2 594	2 761	2 291
Bahrain	1 049	2 915	1 756	1 794	257	156
Egypt	5 376	10 043	11 578	9 495	6 712	6 386
Iraq	515	383	972	1 856	1 452	1 426
Jordan	1 984	3 544	2 622	2 829	2 429	1 703
Kuwait	234	122	112	-6	1 114	81
Lebanon	3 321	3 132	3 376	4 333	4 804	4 955
Morocco	1 653	2 449	2 805	2 487	1 952	1 304
Oman	1 538	1 588	3 431	2 528	1 471	2 045
Qatar	2 500	3 500	4 700	3 779	8 125	5 534
Saudi Arabia	12 097	17 140	22 821	38 151	32 100	28 105
Tunisia	782	3 308	1 616	2 758	1 688	1 513
United Arab Emirates	10 900	12 806	14 187	13 724	4 003	3 948
Total	45 035	64 731	73 645	86 322	68 868	59 447

Source: Author's elaboration according to (UNCTAD).

In the United Arab Emirates, the foreign direct investment increased from 8.4 US $ billion in 2004, to US $ 12 billion in 2005. In Egypt, the foreign direct investment increased from US $ 2.2 billion in 2004, to US $ 5.4 billion in 2005. Saudi Arabia foreign direct investment increased from US $ 1.9 to 12 US $ billion in 2005. The foreign direct investment in Morocco was US $ 1 billion in 2004, increased to US $ 1.6 billion in 2005. Jordan foreign direct investment was US $ 651 million in 2004, increased to US $ 1.9 billion in 2005. In Lebanon, the foreign direct investment increased from US $ 1.9 billion in 2004, to US $ 3.3 billion in 2005. Oman foreign direct investment was US $ 200 million in 2004, increased to US $ 1.5 billion in 2005. In Qatar, the foreign direct investment increased from US $ 1.2 billion to US $ 2.5 billion in the same period. Algeria foreign direct investment was US $ 882 million in 2004, increased to US $ one billion in 2005. In Bahrain, the Foreign direct investment increased from US $ 865 million in 2004, to US $ one billion in the subsequent year. Tunisia foreign direct investment was US $ 936 million in 2004, increased to US $ 782 million. In Kuwait, the foreign direct investment increased from US $ 24 million in 2004, to US $ 234 million in 2005. Iraq noticed an increase in foreign direct investment from US $ 90 million in the year 2004, to US $ 515 million in the subsequent year. Table 3-2 shows the inflow of FDI to Arab countries for the period 2005-2010.

Three Arab countries have received an inflow of foreign direct investment in 2005 in value that surpassed US $ 5 billion each. These were Saudi Arabia US $ 12 billion, United Arab Emirates US $ 11 billion and Egypt about US $ 5.4 billion. The inflow of foreign direct investments to the United Arab Emirates, Saudi Arabia, and Egypt was about 59 percent of the total inflow of foreign direct investment to the Arab countries in 2005. Other two countries received an inflow of FDI that surpassed the US $ two billion. These were Morocco US $ 1.6 billion, and Lebanon US $ 3.3 billion. These countries represented a rate of 11 percent of the total inflow of foreign direct investment to the Arab countries in 2005.

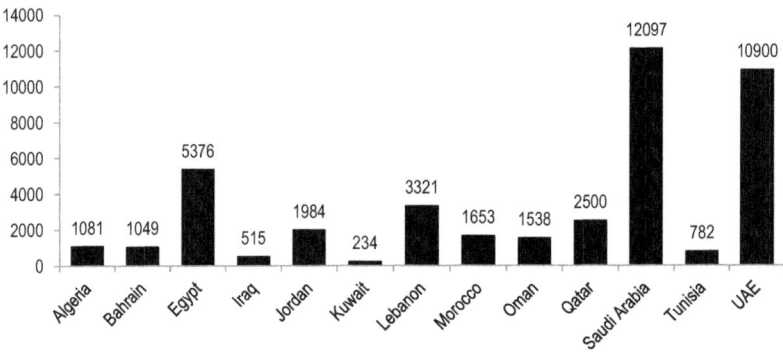

Figure 3-1. FDI inflows in Arab Countries, 2005(US $ Million)

Source: Author's elaboration according to the Table 3-2.

Four Arab countries have attracted an inflow of foreign direct investment that surpassed the US $ 1 billion in 2005. These countries were Jordan US $ 1.9 billion, Qatar US $ 2.5 billion, Algeria US $ 1 billion and Bahrain US $ 1 billion. These four countries represented 13.4 percent of the total inflow of foreign direct investment to the Arab countries in 2005. Figure 3-1 illustrates the FDI in Arab Country in 2005.

In 2006, the FDI inflows to the Arab countries out of the total world investment were US $ 70.1 billion. The inflow increased in eight Arab Countries, that is United Arab Emirates, Egypt, Algeria, Bahrain, Morocco, Tunisia, Jordan, Oman. Instead, the inflows experienced a regression in three Arab countries, which were Kuwait, Iraq, and Lebanon. Saudi Arabia led the rank of the Arab countries; the investment coming there was about 29.4 percent in the year 2005 to reach US $ 17.1 billion in 2006. The United Arab Emirates followed them in less inflow of 23 percent amounting to US $ 12.8 billion, which was mainly in 15 free zones. Besides that, the United Arab Emirates has conducted merger transactions, acquisition, and the increase in new investment projects (Singh & Rahim, 2012, p. 664). The government of the United Arab Emirates founded the free zones; they are encouraged foreign direct investments into the UAE, and direct them to the industrial sector. Many of the commercial or industrial free zones gave an impulse to the investors' to form industrial institutions. It became possible for the foreigners to own a 100 percent of the project capital in these zones not as it was before, where UAE citizens were typically required to own at least 51 percent of the company's capital (LLP, 2011, p. 1). The Jebel Ali Free Zone in UAE is one of the world's fastest and largest growing free zones in the world (Foreign Investment Office of Dubai, 2012).

Egypt has become third in rank with the FDI inflow reaching US $ 10.0 billion. The FDI inflows coming to Jordan amounted to US $ 3.5 billion, especially in the telecommunications sector. The economic laws and special incentives helped to attract the foreign direct investment, which took advantage of the facilities. The value of investment in the Jordanian Qualified Industrial Zones (QIZ) was US $ 13.7 billion, with over 48303 jobs in 2004 (Khasawneh, 2010, p. 104).

Due to geopolitical reasons Iraq and Lebanon has attracted only limited investment. It decreased in Iraq at the rate of 47 percent, amounting to US $ 383 million. The inflow to Lebanon increased by a small percentage, which amounted to 2 percent to reach US $ 3.1 billion.
The inflows to Arab countries within the region of North Africa increased. The inflows to Arab countries within the region of North Africa increased due to the reforms undertaken by countries to open their economies to foreign direct investment. Including liberalization of banking services, allowing foreigners to own large areas of land, and the fact that trans-national companies from the EU countries bought important assets, especially in Morocco and Egypt, within the framework of the privatization program, which was applied since the 1980s. Also, the investors from these countries own companies operating in the European Union, including Orascom Telecom (Egypt), which acquired Wind Telecomunicazioni SPA (WIND, Italy) worth of US $ 12.8 billion, and Marco company from Morocco (The Arab Investment and Export Credit Guarantee Corporation, 2005).

In Tunisia, inflows increased at unprecedented rates for 2005 amounted to 324 percent to reach US $ 3.3 billion. As part of these policies, Tunisia opened its economy to foreign franchises in certain sectors. Tunisia entered into various regional trade agreements. These agreements were:; in 1995 Association Agreement with the European Union, in 2002 Trade, and Investment Framework Agreement (TIFA) with the United States, and in 2004 Agadir Agreement, and multilateral trade agreement with Egypt, Jordan, and Morocco (Bank Information Center, 2013, p. 4). Algeria has grown in investment inflows by 66 percent from their value in 2005 to US $ 1.8 billion in 2006. Besides, Algeria ended the ownership of most of the foreign oil and gas industries in the country according to the oil and gas Act of 2005 (Independent Statistics & Analysis, 2014, p. 3). In 2006, Morocco FDI inflows increased to US $ 2.4 billion. Figure 3-2; illustrates the FDI inflows to Arab Countries in 2006.

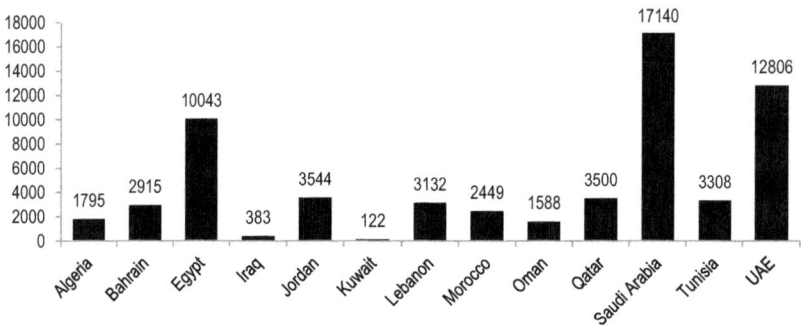

Figure 3-2. FDI in Arab Countries, 2006(US $ Million)

Source: Author's elaboration according to the Table 3-2.

The percentage of investment inflows coming into the GCC Arab Gulf (Kuwait, Bahrain, Oman, Qatar, Saudi Arabia, and the United Arab Emirates) was 54 percent of the total inflows to the Arab region in 2006 and increased to 69 percent in the year 2008. This is a high percent from the total Arab countries. This could be due to the investments in the oil and gas sector. Figure 3-3 shows the Share of the Arab Gulf countries of the Total FDI in Arab countries 2005-2010 (Percent). The significant increase was experienced by Saudi Arabia as the largest host of investment within the group of Arab countries with about US $ 150.4 billion in the period 2005-2010.

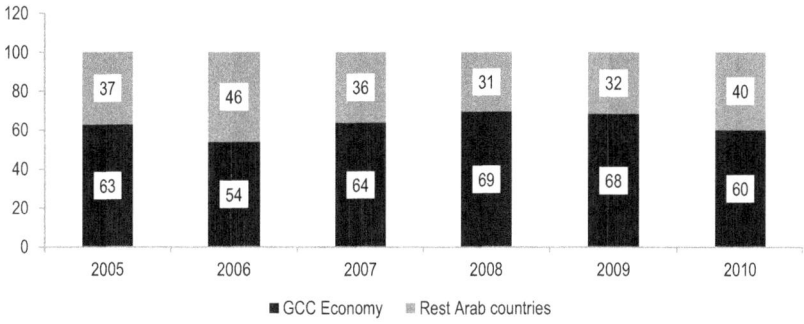

Figure 3-3. Share of the Arab Gulf Countries of the Total FDI in Arab Countries 2005-2010 (Percent)

Source: Author's elaboration according to the Table 3-2.

The United Arab Emirates remained at the second place, with US $ 59.5 billion in the period 2005-2010. Qatar was at third place with US $ 28.1 billion in the same period 2005-2010. The Arab Gulf countries got over 60 percent from the total FDI inflows as an annual average through the period 2005-2010.

The inflows of the foreign direct investments in the Arab countries in 2007 have increased for the subsequent eighth year, according to the report of the international investment 2008 (UNCTAD, 2008b). According to the detailed data, the total foreign direct investment inflows to Arab countries being reviewed in 2007 was about US $ 73.6 billion in contrary to US $ 64.7 billion in 2006, with a limited increase amounted to 13.7 percent. This increase was attributed to the improvement of legislative frameworks for investment in many countries of the region, particularly in financial services, construction, communications, and tourism. Moreover, the rise in oil, and other minerals prices, which led to attracting more investment to the industries related to the oil and gas sector (The Arab Investment and Export Credit Guarantee Corporation, 2007). Despite this increase, the share of Arab countries of these inflows reduces to 3.7 percent of the global total.

The increase in the total inflows was caused by the inflows of 8 Arab countries. Saudi Arabia occupied the first position among the Arab countries. The inflows have grown at 33 percent to reach US $ 22.8 billion in 2007. The United Arab Emirates was ranked the second. While the inflows coming to the United Arab Emirates rose to a rate of 10.7 percent to reach a value of US $ 14.1 billion, followed by Egypt, to which the inflows remained at high levels, as it received a noticeable increase by 15 percent to reach US $ 11.5 billion. These inflows mostly went to several sectors of the economy, the most important were: petroleum sector and the textile industry and the chemical and medical industries. In Qatar investment rose from US $ 3.5 billion in 2006 to US $ 4.7 billion in 2007. While inflows to Oman doubled to US $ 3.4 billion, Iraq attracted US $ 972 million, concentrated in the oil and petrochemical projects despite the difficult political situation (The Arab Investment and Export Credit Guarantee Corporation, 2007). The inflows to each of Lebanon and Morocco have increased in a very limited extend. The foreign direct investment inflows coming to 5 Arab countries witnessed a decline. In Tunisia, it has fallen down by 51 percent to reach US $ 1.6 billion, and then Jordan and Bahrain by 43 percent, 40 percent, respectively. It reduced to a limited extent in Algeria contributing 7 percent to US $ 1.6 billion. Kuwait also witnessed a decline to US $ 112 million. Figure 3-4, illustrates the FDI in Arab Countries in 2007 (US $ Million).

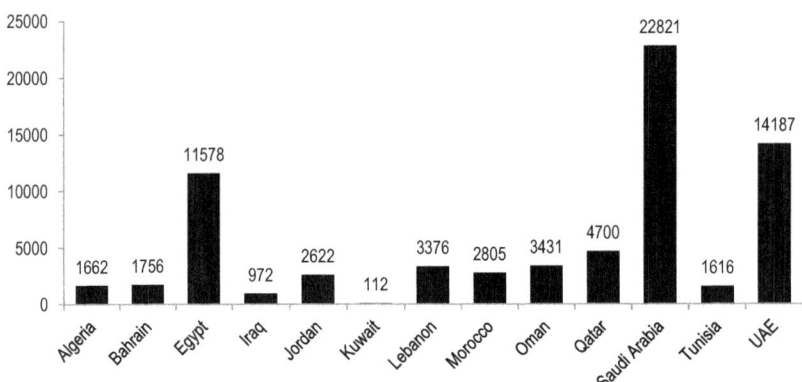

Figure 3-4. FDI in Arab Countries, 2007(US $ Million)

Source: Author's elaboration according to the Table 3-2.

In 2008, the inflows of foreign direct investment to 22 Arab countries increased to US $ 97.6 billion, compared with US $ 82 billion in 2007. These inflows to Arab countries represent 5.7 percent of the total inflows of US $ 1.7 trillion (UNCTAD, 2011b). The share of the Arab countries of the global inflows featured fluctuations during the last period where it increased slightly from 4.8 percent in 2005 to 4.9 percent and then declined to 4.1 percent in 2007, before re-boarding strongly to 5.7 percent in 2008.

The inflows FDI into seven Arab countries (Jordan, Bahrain, Algeria, Saudi Arabia, Iraq, Tunisia, and Lebanon) have increased at rates ranging from 0.21 percent to Jordan and 70.64 percent to Tunisia. While decreased in six countries (Qatar, Kuwait, Morocco, Oman, Egypt, and the United Arab Emirates). Saudi Arabia occupied the first rank among Arab countries, being the largest host country for FDI to reach US $ 38.1 billion, with a share of 39.6 percent of the total Arab FDI. The United Arab Emirates was in the second place with US $ 13.7 billion and a share of 14.2 percent, and then Egypt in third place with US $ 9.5 billion and a share of 9.8 percent. Figure 3-5, illustrates the FDI in Arab countries in 2008(US $ Million).

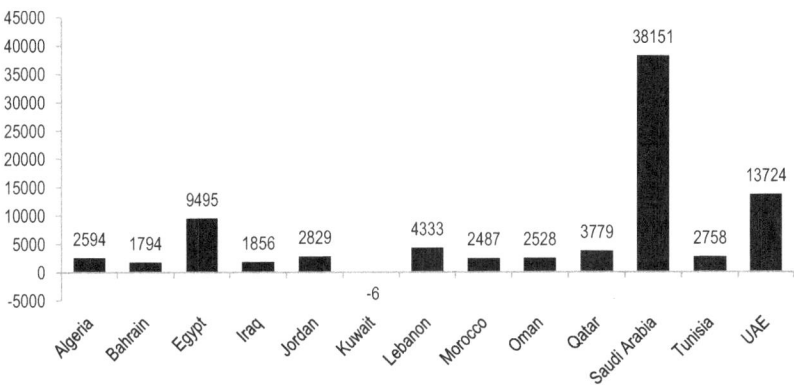

Figure 3-5. FDI in Arab Countries, 2008(US $ Million)

Source: Author's elaboration according to the Table 3-2.

In 2009, the all-Arab countries attracted FDI inflows of about US $ 82.4 billion compared with US $ 97.6 billion attracted in 2008. That means the foreign direct investment inflows received by the Arab countries for 2009 has decreased by about US $ 15.2 billion, or a rate of -16 percent. This decline in FDI inflows was attributed to the continuing impact of the global economic and financial crises on global foreign direct investment inflows. Note that all international economic blocs have seen rates drop in foreign direct investment inflows during the year 2009, and this has been referred to in the first chapter of this dissertation. The Arab world recorded the lowest rate of economic decline compared to other groups. Arab region recorded a rate of -16 percent, compared to: developing countries with a rate of -22 percent, transition economies with a rate of -40 percent, developed countries with a rate of -40 percent, and a rate of -32 percent worldwide.

Kingdom of Saudi Arabia has led the list of host countries for foreign direct investment inflows received in 2009, at a value US $ 32.1 billion and 44 percent of the total foreign direct investment inflows to the group of the Arab countries, subject to our study, during the year 2009. Despite falling slightly by 6.9 percent during that year compared to data recorded in 2008. Most of the incoming foreign direct investments to the Kingdom of Saudi Arabia were in the sectors of industry and services, with the total inflows of about 32.9 percent, to reach US $ 11.7 billion in 2009 (National Competitiveness Center, 2010, p. 9).

Qatar took the second place in rank, after Saudi Arabia. In 2009 Qatar received about US $ 8.1 billion as foreign direct investments. . Most FDI was in the gas sector, i.e. with an increase of 115 percent compared to the rate of inflows recorded in 2008, this is about 50.7 percent of total FDI inflows (Qatar Statistics Authority, 2009). However, the achieved inflows to the United Arab Emirates in 2009 recorded a decline of 70.8 percent from 2009 to US $ 4 billion compared with US $ 13.7 billion in 2008. In Egypt, there was a decrease of the total inflows from US $ 9.5 billion in 2008 to US $ 6.7 billion in 2009, a net reduction of 29.3 percent. In Lebanon, the received foreign direct investment inflows increased from US $ 4.3 billion in 2008 to US $ 4.8 billion in 2009 mostly concentrated in the real estate sector (The Arab Investment and Export Credit Guarantee Corporation, 2010). In Morocco, the inflows of foreign direct investment in the Kingdom of Morocco reduced over the year 2009 to reach US $ 1.9 billion, compared to about US $ 2.4 billion in 2008. In Jordan, the foreign direct investment inflows have fallen to a limited extent, which amounted to US $ 2.4 billion in 2009 compared to about US $ 2.8 billion in 2008.

Instead, the achieved inflows to Algeria in 2009 recorded a slight increase of 6.4 percent to amount the value of US $ 2.7 billion compared with US $ 2.6 billion in 2008. In Kuwait, the inflows of foreign direct investment received during the year 2009 increased to US $ 1.1 billion in 2009 from negative inflows amounted to US $ 6 million during the year 2008. As for Tunisia, the flow of foreign direct investment inflows decreased by 35.2 percent during 2009, to reach a value of US $ 1.7 billion compared with US $ 2.7 billion in 2008. Most of these come mostly from the EU, which is worth of US $ 1.6 billion, at about 90 percent of the total inflows. The Arab investments were confined to only US $ 164 million, comprising only 9.3 percent out of the total. The most concentrated influx of foreign direct investments in the energy sector valued at US $ 1.03 billion and 58.2 percent of the total (The Arab Investment and Export Credit Guarantee Corporation, 2009, p. 83). In Iraq, the foreign direct investment inflows decreased at a rate of - 21.7 percent to reach about US $ 1.4 billion in 2009, compared to about US $ 1.8 billion in 2008. In Oman, also, the flow of foreign direct investment regressed from US $ 2.5 billion in 2008 to US $ 1.4 billion in 2009. The foreign direct investment inflows to Bahrain's economy has decline greatly to 85.7 percent, i.e. US $ 257 million in 2009, compared to US $ 1794 million in 2008.

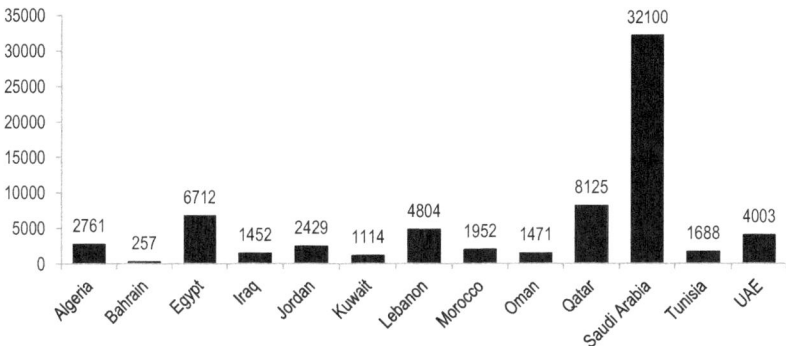

Figure 3-6. FDI in Arab Countries, 2009(US $ Million)

Source: Author's elaboration according to the Table 3-2.

By comparing the incoming foreign direct investments to the Arab countries during 2008 and 2009, only four Arab countries among the countries of the study group, an increase was recorded in investment inflows that contained Qatar, Lebanon, Algeria, and Kuwait. Meanwhile the foreign investments value for Saudi Arabia, Egypt, Iraq, Oman, United Arab Emirates, Morocco, Jordan, Tunisia, and Bahrain, was reduced in 2009 in comparison to inflows of 2008. Figure 3-6, illustrates the FDI in Arab countries in 2009 (US $ Million).

All Arab countries attracted about US $ 64.3 billion in 2010, in comparison with US $ 83.9 billion attracted in 2009. The reason for this decrease in the FDI inflows was the reduction of FDI inflow to the major receiving countries such as Saudi Arabia, with the two third of inflows in about 41 percent, also due to the decrease of inflows to United Arab Emirates, Qatar, and Egypt. Saudi Arabia took the lead in the host countries of the foreign direct investments in 2010 with a value of 28.1 US $ billion, in average 43.7 percent of gross foreign direct investments' inflow to Arab countries. Comparing to data of 2009 there was a reduction of inflows. This reduction was because of deletion of some big projects in oil sector (The Arab Investment and Export Credit Guarantee Corporation, 2010). Qatar took the third position after Egypt, in the lead of the host countries of the foreign direct investments in 2010. In Egypt, the gross of FDI inflows dropped from US $ 6.7 billion in 2009, to US $ 6.4 billion during 2010. According to official statics reduction was with the rate 4.9 percent (Central Bank of Egypt). The foreign direct investments inflows in Qatar were US $ 5.5 billion in 2010 that means a decreasing rate of 31.88 percent in comparison with inflows in 2009. The inflows to the United Arab Emirates had a slight reduction in average 1.4 percent during 2010, to reach US $ 3.9 billion compared with US $ 4 billion on 2009, according to the data of Emirates Central Banks Payments (Central Department of Statistics and Information).

The inflows of foreign direct investments in Lebanon increased from US $ 4.8 billion on 2009 to reach US $ 4.95 billion in 2010, according to payment balance statics published by Central Bank of Lebanon (Banque du Liban). In Morocco, reduced inflows of foreign direct investment in the Kingdom during the year 2010 was recorded, to reach US $ 1.3 billion, compared to about US $ 1.9 billion in 2009. Jordan, presented reduced FDI inflows of US $ 1.7 billion in 2010, compared to US $ 2.4 billion in 2009, with a decline of 29.9 percent.

The inflows to Algeria has decreased during the year, demonstrating a rate of 19.3 percent, according to the BOP data released by the Central Bank of Algeria, to reach a value of US $ 2.2 billion compared with US $ 2.7 billion in 2009 (Bank Of Algeria). In Tunisia, the inflows declined by 10.4 percent during 2010, to reach about US $ 1.6 billion compared with US $ 1.7 billion in 2009. Inflows to Iraq has reduced, had a rate of 1.7 percent to reach about US $ 1.42 billion in 2010, compared to US $ 1.45 billion in 2009 (Central Statistical Organization).

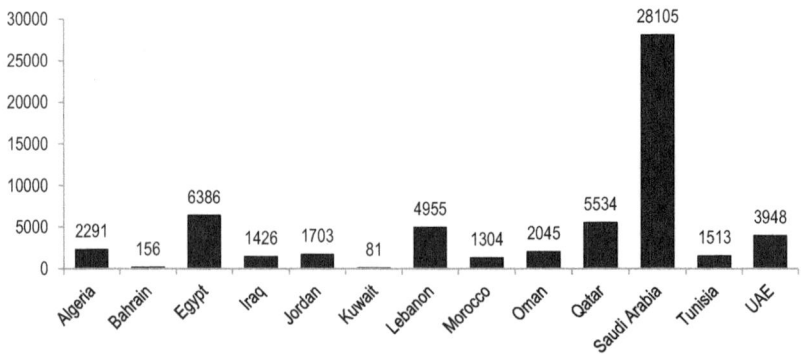

Figure 3-7. FDI in Arab Countries, 2010(US $ Million)

Source: Author's elaboration according to the Table 3-2.

In Bahrain, the data from the balance of payments issued by the Central Bank of Bahrain, shows that FDI inflows coming to Bahrain's economy have declined by 39.4 percent to reach US $ 156 million during 2010, compared to US $ 257 million during the year 2009 (Central Bank of Bahrain). In Kuwait, FDI inflows received under the statistics of the balance of payments during the year 2010 issued by the Central Bank of Kuwait, reduced from US $ 1.1 billion in 2009, to reach US $ 81 million during 2010 (Central Bank of Kuwait). Figure 3-7, illustrates the FDI in Arab countries in 2010 (US $ million).

The FDI is concentrated in a few countries. For instance, about 80 percent of the FDI in 2010 was concentrated in six of Arab countries: Saudi Arabia 42 percent, Egypt 10 percent, Qatar 8 percent, Lebanon 7 percent, and on the United Arab Emirates 6 percent. Oil and gas industry, the hotel sector, and the real economy got most foreign direct investment in the Arab countries (Hasen & Gianluigi, 2007).

3.2.2. The Inter-Arab Direct Investment and Sectoral Distribution of Arabic Countries

We do not have detailed data on the sectoral distribution of foreign direct investment in the countries of our study sample. The available data was for FDI in Inter-Arab countries only. The investment climate in Arab countries report for 2010 refers to the lack of inter-Arab investment data supplied to the institution by the Arab countries.

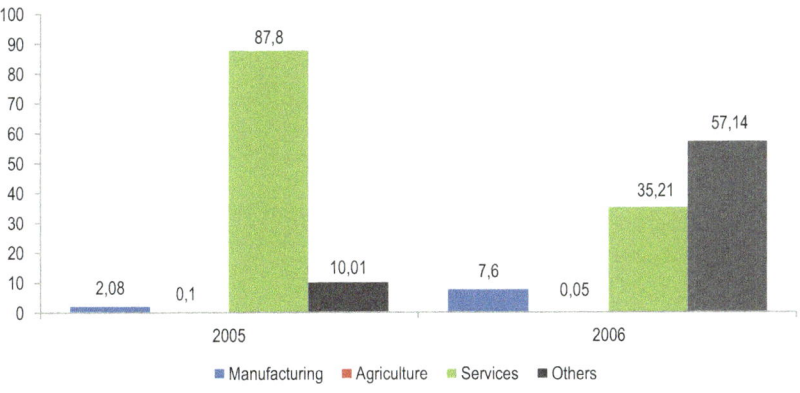

Figure 3-8. Sectoral Distribution of Inter-Arab Direct Investments 2005-2006(Percent)

Source: Author's elaboration according to (The Arab Investment and Export Credit Guarantee Corporation, 2005; The Arab Investment and Export Credit Guarantee Corporation, 2006).

The share of total inter-Arab investments of the total investment of the world was about 24.26 percent in 2005. This percentage decreased to 18.26 percent in 2010 (El-Seretty & Shabbara, 2014, p. 1280). The services sector dominated the Inter-Arab direct investments contributing up to 87.8 percent of total Inter-Arab direct investments in 2005, followed by 10.01 percent of the other sectors. The manufacturing sector was 2.08 percent, and last was the agricultural sector with 0.11 percent. In 2006, in Inter-Arab investments the services sector ranked second at 35.21 percent after the other sectors, which contributed 57.14 percent of these investments. Later, there was the manufacturing sector by about 7.6 percent. Finally, the agricultural sector was about 0.05 percent. Figure 3-8, depicts the sectoral distribution of Inter-Arab direct investments over the years 2005, 2006.

The geographical distribution of Inter-Arab investments for the period 2005-2006 is shown in Table 3-3. It is evident there that Morocco ranked first in the value of direct Inter-Arab investments in the manufacturing sector among the rest of the Arab countries in 2005. Egypt ranked first in the agricultural sector in the same year. Saudi Arabia ranked first among the Arab countries in the value of Inter-Arab investments in both of services, and other sectors (real estate, trade, and tourism) in 2005.

Table 3-3. Geographical Distribution of Inter-Arab Direct Investments to Arab Countries, 2005-2006 (US $ Million)

Region /Economy	Manufacturing		Agricultural		Services		Others		Total	
	2005	2006	2005	2006	2005	2006	2005	2006	2005	2006
Algeria	36	0	0	0	215	0	10	0	261	0
Egypt	307	0	33	0	307	0	180	3 265	827	3 265
Jordan	133	1 035	2	6	168	57	0	0	302	1 098
Lebanon	13	25	0	0	767	970	1 000	1340	1 780	2335
Morocco	160	0	1.2	0	953	0	8	350	1 121	350
Saudi Arabia	0	19	0	0	26 666	1 630	2 131	3 188	28 797	4837
Tunisia	45	5	0	1	151	2 361	4	0	200	2 367
Total	694	1 084	36	7	29 226	5 018	3 333	8 144	33 288	14 252
Percent	2.08	7.60	0.11	0.05	87.80	35.21	10.01	57.14	100	100

Source: Author's elaboration according to (The Arab Investment and Export Credit Guarantee Corporation, 2005; The Arab Investment and Export Credit Guarantee Corporation, 2006)

In 2006, Jordan ranked first among the Arab countries in the value of Inter-Arab investments in both manufacturing and agricultural sectors. Tunisia ranked first among the Arab countries in the value of Inter-Arab investments in the services sector in 2006. In other sectors, Egypt ranked first among Arab countries in Inter-Arab direct investments in 2006.

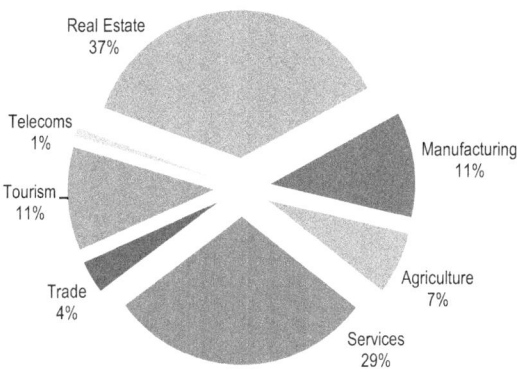

Figure 3-9. Sectoral Distribution of Inter-Arab Direct Investments, 2007(Percent)

Source: Author's elaboration according to (The Arab Investment and Export Credit Guarantee Corporation, 2007).

In 2007, the majority of Inter-Arab investments were directed towards projects in the service, and real estate sectors. Figure 3-9 depicts that the sectoral distribution of Inter-Arab direct investments is dominated by the real estate sector contribute for 36.7 percent of total Arab direct investments, followed by services sector 29.4 percent and manufacturing sector 11.5 percent, and the agricultural sector with 6.8 percent. The last were the tourism sector with 11.3 percent, trade sector with 3.5 percent, and the telecoms' sector with 0.9 percent of all Inter-Arab investments.

According to the data collected from four Arab countries, Inter-Arab investments totaled US $ 6.1 billion in 2007, compared to US $ 14.2 billion received by seven Arab countries in 2006. In one Arab country the investment increased while declined in the other three. Investments in Jordan and Egypt dropped from their 2006 levels, but the most dramatic decline was in Tunisia where it decreased by more than US $ 2 billion. While in Lebanon Inter-Arab investments increased from US $ 2335 million in 2006, to US $ 3342.8 million in 2007.

Geographical distribution of Inter-Arab investments for the year 2007 is shown in the Table 3-4. In the table it is evident that Egypt ranked first in the value of direct Inter-Arab investments in the manufacturing, services, and agricultural sectors among the rests of the Arab countries in 2007. Jordan ranked first in the value of direct Inter-Arab investments in the trade sector among the rests of the Arab countries in the same year. While Lebanon ranked first in the value in both tourism, and real estate sectors in 2007. Tunisia was ranked first among Arab countries in 2007, in the telecommunications' sector.

Table 3-4. Geographical Distribution to Inter-Arab Direct Investments to Arab Countries, 2007
(US $ Million)

Region/Economy	Manufacturing	Agricultural	Services	Trade	Tourism	Telecoms	Real Estate	Total
Egypt	393.5	208	835.8	0	172.4	5.6	258.6	1 874
Jordan	187.8	159.9	274.9	214	0	0	9.3	845.9
Lebanon	100.3	50.1	712.0	0	474.7	0	2 005.7	3 342.8
Tunisia	27.4	1	0	0	51.5	47.4	0	127.3
Total	709	419	1 822.7	214	698.6	53	2 273.6	6 190
Percent	11.5	6.8	29.4	3.5	11.3	0.9	36.7	100.0

Source: Author's elaboration according to (The Arab Investment and Export Credit Guarantee Corporation, 2007).

The share of the service sector was 54.3 percent of the total inter-Arab direct investment in 2008, followed by manufacturing sector with about 35 percent. The other sectors had 10.5 percent, and the last was the agricultural sector with 0.2 percent in 2008. In 2009, in Inter-Arab investments the services sector ranked second with 12.2 percent after the manufacturing sector that contributes for 82.5 percent of these investments. The other sectors were below, with share of about 5.2 percent. Finally, agricultural sector was about 0.1 percent in 2009. Figure 3-10, depicts the sectoral distribution of Inter-Arab direct investments over the years 2008, 2009.

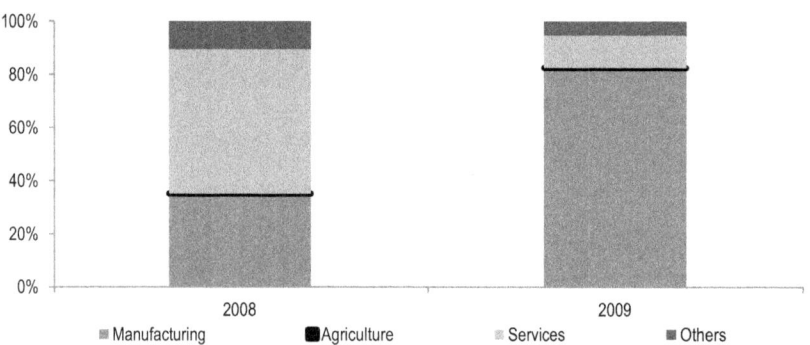

Figure 3-10. Sectoral Distribution of Inter-Arab Direct Investments, 2008-2009(Percent)

Source: Author's elaboration according to (The Arab Investment and Export Credit Guarantee Corporation, 2008; The Arab Investment and Export Credit Guarantee Corporation, 2009).

Depending on the available geographically distributed data on the Inter-Arab, direct investment, reported by five Arab countries. Inter-Arab direct investments totaled US $ 920 million in 2009, compared to US $ 22 billion received by the same five countries in 2008. Each of the Dubai crisis[*], the global economic, and financial crisis, played a key role in the decline in FDI inflows to Arab countries (The Arab Investment and Export Credit Guarantee Corporation, 2009).

Table 3-5. Inter-Arab Direct Investments, 2008-2009 (US $ Million)

Region/Economy	Manufacturing		Agricultural		Services		Others		Total	
	2008	2009	2008	2009	2008	2009	2008	2009	2008	2009
Algeria	5 654	0	0	0	3	0	9	0	5 666	0
Jordan	403.9	717.2	1	1	28.7	21.4	0	16.8	433.5	756.4
Lebanon	21.3	0	41.9	0	403.6	0	2 194.3	0	2 661.1	0
Saudi Arabia	1 618	0	0	0	11 233	0	101	0	12 952	0
Tunisia	10	41.8	0	0	296.5	90.5	14	31.4	320.5	163.7
Total	7 707.2	759	42.9	1	11 964.8	111.9	2 318.3	48.2	22 033.1	920.1
Percent	35.0	82.5	0.2	0.1	54.3	12.2	10.5	5.2	100.0	100.0

Source: (The Arab Investment and Export Credit Guarantee Corporation, 2008; The Arab Investment and Export Credit Guarantee Corporation, 2009).

The geographical distribution of Inter-Arab investments for the period 2008-2009 is shown in the Table 3-5. In the table it is evident that Saudi Arabia ranked first in the value of direct Inter-Arab investments in the services sector among the rests of the Arab countries in 2008. Lebanon ranked first in the agricultural sector in the same year. Algeria ranked first in the manufacturing sector in 2008. In the other sectors, Lebanon ranked first among the Arab countries in the value of Inter-Arab investments in these sectors in 2008.

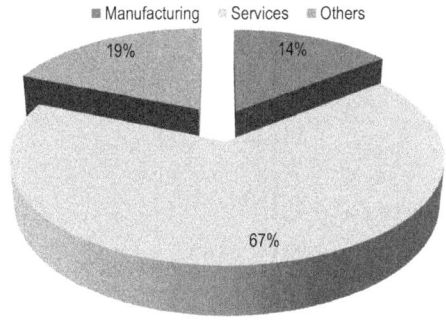

Figure 3-11. Sectoral Distribution of Inter-Arab Direct Investments, 2010(Percent)

Source: Author's elaboration according to (The Arab Investment and Export Credit Guarantee Corporation, 2010).

---

[*]The United Arab Emirates has seen an economic crisis in the November 26, 2009 due to the global financial crisis, the drop in oil prices, and the crisis in the real estate sector in Dubai in 2009.

In 2009, Jordan ranked first in each of manufacturing and agricultural sector in 2009. Tunisia ranked first among the Arab countries in the value of Inter-Arab investments in both others sectors and the services sector in 2009. In 2010, Figure 3-11 depicts that the sectoral distribution of Inter-Arab direct investments is dominated by services sector which contributed for 66.7 percent of total Arab direct investments, followed by manufacturing sector contributing for 14.5 percent and the other sectors with 18.8 percent.

Inter-Arab direct investments totaled only US $ 782 million in 2010, to five countries, compared to US $ 920 million in 2009, with available data only to two countries in this year: Morocco, and Tunisia. Geographical distribution of Inter-Arab investments for the year 2010 is shown in the Table 3-6. In the table, it is evident that Morocco ranked first in the value of direct Inter-Arab investments in the manufacturing, agricultural, and services sectors compared to Tunisia.

Table 3-6. Inter-Arab Direct Investments, 2010 (US $ Million)

Region/Economy	Manufacturing	Services	Others	Total
Morocco	90.5	397	128.3	615.8
Tunisia	22.9	125	18.5	166.4
Total	113.4	522	146.8	782.2
Percent	14.5	66.7	18.8	100

Source: Author's elaboration according to (The Arab Investment and Export Credit Guarantee Corporation, 2010).

3.3. Analyses of Indicators of Investments Climate in Arab Countries

Investors often cite economic and political stability as a key factor in their location decisions. Some countries are sometimes politically unstable and get relatively small amounts of foreign direct investment. This rule has an exception in countries rich in natural resources. These countries, despite the instability, have been able to attract significant amounts of foreign direct investment (Burger, Ianchovichina, & Rijkers, 2013, pp. 2-3).

Following what was discussed in Chapter 2 that is a range of ways of attracting investment and measurable indicators, in this chapter we will present several indicators, which relationships we believe to provide a favourable investment climate. We have selected below indicators from over 82 indicators (Composite Indicators Research Group), because they provide data for all or some of the countries, which are the subject of this section, and because we will compare our results with some of them.

1. Global Competitiveness Index (GCI)

The importance of the concept of competitiveness has increased in recent years in a globalized world. There is no accepted definition of competitiveness, and there is no accepted theory that explains this category (Notta, Vlachvei, & Samathrakis, 2010). The concept of competitiveness is associated with the standard of living on any country level (Porter, 2005).

The competitiveness of a country is the ability of a country to produce goods and services that meet the test of the international markets to raise the level of welfare of its citizens and maintain and expand the real income (Haque, 1995). The international competitiveness is defined as the ability to sustain in a global economy at the acceptable growth level in the standard of living of the people in a country. With an acceptably fair distribution, with providing jobs for substantially all people who intend and can work and doing so without reducing the growth potential in the standards of living of future generations (Hickman, 1992).

The Global Competitiveness Index is published annually by the world economic forum. In 2004, Xavier Sala-I-Martin and Elsa V. Artadi released the index. It is reliable for countries due to submission valuable insights about the economic policies, institutions, and factors stimulating production that lead to continued economic growth. Whereas the global competitiveness index through annually report focuses on economic welfare and increasing standards of living (Arslan & Tathdil, 2012, p. 34).

The index is based on data from leading international sources and the results of annual surveys conducted by the world economic forum. These surveys include the views of thousands of business on topics related to national competitiveness. The index depends on a weighted average of many elements, which includes 12, different pillars that call the 12 pillars of competitiveness. Each of which reflects one aspect of the complex reality that call the competitiveness (The World Economic Forum, 2007-2008). The range of score is between 1-7, and the higher average score means higher competitiveness. Figure 3-12 depicts the 12 pillars of competitiveness.

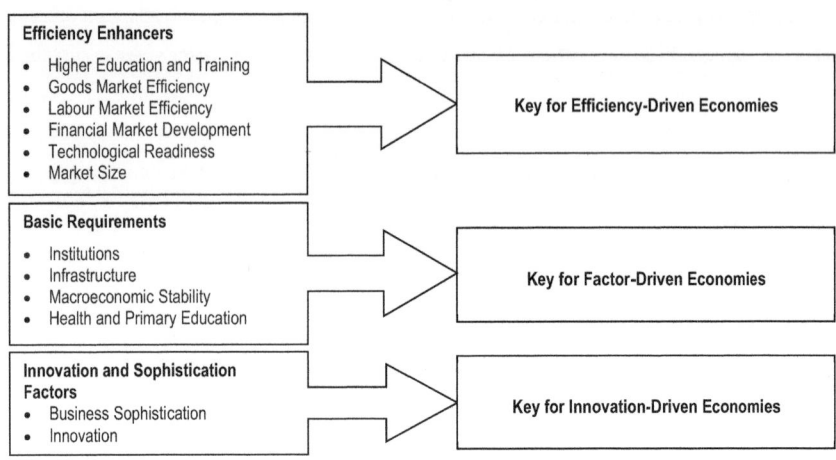

Figure 3-12. The 12 Pillars of Competitiveness

Source: (The World Economic Forum, 2011, p. 13).

The data about Global Competitiveness Index that are available to the Arab countries shows that in 2005 United Arab Emirates topped the Arab countries with its global ranking 18 and Algeria was in the last list of the Arab countries with rank 78. In 2005 data were not available to Oman, and Saudi Arabia. In 2006, Tunisia made substantial progress towards the topped Arab countries with its global ranking 30, reaching a score 4.71. Algeria was in the last position of the Arab countries with rank 90 in the world. This year, data were also not available to Oman, and Saudi Arabia.

In 2007, Kuwait had made substantial progress and jumped over 14 positions in the world ranking to occupy the 30th place in the world. Kuwait with this rank is at the first position among the Arab countries. Saudi Arabia was added to the report for the first time this year and reached the rank 35 in the world, and the fourth among Arab countries. Algeria stays at the same last position among the Arab countries and ranking 81 in the world. In 2008, Qatar jumped over five positions in the world ranking to occupy the rank 26, and topped the Arab countries with this global ranking. Algeria was at the same 11 rank among the Arab countries and ranked 99 in the world.

Table 3-7. Global Competitiveness Index in Arab Countries, 2005-2010

Country	2005 Score	2005 Rank	2006 Score	2006 Rank	2007 Score	2007 Rank	2008 Score	2008 Rank	2009 Score	2009 Rank	2010 Score	2010 Rank
Algeria	3.46	78	3.9	76	3.91	81	3.71	99	3.95	83	3.96	86
Bahrain	4.48	37	4.28	49	4.42	43	4.57	37	4.54	38	4.54	37
Egypt	3.96	53	4.07	63	3.96	77	3.98	81	4.04	70	4	81
Jordan	4.28	45	4.25	52	4.32	49	4.37	48	4.3	50	4.21	65
Kuwait	4.58	33	4.41	44	4.66	30	4.58	35	4.53	39	4.59	35
Morocco	3.49	76	4.01	70	4.08	64	4.08	73	4.03	73	4.08	75
Oman	-	-	-	-	4.43	42	4.55	38	4.49	41	4.61	34
Qatar	4.97	19	4.55	38	4.63	31	4.83	26	4.95	22	5.1	17
Saudi Arabia	-	-	-	-	4.55	35	4.72	27	4.75	28	4.95	21
Tunisia	4.32	40	4.71	30	4.59	32	4.58	36	4.5	40	4.65	32
UAE	4.99	18	4.66	32	4.5	37	4.68	31	4.92	23	4.89	25

Source: Author's elaboration according to (The World Economic Forum).

Qatar, in 2009 jumped over four positions in the world ranking to occupy the rank 22, and with this position it was the first among the Arab countries. Algeria at the end of the list of Arab countries and its position jumped to rank 83 in the world. Qatar during the year 2010 jumped over five positions in the world ranking to occupy the rank 17, and with this position it was the first among the Arab countries for the fourth year.

Algeria was at the same ranking - 11, among the Arab countries for the fourth year and ranking 86 in the world. The Table 3-7 shows the Global Competitiveness Index in Arab Countries for the period 2005-2010. Data regarding Iraq and Lebanon are not available from this source.

2. Enabling Trade Index, (ETI)

The Global Enabling Trade report for 2010, published for the first time in 2008, covers 125 major and emerging economies. The report ranks the countries using data from different sources such as World Economic Forum's Executive Opinion Survey, UNCTAD, International Trade Centre, World Bank, IATA, ITU, and Global Express Association (The World Economic Forum, 2012, p. Xiii).

The enabling trade index measures the factors, policies, and services that help to trade goods across borders and to the destination. It is made up of four subs-indices (The World Economic Forum, 2010, pp. 10-13):

- market access,
- border administration,

- transport and communications infrastructure,

- business environment,

Each of these sub-indices has two to three pillars that assess different aspects of a country's trade environment.

The report starts to cover the area of Arab World from 2009. In 2009, the report covered 11 Arab countries. The Table 3-8 shows the score and ranks for these countries for the period 2009-2010. The author could not find the range of score to the Enabling Trade Index from this source, but the highest score was 6.06 for Singapore and the lowest 2.79 for Burundi in 2010. Data to Iraq and Lebanon are not available from this source.

Table 3-8. Enabling Trade Index in Arab Countries, 2009-2010

Country	2009		2010	
	Score	Rank	Score	Rank
Algeria	3.18	112	3.14	119
Bahrain	4.76	24	4.95	22
Egypt	3.72	75	3.88	76
Jordan	4.39	37	4.55	39
Kuwait	3.96	59	4.01	65
Morocco	4.01	55	3.9	75
Oman	4.52	34	4.71	29
Qatar	4.5	35	4.68	34
Saudi Arabia	4.36	42	4.54	40
Tunisia	4.36	41	4.57	38
United Arab Emirates	4.97	18	5.12	16

Source: Author's elaboration according to (The World Bank).

The table shows five countries, that is Algeria, Egypt, Jordan, Kuwait, and Morocco, which deceased in the ranking in the year 2010 compared to 2009. Algeria dropped from the ranking at the level 112 in 2009, to the rank 119 in 2010. Egypt fell from the rank 75 in 2009, to the rank 76 in 2010. The index of enabling trade to Jordan dropped down from rank 36 in 2009to the rank 39 compared to in 2009.

Kuwait rank fell from the rank 59 in 2009, to occupy the rank 65 in 2010, in the world. Finally, in Morocco the index of enabling trade declined from the rank 55 in 2009, to occupy the rank 75 in 2010. The ranks of enabling trade index in Oman, Qatar, Saudi Arabia, Tunisia, and the United Arab Emirates increased from 2009 to 2010. The rank of enabling trade index Oman increased from the rank 34 in 2009, to occupy the rank 29 in 2010.

Qatar rank increased from the rank 35 in 2009, to occupy the rank 34 in 2010. Saudi Arabia rank of enabling trade index increased from the rank 42 in 2009, to occupy the rank 40 in 2010. The enabling trade index of Tunisia increased from the rank 41 in 2009, to occupy the rank 38 in 2010 in the whole world ranks. In the both years 2009, and 2010, United Arab Emirates ranked first among Arab countries in the index, to occupy the rank 18 in 2009, and to occupy the rank 16 in 2010, globally.

3. Index of Economic Freedom

Economic freedom is related to that part of the freedom concerned with the physical autonomy of the individual regarding the state and other organized groups (Beach & Kane, 2008). Each of the Heritage Foundation and the Wall Street Journal put Index of Economic Freedom, in 1995. The index aims to provide a measure of economic freedom for every economy in the world (Hristova, 2012, p. 5). Since 1995, the index provides data for 185 countries in the world, ranking 179 of them. The index uses data from external sources such as the World Bank, the International Monetary Fund, and the World Economic Forum. It provides much data to a great number of countries (Gwartney, Lawson, & Hall, 2013, p. 2). Measures ten elements of economic freedom, assigning a grade in each using a scale from zero to 100, where 100 represents the largest freedom. The scales are free 80-100, mostly free 70.0-79.9, moderately free 60.0-69.9, mostly un-free 50.0-59.9, and repressed 0-49.9. In the measurement of economic freedom, the index analysed countries' commitment grouped into four broad categories or pillars of economic freedom. First is the rule of law (property rights, and freedom from corruption). Second is the principles of limited government (fiscal freedom, and government spending). Third is regulatory efficiency (business freedom, labour freedom, monetary freedom). The last refers to open market (trade freedom, investments freedom, and financial freedom) (Miller, Kim, & Holmes, 2014).

The data regarding Index of Economic Freedom that are available to the Arab countries are shown in the Table 3-9; the United Arab Emirates topped the Arab countries with its global ranking 15 in 2005. Algeria ranked 127 in the world and the last among the Arab countries with a rank 9. In 2006, Kuwait had the top rank among the Arab countries to occupy the rank 19 in the world. Algeria ranked 124 in the world and ranked 9 among the Arab countries.

In 2007, United Arab Emirates topped the Arab countries with its global ranking 19. Algeria ranked 131 in the world and ranked 9 among the Arab countries. In 2008, for the second year respectively, the United Arab Emirates topped the Arab countries with its global ranking 12.

Algeria ranked 132 in the world and ranked 9 among the Arab countries and for the fourth year, it is at the end of the list of Arab countries.

Table 3-9. Index of Economic Freedom in Arab Countries, 2005-2010

Country	2005		2006		2007		2008		2009		2010	
	Score	Rank	Score	Rank	Score	Rank	Score	Rank	Score	Rank	Score	Rank
Algeria	5.3	127	5.57	124	5.34	131	5	132	3.18	112	5.33	136
Bahrain	7.1	44	7.32	37	7.56	20	7.58	18	4.76	24	7.96	7
Egypt	6.5	76	6.65	75	6.68	79	6.68	80	3.72	75	6.48	99
Jordan	7	52	7.19	45	7.4	34	7.24	42	4.39	37	7.65	21
Kuwait	7.3	32	7.62	19	7.46	30	7.46	24	3.96	59	7.63	23
Morocco	5.9	107	6.24	95	6.16	104	6.2	100	4.01	55	6.42	102
Oman	7.6	18	7.32	37	7.36	36	7.22	43	4.52	34	7.65	21
Qatar	-	-	-	-	-	-	-	-	4.5	35	7.69	18
Saudi Arabia	-	-	-	-	-	-	-	-	4.36	42	7.1	64
Tunisia	6.6	69	6.44	82	6.39	90	6.44	90	4.36	41	6.82	79
United Arab Emirates	7.7	15	7.49	26	7.58	19	7.73	12	4.97	18	7.89	10

-Data are not available

Source: Author's elaboration according to (Wall Street Journal).

In 2009, for the third year, respectively, the United Arab Emirates topped the Arab countries with its global ranking 18. Saudi Arabia was added this year to the ranking for the first time and reached the rank 42 in the world, and the 7 among Arab countries. Algeria ranked 112 in the world and ranked 11 among the Arab countries. In 2010, Bahrain for the first year topped the Arab countries with its global ranking 7. Algeria ranked 136 in the world and ranked 11 among the Arab countries.

4. Transparency Index (Corruption)

There is no universal standard definition of corruption because it is subject to many factors: sectoral, legal, and ethical (Cederlöf & Ålander, 2013). The transparency is defined as the dissemination the accurate and regular information (Mitchell, 1998, p. 109). Other's are define the transparency as the "increased flow of timely and reliable economic, social and political information, which is accessible to all relevant stakeholders" (Daniel & Tara, 1999). Another definition goes further and perceive the transparency as the announcement by the government the information used to make the decision, not only announcement for the policy-decision (Hollyer, Rosendorff, & Vreeland, 2011, p. 9). Transparency International has defined it, as "Corruption is the abuse of entrusted power for private gain, it hurts everyone whose life, and livelihood or happiness depends on the integrity of people in a position of authority" (Transparency International UK's Defence and Security Programme).

Johann Graf Lambsdorff designed the Transparency International Index (CPI) (Lambsdorff, 2007). The index ranks 183 countries regarding corruption among politicians and government officials (Eiras, 2003). It is a composite index, based on polls, conducted by several reputable independent institutions.

Table 3-10. Transparency Index in Arab Countries, 2005-2010

Country	2005		2006		2007		2008		2009		2010	
	Score	Rank	Score	Rank	Score	Rank	Score	Rank	Score	Rank	Score	Rank
Algeria	2.8	97	3.1	84	3	99	3.2	92	2.8	111	2.9	105
Bahrain	5.8	36	5.7	36	5	46	5.4	43	5.1	46	4.9	48
Egypt	3.4	70	3.3	70	2.9	105	2.8	115	2.8	111	3.1	98
Iraq	2.2	137	1.9	160	1.5	178	1.3	178	1.5	176	1.5	175
Jordan	5.7	37	5.3	40	4.7	53	5.1	47	5	49	4.7	50
Kuwait	4.7	45	4.8	46	4.3	60	4.3	65	4.1	66	4.5	54
Lebanon	3.1	83	3.6	63	3	99	3	102	2.5	130	2.5	127
Morocco	3.2	78	3.2	79	3.5	72	3.5	80	3.3	89	3.4	85
Oman	6.3	28	5.4	39	4.7	53	5.5	41	5.5	39	5.3	41
Qatar	5.9	32	6	32	6	32	6.5	28	7	22	7.7	19
Saudi Arabia	3.4	70	3.3	70	3.4	79	3.5	80	4.3	63	4.7	50
Tunisia	4.9	43	4.6	51	4.2	61	3.5	62	4.2	65	4.3	59
UAE	6.2	30	6.2	31	5.7	34	4.4	35	6.5	30	6.3	28

Source: Author's elaboration according to (Transparency International).

The CPI focuses on corruption in the public sector and corruption as the abuse of public office for private gain (The Internet Center for Corruption Research). Surveys used to ask questions relating to the misuse of public power for private benefit, for example, embezzlement, bribery, administrative and political corruption (Dragon). Transparency International Index (CPI) is a composite of various corruption indicators (Thompson & Shah, 2005). The degree of corruption as the index ranges between 10 (highly clean) and zero (very bad).

Table 3-10 shows the Transparency Index in Arab countries for the period 2005-2010. In 2005, the Oman topped the Arab countries in the Transparency International Index and ranked 28 in the world. Iraq ranked 137 in the world and the end of the list among Arab countries with position 12. In 2006, the United Arab Emirates topped the Arab countries with rank 31 in the world. Iraq ranked 160 in the world and the end of the Arabic countries list. In 2007, Qatar topped the Arab countries with rank 32 in the world. Finally, Iraq ranked 178 in the world and was at the end of the Arabic countries list. In 2008, Qatar was at the top of the Arab countries for the second year ranked 28 in the world. Iraq ranked 178 in the world, at the end of the Arabic countries list. In 2009, Qatar topped the Arab countries in the Transparency International Index for the third year and ranked 22 in the world. Iraq ranked 176 in the world and the end of the Arabic countries list. In 2010, Qatar topped the Arab countries for the fourth year and ranked 19 in the world. Iraq ranked 175 in the world and the end of the Arabic countries list.

5. Doing Business Index

Bureaucratic quality can be measured through the World Bank Ease of Doing Business Index. The Doing Business project was launched in 2001 (Foa & Tanner, 2012). The first report of Doing Business was published in 2003. It looks at the local small and medium-sized businesses through data collection and analyses of comprehensive quantitative comparison between the business organization environments activities. The Ease of Doing Business index includes the ten following topics. Each topic is itself an aggregate of a set of indicators (Manuel, et al., 2013, p. 14):

- starting a business,
- paying taxes,
- enforcing contracts,
- getting electricity,
- trading across borders,
- protecting investors,
- dealing with construction permits,
- registering property,
- getting credit,
- resolving insolvency.

The data concerning Doing Business Index that are available to the Arab countries are shown in the Table 3-11, Saudi Arabia had the top rank among the Arab countries for the period 2005-2010. In 2005, Kuwait occupied the high rank among the Arab countries, after Saudi Arabia that is the rank 47 in the world. Egypt ranked 141 in the world and 11 among Arab countries.

In 2006, Kuwait occupied the top rank among the Arab countries to occupy the rank 46 in the world, and Egypt ranked 165 in the world and 11 among Arab countries for the second year.

Table 3-11. Doing Business Index in Arab Countries, 2005-2010

Country	2005 Rank	2006 Rank	2007 Rank	2008 Rank	2009 Rank	2010 Rank
Algeria	128	116	125	132	136	136
Bahrain	-	-	-	18	20	28
Egypt	141	165	126	114	106	94
Iraq	114	145	141	152	153	166
Jordan	74	78	80	101	100	111
Kuwait	47	46	40	52	61	74
Lebanon	95	86	85	99	108	113
Morocco	102	115	129	128	128	114
Oman	51	55	49	57	65	57
Qatar	-	-	-	37	39	50
Saudi Arabia	38	38	23	16	13	11
Tunisia	58	80	88	73	69	55
United Arab Emirates	69	77	68	46	33	40

-Data are not available.

Source: Author's elaboration according to (The World Bank, 2006; The World Bank, 2007; The World Bank, 2008; The World Bank, 2009; The World Bank, 2010).

In 2007, Kuwait occupied the top rank among the Arab countries, to occupy the rank 40 in the world for the third year and Iraq ranked 141 in the world and 11 among Arab countries.

In 2008, United Arab Emirates occupied the top rank among the Arab countries, to occupy the rank 46 in the world. Bahrain for the first time is added and ranked 18 in the world, and ranked as the second among Arab countries. Qatar for the first time is added and ranked 37 in the world and rank as the third among Arab countries. Iraq ranked 152 in the world and 13 among Arab countries.

In 2009, Bahrain is ranked 20 in the world and ranked as the second among Arab countries for the second years. The order of Arab countries in doing business index rank in the world is sorted by the sequence in the Arab countries in 2009. The United Arab Emirates ranks 33, Qatar ranks 39, Kuwait ranks 61, Oman ranks 65, Tunisia ranks 69, Jordan ranks 100, Egypt ranks 106, Lebanon ranks 108, Morocco ranks 128, Algeria ranks 136, and Iraq ranked 153 in the world and 13 among Arab countries. In 2010, Bahrain ranked 28 in the world, and rank the second among Arab countries for the third year, and Iraq ranked 166 in the world and 13 among Arab countries.

6. Worldwide Governance Indicators (WGI)

Since the beginning of the nineties, the researchers on the development focused on 'good governance' to achieve the goal of development (Thomas, 2010, p. 31). The World Bank has identified "good governance" as "the ways public officials and public institutions acquire and exercise authority to provide public goods and services, including basic services, infrastructure, and a sound investment climate" (Maurseth, 2009). The World Bank issued a global indicator of governance ('WGI') as one of a number of governance indicators (Thomas, 2010, p. 31). Traditions and institutions that exercised power in the country are the highlights of the index made up, all over the world (Kaufmann, Daniel; Kraay, Aart; Mastruzzi, Massimo, 2010).

The Worldwide Governance Indicators report on six broad dimensions of governance for 215 countries over the period 1996-2013 (Kaufmann, Daniel; Kraay, Aart, 2007, p. 8):

- voice and accountability,
- political stability and violence,
- government effectiveness,
- regulatory quality,
- rule of law,
- control of corruption.

The WGI compile and summarize information from 32 existing data sources that report the views and experiences of citizens, entrepreneurs, and experts in the public, private and NGO sectors from around the world, on the quality of various aspects of governance.
The WGI draw on four types of source data (Quibria, 2014, p. 9):

- surveys of households and firms,
- commercial business information,
- non-governmental organizations,
- public sector organizations.

The indicators refer to their standard units, ranging from approximately -2.5 to 2.5, and with higher values corresponding to better outcomes (United Nations Development Assistance Framework, 2010, p. 15). Here we will refer to both political stability and the rule of law because of the following reasons:

- available data to Arab countries,
- these two factors are the most important in these countries, and will be among our test in this dissertation
- other factors included in Worldwide Governance Indicators, we refer to them at another indicator, such as Corruption.

Table 3-12. Political Stability Index in Arab Countries, 2005-2010

Region/Economy	Score/ Year					
	2005	2006	2007	2008	2009	2010
Algeria	-0.93	-1.12	-1.13	-1.09	-1.22	-1.26
Bahrain	-0.02	-0.39	-0.24	-0.24	-0.16	-0.51
Egypt	-0.65	-0.87	-0.59	-0.52	-0.62	-0.91
Iraq	-2.72	-2.83	-2.79	-2.48	-2.19	-2.26
Jordan	-0.13	-0.77	-0.31	-0.36	-0.36	-0.31
Kuwait	0.2	0.36	0.56	0.46	0.34	0.44
Lebanon	-1.02	-1.85	-2.13	-1.9	-1.58	-1.63
Morocco	-0.55	-0.47	-0.51	-0.6	-0.41	-0.38
Oman	0.92	0.82	0.91	0.92	0.8	0.59
Qatar	0.99	0.91	0.94	1.1	1.21	1.12
Saudi Arabia	-0.25	-0.54	-0.5	-0.37	-0.51	-0.22
Tunisia	0.05	0.24	0.19	0.12	0.06	-0.04
United Arab Emirates	0.85	0.91	0.97	0.7	0.91	0.79

Source: Author's elaboration according to (The World Bank Group).

Table 3-12 shows the estimates of the indicator of the political stability in Arab countries for the period 2005-2010. In the table, the sequence of the Arab countries according to the political stability index in 2005, respectively, is as follows :Qatar, Oman, United Arab Emirates, Kuwait, Tunisia, Bahrain, Jordan, Saudi Arabia, Morocco, Egypt, Algeria, Lebanon, and in the last was Iraq. In 2010, for example we can see that Bahrain reduces three positions from the position of the year 2009 to rank 9 among the Arab countries. Jordan kept its position in 2007 and maintained the rank 7 among the Arab countries until the end of 2010. Saudi Arabia jumped over three positions from the position of the year 2009 to rank 6 among the Arab countries in 2010 etc. for the other countries. It means there is no continuous stability in the region, and therefore, the quality of various aspects of governance is changing over the time.

From the Table 3-13, the sequence of the Arab countries according to the Rule of Law Index in 2005, respectively, is as follows: Qatar, Bahrain, Kuwait, United Arab Emirates, Jordan, Oman, Saudi Arabia, Tunisia, Egypt, Morocco, Lebanon, Algeria, and the last was Iraq.

Table 3-13. Rule of Law Index in Arab Countries, 2005-2010

Region/Economy	Score/ Year					
	2005	2006	2007	2008	2009	2010
Algeria	-0.7	-0.64	-0.71	-0.71	-0.76	-0.75
Bahrain	0.65	0.42	0.57	0.57	0.55	0.48
Egypt	0.03	-0.2	-0.18	-0.09	-0.06	-0.12
Iraq	-1.77	-1.79	-1.92	-1.84	-1.77	-1.62
Jordan	0.41	0.38	0.45	0.46	0.28	0.2
Kuwait	0.6	0.58	0.65	0.62	0.61	0.6
Lebanon	-0.3	-0.63	-0.71	-0.68	-0.69	-0.69
Morocco	-0.12	-0.25	-0.26	-0.19	-0.19	-0.16
Oman	0.4	0.37	0.51	0.71	0.66	0.64
Qatar	0.7	0.72	0.63	0.79	1.01	0.95
Saudi Arabia	0.1	0.11	0.19	0.19	0.16	0.26
Tunisia	0.1	0.2	0.17	0.14	0.2	0.12
United Arab Emirates	0.48	0.37	0.36	0.49	0.46	0.37

Source: Author's elaboration according to (The World Bank Group).

In 2010, at the end of the period of our study we can see the sequence of the first four Arab countries according to the Rule of Law Index, which is respectively as follows: Qatar, United Arab Emirates, Oman, Kuwait. All these countries are a part of the Gulf Cooperation Council, and it means that this group of the country have the better stability than other Arab countries. As well as we can note these countries are in the first four of Arab countries according to the Rule of Law Index in 2005.

CHAPTER FOUR: Empirical Analysis of the Investment Attractiveness in Arab Countries

In this chapter, the outcomes of the methods and procedures presented in Chapter 2 are applied to the data (determinants of FDI attractiveness) describing 13 Arab countries and Poland, used as a basis for comparison. The scope of this study was all 22 Arab countries. However, we have been restricted to "only" 13 of these Arab countries' data because there is not enough data about the others. For example, for Sudan there is no data about FDI, for the State of Palestine there is no data about inflation and for the Comoros there is no data for GDP. In Somalia, there was a war during this period and an unstable political and economic situation. In some Arab countries there data exists, but it is unreliable. We selected the period 2005-2010 because:

- the years before 2005, the region experienced a long period of instability. That was because of the wars in Iraq, and imposing economic sanctions on Iraq. Therefore, the Arab region has suffered from a state of political and economic stability. As well as the FDI inflows, percentage of world total FDI inflows before 2005 was insignificant and did not exceed 3.4 percent. While this percentage increased to 4.8 percent in 2005 and reached a maximum in 2009, with 7 percent.

- since the beginning of 2011, the Arab world has witnessed a lack of political and economic stability, which lasted until now, because of the Arab Spring or the Arab revolutions. During the period that followed the events of the Arab Spring there is not enough or reliable data for many of the Arab countries.

This study is the first to compare the investment attractiveness of Arab countries in the Middle East and North Africa with that of Poland in the period 2005-2010. We did an investigation in both of database of the Iraqi Ministry of Higher Education and Scientific Research and in different databases on the Internet and there was not a study on the same subject. We selected Poland as the basis for comparison and the reasons for this are as follows:

1. For comparison, we wanted a country, which was a good benchmark for investment attractiveness. We concentrated on Europe because of the change from a centrally planned economy to a market economy, as this is what happened in some of the Arab countries, which were transformed from a centralised system into a market system, such as Iraq. Poland has become the most attractive country for foreign investment in Central Europe since its transformation from communism more than 20 years ago. There is some

instruction of inflows of capital to the country in some Arab countries same like in Poland on communism. Poland has the largest economy in Central Europe and was the only European Union country that recorded economic growth when the other economies declined during the financial crisis in 2009. Poland has one of the strongest stock exchanges, while the financial markets in some Arab countries are characterised by weak or non-existent stock exchanges. Thus, Poland is a good model for countries seeking to develop financial markets. Poland is the largest source of natural resources in Europe, and some Arab countries (such as Saudi Arabia, Iraq, Qatar and others) have huge potential natural resources, such as oil and gas and other minerals (see Chapter 3). Poland may now be at a historical crossroads, in effect becoming one of the leading European countries and a model for Arab economies.

2. In some aspects, Arab countries are comparable to Poland. Poland is a religious society in a similar way to Arab countries. To select other countries for comparison - such as China, India, etc. - would have been misleading because of the large difference between the size of their economies and populations and those of each separate Arab country, and therefore it was sensible to choose Poland. Also, Poland has its own independent currency, as is the case with Arab countries.

Measures of attractiveness are determined on the basis of two sets of data: data for each year (the period 2005 to 2010) separately, and the average data for every factor for the whole period 2005-2010. This will be the procedure adopted in our calculations in this chapter. The period 2005-2010 was selected because: before 2005 some Arab countries experienced a long period of instability such as: the wars in Iraq (1980-1991), the imposition of economic sanctions on Iraq (1991-2003); low oil prices in certain years, some Arab countries having to resort to the IMF as a precondition for the rescheduling of their foreign debt and agreeing to a comprehensive reform programme, and thus being forced to reduce subsidies on the prices of basic living materials, which led to the explosion of popular unrest in Egypt (1977), Tunisia (1984), Morocco (1981 and 1984), Algeria (1988), Jordan (1989), and led to a lack of economic and political stability in these countries. Therefore, the Arab region has suffered from a state of political and economic instability. As well as the FDI inflows, percentage of world total FDI inflows before 2005 was insignificant and did not exceed 3.4 percent. While this percentage increased to 4.8 percent in 2005 and reached a maximum in 2009, with 7 percent. Since the beginning of 2011, the Arab world has witnessed a lack of political and economic stability that persists to this day because of the so-called Arab Spring or the Arab revolutions. During the period that followed the events of the Arab Spring there is not enough or reliable data for many of the Arab countries.

Our data sets are: 1. Economic factors: GDP growth, GDP p/c, GDP p/c growth, tax payment, trade (% of GDP), inflation/ GDP deflator, imports of goods and services (% of GDP), urban population and labour force; 2. Social factors: secondary education, electricity production; 3. Political factors: political stability, rule of law, transparency, time to export and time to import. For each of these we shall use the following attractiveness measuring procedure: a synthetic vector measure, separately for each factor, and a composite measure using the synthetic vector measure for each set of key determinants, i.e. a composite vector measure for vector measures of the economic variables, social variables and political variables. Each kind of measure of attractiveness will be confronted with the actual amount of inward FDI inflows in the particular countries. As a measure of the proposed indicators' adequacy, we used the Pearson correlation. In section 4.1, we shall analyse the attractiveness of Arab countries and Poland using vector methods. In section 4.2, the factors influencing investment attractiveness in Arab countries (in comparison with Poland) will be analysed. In section 4.3, we shall present the changes in the investment attractiveness of Arab countries and Poland in the period 2005-2010. In section 4.4, we shall refer to the propositions for changes in investment attractiveness important in Arab countries, according to the results of our study.

4.1. Analyses of the Attractiveness of Arab Countries and Poland Using Vector Methods

In this chapter, we shall use the input data that we have selected according to three groups of factors. We refer to these groups in detail in Chapter 1 (see input data in appendices 1-14). We try to have our score, and ranks to Arab countries and Poland, using 16 factors from three kinds of groups. Our choice of these factors was on the basis of the theoretical analyses of the problem and grouping was done according to this theoretical restricted by availability of data. These groups can overlap and are sometimes difficult to differentiate. We decided to do a test for each year and we also made a test for the average data over the period 2005-2010. Our test in this section will be of all the Arab countries and Poland as comparing country.

In order to build our composite vector measure, we will adopt the places that we described earlier in section 2.3.1:

1. Selection of variables (see Table 2-1, and appendices 1-14),
2. Elimination of variables (see Table 4-1, and appendices 22-27),

114

3. Normalisation of variables (see figures 4-1, 4-2, 4-3, and appendices 22-27),

4. Determination of the pattern and anti-pattern (see appendices 1-14, and appendices 37-42),

5. Determination of the synthetic measure (see appendices 15-21, and 28-42).

In the first step we shall calculate the statistical parameters of 16 selected variables (determinants), used to represent 13 Arab countries and Poland. Variables are gathered into three groups of parameters (so-called key determinants): economic determinants, social determinants and political determinants. The collected data cover the period from the year 2005 until the year 2010. Table 4-1 shows descriptive statistics of the raw data for the period 2005-2010 average and the rest of the tables for the years 2005-2010 are in appendices 22-27.

Table 4-1. Descriptive Statistics of Raw Average Data for the period 2005-2010

Group Factors		Variable	Minimal Value	Maximal Value	Mean Value	Median Value	Standard Deviation
		GDP growth	2.7667	16.3500	5.8512	5.8250	3.3076
		GDP p/c	1.4085	56.8818	14.2822	7.5829	16.4080
		GDP p/c growth	-10.3833	4.7833	1.6417	3.5250	4.1331
	Economic Factors	Trade (% of GDP)	60.9000	137.9000	96.1607	90.8000	24.1691
		Tax payment	3.0000	38.1667	20.0833	16.5000	10.2450
		Inflation/ GDP deflator	2.4833	15.9500	7.6917	8.5500	3.7527
		Imports of goods and services (% of GDP)	27.5500	83.2833	44.7655	40.1333	16.6329
		Urban population	43.2000	98.2000	75.1881	77.0417	15.9595
Social	Factors	Labour force	0.5700	24.4138	6.7672	3.8622	7.2309
		Secondary education	0.0623	7.9659	1.6018	0.5964	2.1598
		Electricity	5.5616	100.7868	28.5990	14.7887	30.7480
	Political Factors	Political stability	-2.5450	1.0450	-0.2619	-0.3167	1.0316
		Rule of law	-1.7850	0.8000	0.0486	0.2658	0.6956
		Transparency	1.6500	6.5167	4.2488	4.4000	1.3763
		Time to export	8.5000	98.3333	22.3452	16.6667	22.2165
		Time to import	8.6667	98.0000	25.9048	21.8333	21.5937

Source: Author's elaboration.

In this section, we present the results of FDI attractiveness, using the vector measure described in Chapter 2. After presenting the results, a relevant discussion is provided. We use the vector method as the basic method employed for ranking the FDI attractiveness of selected countries. This method provides a multidimensional space for selected economic and demographic determinants to one-dimensional space of the FDI attractiveness scores. We used a Pearson

115

correlation between our vector measure scores and the actual amount of FDI inflows as a vector scores validation method. It is intuitively clear that the measures of FDI attractiveness should significantly correlate with actual inflows of FDI

Because the vector measure is non-linearly connected with the original data, it is impossible to back track from vector measure score to the values of individual determinants and assess their influence on the resulting value of scores. The possibility of such backtracking would be very helpful to suggest which determinants should be improved to increase the country's FDI attractiveness. To ensure such a possibility we introduced some structure to the set of determinants, grouping them into three categories. For each group of determinants we calculated its vector measure score, obtaining in the result the three dimensional description for each country. This procedure we call composite vector measure. This made it possible to compare the scores of individual key determinants with the ranking of the country and assess which of the key determinants should be improved to increase this country's FDI attractiveness.

In the bar plots we used linear scaling of scores in the range 100 to zero. The value 100 is attributed to the maximal value of vector measure score and zero to the minimal value. In the case of composite vector measure, we attribute 100 to the maximal value of the individual key determinant, zero to minimal value, and present this composite measure in the form of a stacked bar plot. This means that a stacked value can be maximally 300, and the smallest value can be as small as zero. Please note that we plot the composite vector measure for individual countries in an order induced by these countries' ranking (determined by the score of the vector measure).

To guarantee comparability we deflate some data series, either by current GDP or by population (data to each of them in appendices 1-14). In Figure 4-1, we show a box plot for deflated data.

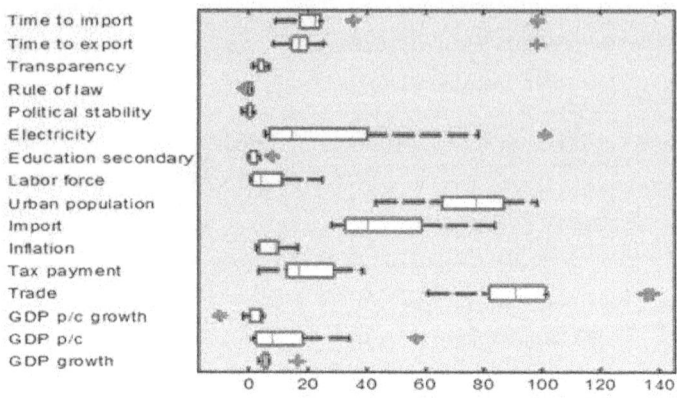

Figure 4-1. Box plot of deflated average data for the period 2005-2010

Source: Author's elaboration.

In order to realise index aggregation, all data points need to be normalised. Prior to weighting and aggregation, the variables are normalised to ensure the same standard among the them. The aim in the normalisation process is to identify the most proper procedure that takes into account the different measurement units and corresponding robustness of possible outliers (JRC Science Hub-European Commission, 2008). The choice of normalisation method depends particularly on the fitness for intended purpose and interpretability. Standardisation and re-scaling are identified as the most commonly used methods (Michela, Giovannini, Hoffman, Tarantola, Saltelli, & Saisana, 2005).

We shall use two common kinds of data normalisation, re-scaling and standardisation (z-scores), to compare the results and choose the proper results for our work. The use of re-scaling (distance from the best and worst performers), where positioning is in relation to the global maximum and minimum and the index takes values between 0 (laggard) and 100 (leader) is for its ability to widen the range of variables lying within small intervals and the ease of interpretability in an index context. A box plot of the data after re-scaling for the period 2005-2010 average is shown in Figure 4-2. Moreover, a box plot for the years 2005-2010 is shown in appendices 22-27. The formula for re-scaling is described in detail in Chapter 2.

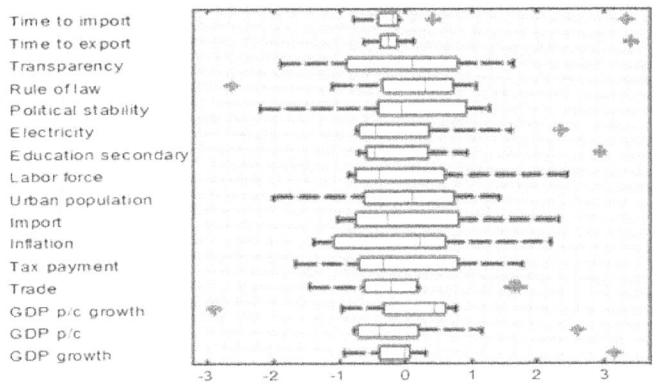

Figure 4-2. Box plot of average data after re-scaling for the period 2005-2010

Source: Author's elaboration.

Standardisation or z-scores (standard deviation from the mean), which imposes a standard normal distribution (i.e. a mean of 0 and a standard deviation of 1), is also commonly used as a normalisation method, where the variables are converted to a common scale with a mean of zero and standard deviation of one.

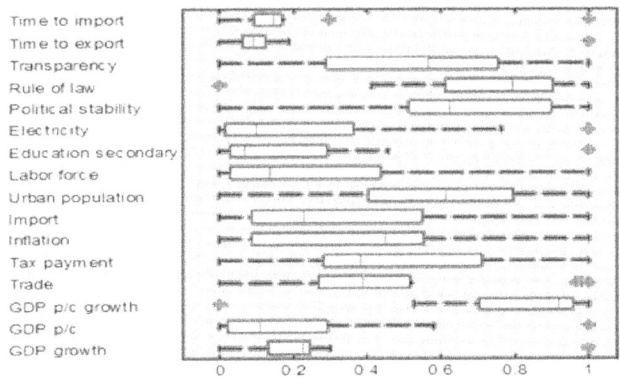

Figure 4-3. Box plot of average data after standardisation (z-scores) for the period 2005-2010

Source: Author's elaboration.

In Figure 4-3, a box plot of the data after standardisation for the period 2005-2010 average is shown above, while the box plot of data for the years 2005-2010 separately is shown in appendices 22-27. The method used in our work was the standard deviation approach (z-score); the reason for choosing this method is its available features in variable aggregation, and because the results of z-score were better than the results of the re-scaling

First of all, we tried to make a calculated to scores and ranks by using vector measure to all the 16 factors separately. Our results (appendixes 15-20) shows that it is impossible to backtrack from vector measure score to values of individual determinants and assess their influence on resulting value of scores. As we aimed to assist decision makers in improving the investment attractiveness, so we introduced the multi-level structure of vector measure, by making a hierarchy: individual determinants are grouped into three key determinants. The final measure is calculated based on the measures of these key determinants, i.e. we calculate vector measure for a group of determinants consisting the key determinants and in next step we calculate final measure based on measures for key determinants.

Our analyses of the results of scores composite vector measure in Figure 4-4 show that, in the year 2005, the composite vector measure of Egypt had the highest value score of vector measure (100). Poland was in the second rank with a score of 99.40. Kuwait was in the third rank with a score of 98.05. Saudi was in the fourth rank with a score of 92.86, followed by Jordan with a score of 87.34. In the sixth rank was Bahrain with a score of 78.89, followed by Algeria with a score of 74.78 and the UAE with a score of 74.09. In ninth place was Qatar with a score of 71.38, followed by Tunisia with a score of 60.54. In eleventh place was Oman with a score of 59.91, followed by Morocco with a score of 53.67. In the last two positions were Lebanon and Iraq with 42.30 and zero scores respectively (see Appendix 28).

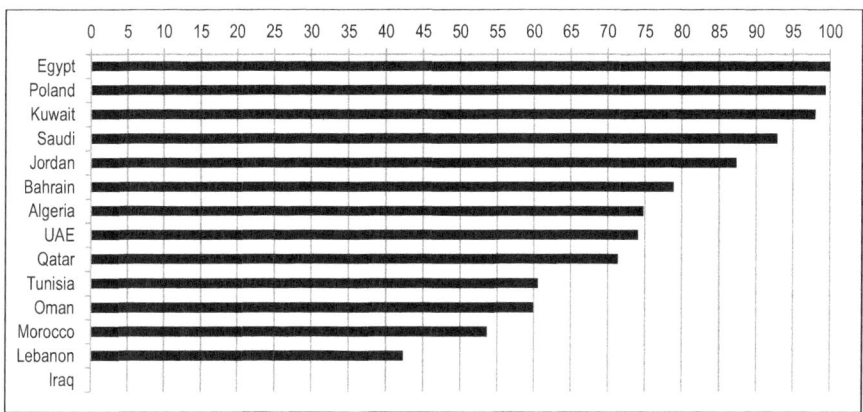

Figure 4-4. FDI attractiveness scores composite vector measures for the year 2005

Source: Author's elaboration.

The analyses of the FDI attractiveness scores of key determinants in the year 2005 for the Arab countries and Poland (see Figure 4-5) show that in the key economic determinants Kuwait, Jordan, and Poland were in the top three positions respectively. This could be due to the highest GDP growth of Kuwait which achieved 10.1 percent, and Jordan which achieved 8.1 percent, while in the case of Poland the value of both GDP growth and GDP growth per capita could be the reasons for this high position. The last three positions were occupied by Oman, Lebanon and, in last place, Iraq. This is a natural result because of the high inflation in these countries and the unstable economic situations in Lebanon and Iraq. In the key social determinants the first three positions were occupied by Egypt and Poland, with Saudi in the third position. These positions are attributable to demographic reasons. The last three positions are occupied by Oman, Qatar and Bahrain. These positions could also be due to demographic reasons. In the key political determinants, the first three positions were the UAE, Oman and Qatar. These positions were owing to these countries having the highest scores in political stability and a high score in the rule of law compared with the other countries. The last three positions were occupied by Lebanon, Algeria and Iraq. These are expected results because these countries had the lowest score in political stability, rule of law and transparency compared with the other countries. In addition, the times to export and import in both Lebanon and Iraq were the highest compared with the other countries.

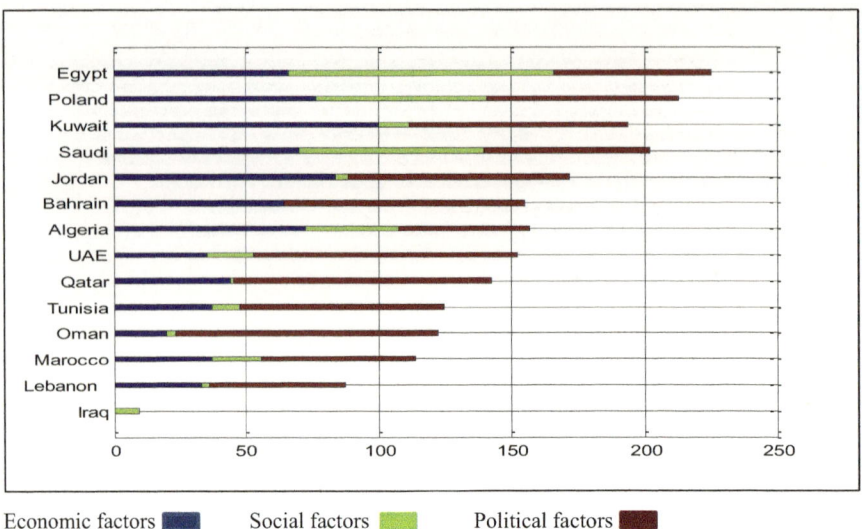

Economic factors ▮ Social factors ▮ Political factors ▮

Figure 4-5. FDI attractiveness score of key determinants for the year 2005

Source: Author's elaboration.

In the year 2006, the composite vector measure shows that Egypt lost its first position to Poland. The highest value score of the vector measure was 100 to Poland. Egypt was ranked third with a score of 85.34 (see Appendix 29). Qatar's position had changed by seven places from ninth in 2005 to the rank of 2 in 2006, with a score of 86.78. Saudi stayed in fourth place for the second year, though its score fell from 92.86 in 2005 to 65.47. It was followed by Morocco, whose score rose from 53.67 in 2005 to 59.57 and its rank changed from 12 to 5 in the same years respectively. Kuwait in this year fell 6 places from the rank of 3 in 2005 to the rank of 6 with a score of 52.20 in 2006. Tunisia jumped from the rank of 10 in 2005 to the rank of 7 in 2006, although its score fell from 60.54 to 50.00 in the same years Algeria dropped one position from the rank of 7 in 2005 to the rank of 8 in 2006, with a score of 46.68. It was the same situation with the UAE: in 2006 its rank was 9 with a score of 40.92, but it declined one rank from the previous year. Jordan's score fell from 87.34 in 2005 to 40.15 in 2006, and its rank declined to 10. In the eleventh rank was Oman for the second year, while its score fell from 59.91 in 2005 to 39.84 in 2006. Bahrain's rank fell from 6 in the year 2005 to the rank of 12 with a score of 37.78 in 2006. Lebanon was in the same rank, 13, for the second year, while its score fell to 28.57. Iraq stood for the second year in the last rank, 14, with the same score of 0. Figure 4-6 shows the FDI attractiveness ranks and scores according to the key determinants.

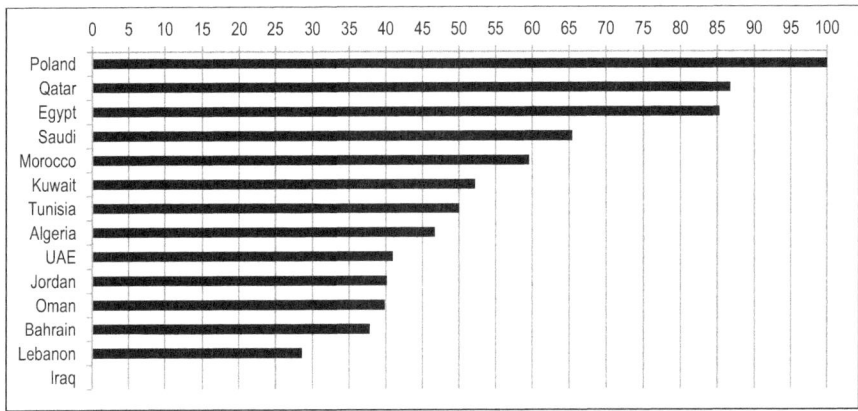

Figure 4-6. FDI attractiveness scores composite vector measures for the year 2006

Source: Author's elaboration.

The analyses of the FDI attractiveness scores of key determinants in the year 2006 for the Arab countries and Poland (see Figure 4-7) show that in economic key determinants Poland, Qatar, and Egypt were in the top three positions respectively. This could be due to the increase of the value to the following factors: GDP growth, GDP per capita growth and inflation, all compared to what was achieved in the other countries. In the last three positions were Oman, Iraq and the UAE. This is a natural result because of the high inflation and the unstable economic situation in Lebanon and Iraq, and because of the negative GDP per capita growth in the UAE (we will refer to this in detail in the next section). In the key social determinants the first three positions were Egypt, Saudi and Poland. We can see that the same countries retained the first three positions for the second year. In the last three positions were Oman, Lebanon, and Bahrain. These positions can be attributed to demographic reasons, and we can see that both Oman and Bahrain had the three lowest scores for the second year. In the key political determinants the first three positions were the UAE, Qatar and Oman. These positions were owing to these countries having the highest scores in political stability and high scores in the rule of law compared with the other countries. We can see that the same countries retained the first three positions for the second year. In the last three positions were Algeria, Lebanon and Iraq. This is a natural result because these countries had the lowest scores for political stability, rule of law and transparency compared with the other countries for the second year. Also the times to export and import in Lebanon and Iraq were the highest compared with the other countries.

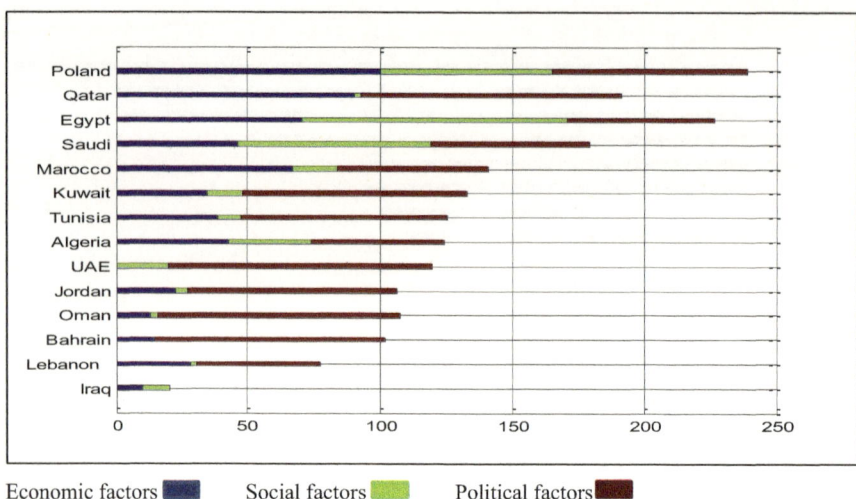

Economic factors ▬   Social factors ▬   Political factors ▬

Figure 4-7. FDI attractiveness score of key determinants for the year 2006

Source: Author's elaboration.

In the year 2007, the highest value score of vector measure was 100 to Poland for the second year (see Appendix 30). Saudi had moved to the second place with a score 86.75 compared with fourth place in the year 2006. Egypt ranked the third with a score of 85.34 for the second year. Qatar's position fell to fourth place with a score of 76.57. Kuwait in this year jumped one-step from sixth place in 2006 to fifth place with a score of 73.02 in 2007. Oman jumped to the rank of 6 with a score of 61.24. Also Jordan jumped from the rank of 10 in 2006, to the rank of 7 with a score of 61.20 in 2007. Tunisia fell from the rank of 7 in 2006 to the rank of 8 in 2007, although its score rose from 50.00 to 61.01 in the same years respectively. Bahrain's score rose from 37.78 in 2006 to 57.77 in 2007, and its rank has changed from rank 12 to 9 in the same years respectively. Algeria fell for the second year from the rank of 8 in 2006 to the rank of 10 in 2006, although its score rose from 46.68 to 57.40 for the same years respectively. It was the same situation with the UAE: in 2006 its rank was 9 with a score 40.92 but this declined to the rank of 11 with a score 55.64 in 2007. It was followed by Morocco. The country's score fell from 59.57 in 2006 to 53.26 in 2007, and its rank fell from 5 to 12 in the same years respectively. Lebanon was in the same rank of 13 for the third year while its score rose to 46.66. Iraq, for the third year, remained in the last rank with 14 and the same score of 0. Figure 4-8 shows the FDI attractiveness scores composite vector measures for the year 2007.

123

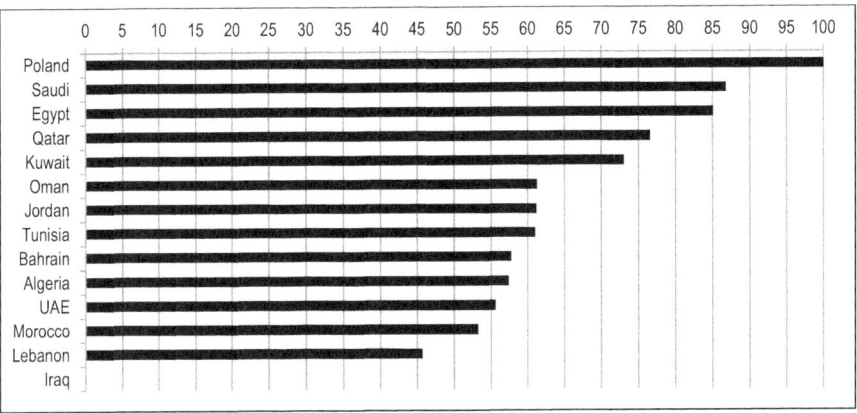

Figure 4-8. FDI attractiveness scores composite vector measures for the year 2007

Source: Author's elaboration.

The analyses of the FDI attractiveness scores of key determinants in the year 2007 for the Arab countries and Poland (see Figure 4-9) show that in the key economic determinants Poland, Kuwait, and Qatar were in top three positions respectively. In this year, Kuwait's position was in the top three and this could be because of the decrease in inflation from 2.1 percent in 2006 to 0.3 percent in 2007. In the last three positions were Morocco, the UAE and Iraq. This is a natural result because of the increase in inflation in Morocco and the decrease in GDP growth in both Morocco and Iraq. The negative GDP per capita growth in the UAE increased in this year compared with 2005 and 2006. In the key social determinants the first three positions were occupied by Egypt, Saudi and Poland and it was the same positions in the year 2006. In the last three positions were Qatar, Lebanon and Bahrain. These positions could be due to demographic reasons, and we can see that both Lebanon and Bahrain were in the same position as in 2006. In the key political determinants the first three positions were occupied by Qatar, the UAE and Oman. These positions were owing to these countries having the highest score in political stability and high scores in the rule of law compared with other countries. We can see that the same countries retained the first three positions for the third year. In the last three positions were Algeria, Lebanon and Iraq. This is a natural result because these countries had the lowest scores in political stability, rule of law and transparency compared with the other countries for the third year. Also the times to export and import in both Lebanon and Iraq were still the highest.

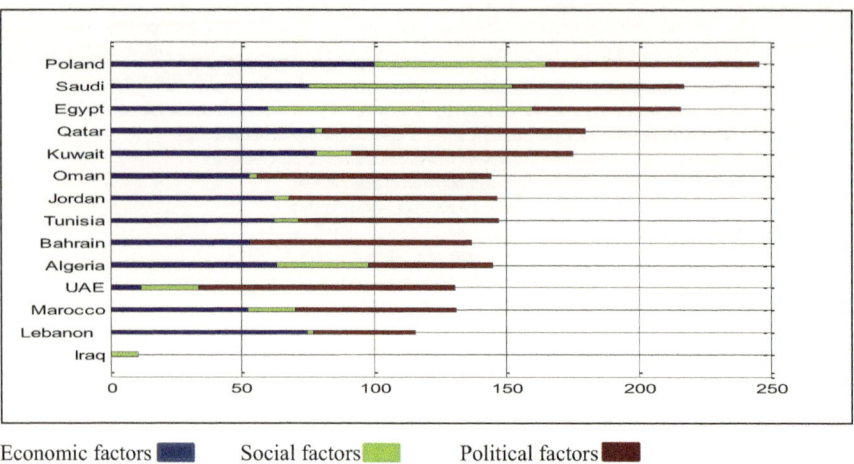

Economic factors ███   Social factors ▦   Political factors ███

Figure 4-9. FDI attractiveness score of key determinants for the year 2007

Source: Author's elaboration.

In the year 2008, the highest value score for vector measure was 100 to Poland for the third year. Egypt jumped to the second rank with a score of 81.65. Nevertheless, its score was less than in the previous year (see Appendix 31). Saudi fell to the third rank with a score of 81.59. Qatar's position was the same at 4 with a lower score of 73.60. Kuwait in this year was at the same rank of 6 that it was in 2007, with a lower score of 55.85. Also Oman was ranked the same at 6 with a lower score of 54.60, followed by Morocco's score, which fell from 53.26 in 2007 to 51.30 in 2008, although its rank rose from 12 to 7 in the same years. This was followed by Bahrain's score, which fell from 57.77 in 2007 to 50.83 in 2008, while its rank changed from 9 to 8 in the same year. The UAE was in the same situation. In 2007, its rank was 11 with a score of 55.64, bit it rose to the rank of 9 with a score 50.39 in 2008. For the second year, Algeria was in the same rank of 10, but its score fell from 57.40 in 2007 to 49.75 in 2008. Tunisia fell from the rank of 8 in 2007, to the rank of 11 in 2008 with a score of 48.58 for the same year. Jordan also fell from the rank of 7 in 2007 to the rank of 12 with a score of 43.46 in 2008. Lebanon was in the same rank, 13, for the fourth year with a score of 37.15. Iraq, for the fourth year, was in the lowest rank of 14 with the same score of 0. Figure 4-10 shows the FDI attractiveness score composite vector measures for the year 2008.

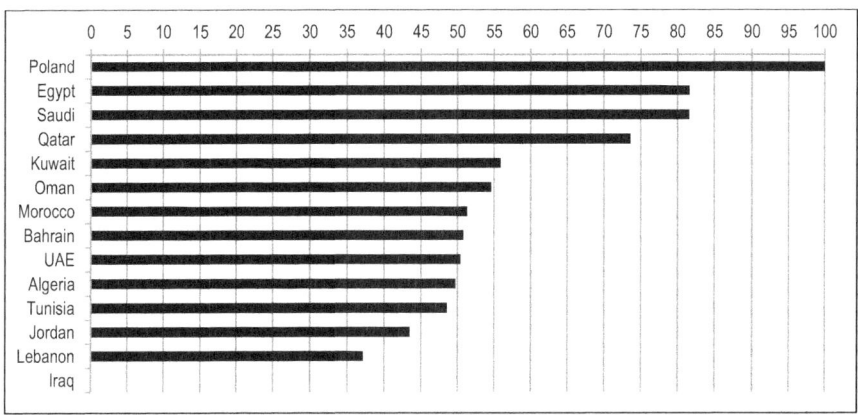

Figure 4-10. FDI attractiveness scores composite vector measures for the year 2008

Source: Author's elaboration.

The analyses of the FDI attractiveness scores of key determinants in the year 2008 for the Arab countries and Poland (see Figure 4-11) show that, in the key economic determinants, Poland, Qatar and Saudi were in the top three positions respectively. In this year, Saudi's position was in the top three and this could be because of the increase in GDP growth from 6 percent in 2007 to 8.4 percent in 2008. The last three positions were occupied by Jordan, the UAE and Iraq. This is a natural result because of the high inflation rates in Jordan, the UAE and Iraq, although the negative GDP per capita growth in the UAE decreased over this year compared with 2007. In the key social determinants, the first three positions went to Egypt, Saudi and Poland and the same positions applied in the year 2007. In the last three positions were Oman, Lebanon and Bahrain. These positions could be attributable to demographic reasons, and we can see that both Lebanon and Bahrain were in the same position from 2006. In key political determinants scores the first three positions are Qatar, Oman and the UAE. These positions were because these countries had the highest scores in political stability and high scores in the rule of law compared with the other countries. The last three positions went to Algeria, Lebanon and Iraq. These are natural results because these countries still had the lowest scores in political stability, rule of law and transparency from last few years. Also the times to export and import in both Lebanon and Iraq were still the same as in 2007.

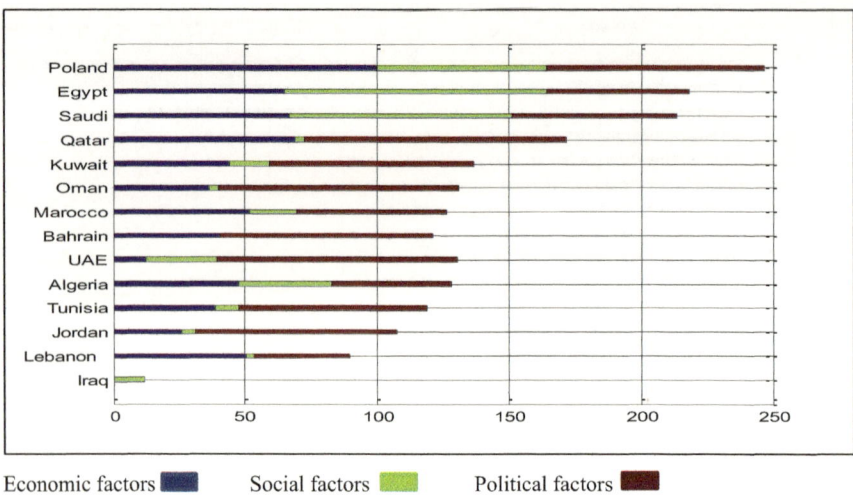

Figure 4-11. FDI attractiveness score of key determinants for the year 2008

Source: Author's elaboration.

Figure 4-12 shows the FDI attractiveness scores composite vector measures for the year 2009. In the year 2009, the high value score of the vector measure was 100 to Qatar after it jumped from the fourth rank in the previous year (see Appendix 32). Poland fell to the second rank with a score of 93.03. Saudi was in the third rank for the second year with a score of 88.60, and this was a higher score than it had in 2008. Egypt fell from the second rank to the fourth rank with a score of 64.68. Algeria's rank changed to 5 with a score of 51.16 compared with the rank of 10 in the previous year. Oman was at the same rank, 6, for the third year with a lower score of 45.89. Kuwait fell to the rank of 7 in 2009, with a score of 42.45. The UAE, in 2009, had changed by one place to the rank of 8 with a score of 36.66 and this was lower than the score of 50.39 in 2008. It was followed by Bahrain's score which fell from 50.38 in 2008 to 33.98 in 2009; also its rank fell from 8 to 9 in the same years respectively. This was followed by Morocco's score which fell from 51.30 in 2008 to 28.33 in 2009, although its rank fell from 7 in 2008 to 10 in the year 2009. Jordan rose from the rank of 12 in 2008 to the rank of 11 with a score of 22.02 in 2009. Tunisia fell from the ranking of 11 in 2008 to a ranking of 12 in 2009, with a lower score of 14.07 in the same year compared with a score of 48.58 in the previous year. In 2009, Iraq had changed for the first time to the rank of 13, with a score of 7.22. Lebanon, for the first time, was in the last of the list with a rank of 14 with a score of 0 in the year 2009.

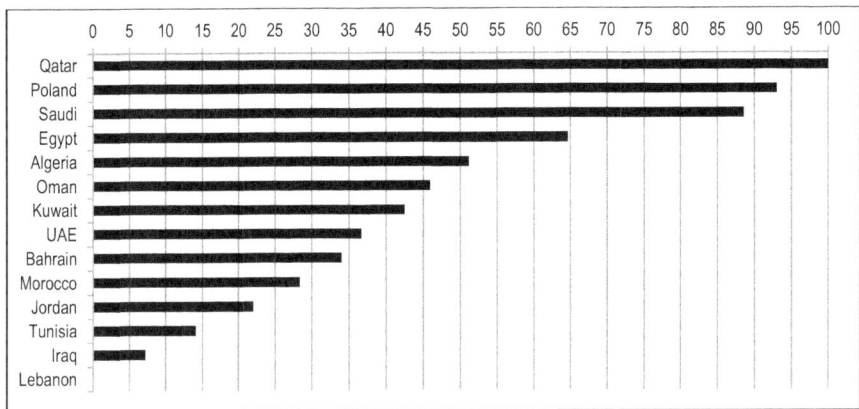

Figure 4-12. FDI attractiveness scores composite vector measures for the year 2009

Source: Author's elaboration.

Figure 4-13 shows the analyses of FDI attractiveness scores of the key determinants in the year 2009, for the Arab countries and Poland. In the key economic determinants, Qatar, Poland and Saudi were in the top three positions respectively. In this year, Poland took the second position because of the decrease in both GDP growth and GDP per capita growth compared with 2008. The last three positions went to Jordan, Tunisia and the UAE. This is a natural result because of the decrease in rates of GDP growth in Jordan and Tunisia, and because of the negative GDP growth and GDP per capita growth in the UAE. In the key social determinants the first three positions went to Egypt, Saudi and Poland and the positions were the same in the year 2008. In the last three positions were Oman, Lebanon and Bahrain. These were the same positions in 2008. In the key political determinants the first three positions went to Qatar, Oman and the UAE. These positions were the same as in 2008 and, for the same reasons as in 2008, these countries had the highest scores compared with the other countries. The last three positions went to Algeria, Lebanon and Iraq and these were the same rankings in 2008. Despite the fact that Lebanon has reduced the number of days that are necessary to complete its export-import operations, it was still in final place.

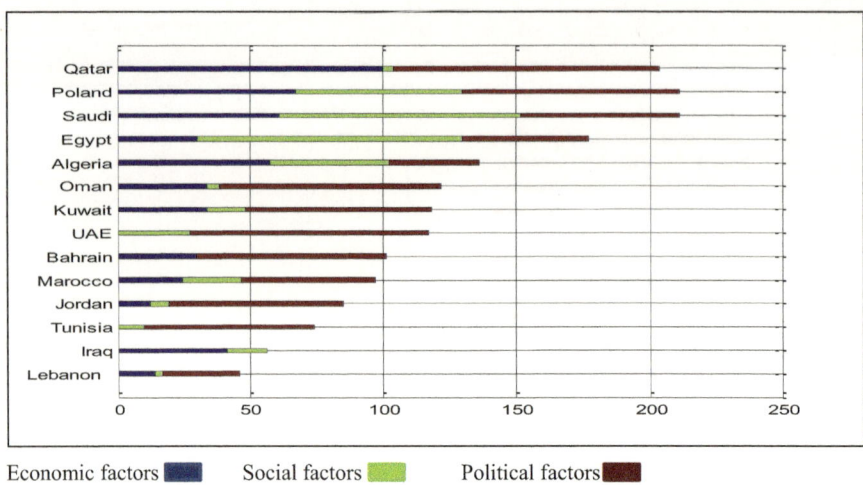

Economic factors ■   Social factors ▢   Political factors ■

Figure 4-13. FDI attractiveness score of key determinants for the year 2009

Source: Author's elaboration.

In the year 2010, Poland returned to the top of the list with the high value score of vector measure 100. Qatar fell one step to the rank of 2 with a score of 86.28 (see Appendix 33). Saudi was in the third rank for the third year with a score of 81.71 and this was a lower score than it was in 2009. Egypt was in the fourth rank for the second year with a score of 80.90 and this was higher than the score in the year 2009. It was followed by Morocco, whose rank rose from 10 in the year 2009 to that of 5 with a score of 59.74 in 2010. It was the same situation with the UAE: in 2009, its rank was 8 with a score of 36.66 which rose to the ranking of 6 with a score of 49.66 in 2010. Algeria fell to the rank of 7 with a score of 47.74 from its ranking of 5 in 2009. It was followed by Bahrain, whose score rose to 44.41 in 2010, from 28.33 in the year 2009, and its rank rose one-step to the rank of 8 in 2010, compared with the year 2009. Lebanon achieved significant growth in 2010, reaching the rank of 9 with a score of 44.05 after it had been in the lowest rank in 2009. Jordan rose from the rank of 11 in 2009 to the rank of 10 with a score of 41.04 in 2010. Oman fell five places to the rank of 11 with a score of 38.67. Also in the year 2010, Kuwait fell five places to the rank of 12 with a score of 37.55. Tunisia fell from the rank of 12 in 2009 to the rank of 13 in 2010 with a score of 34.34 for the same year. Iraq returned to the last ranking of 14 with the same score of 0 in the year 2010.

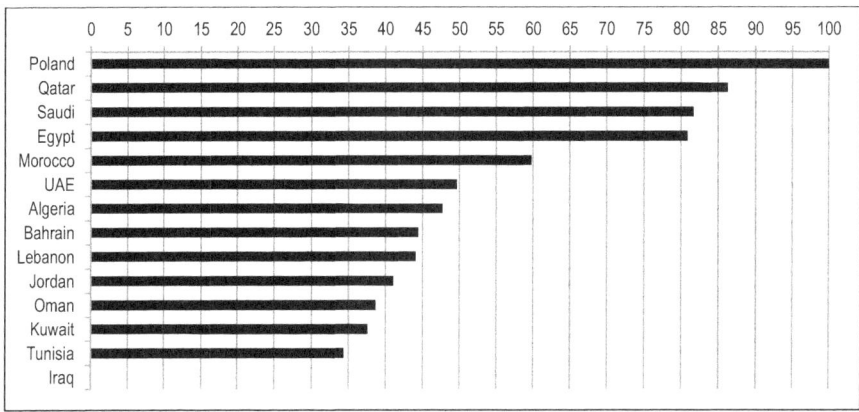

Figure 4-14. FDI attractiveness scores composite vector measures for the year 2010

Source: Author's elaboration.

The analyses of FDI attractiveness scores for the key determinants in the year 2010 for the Arab countries and Poland (see Figure 4-15) show that in the key economic determinants Poland, Qatar and Lebanon were in the top three positions respectively. In this year, Lebanon's position moved from the top three and this could be because of the big decrease in inflation from 10.5 percent in 2009 to 0.2 percent in 2010. The last three positions went to Oman, Kuwait and Iraq. This result is due to the high inflation rates in Oman, Kuwait and Iraq. The negative GDP per capita growth in the UAE decreased in this year compared with 2009, and for that reason the UAE's position changed from the ranking at 14 in 2009 to a ranking of 11 in 2010. In the key social determinants the first three positions went to Egypt, Saudi and Poland and it was the same positions in the year 2010. The last three positions were occupied by Oman, Lebanon and Bahrain and these were the same positions as in 2008 and 2009. In the key political determinants the first three positions went to Qatar, the UAE and Oman. These positions were because these countries still had the highest scores in the factors of the key political determinant group compared with other countries. The last three positions went to Algeria, Lebanon and Iraq.

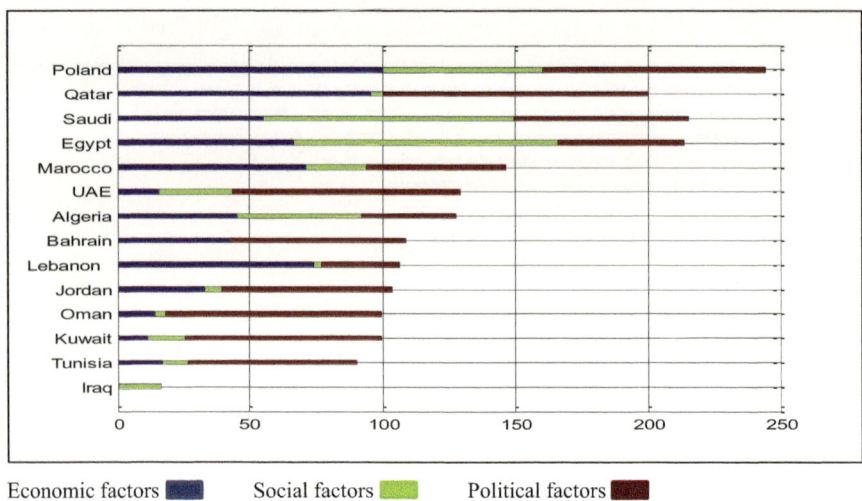

Economic factors ■   Social factors ▨   Political factors ■

Figure 4-15. FDI attractiveness score of key determinants for the year 2010

Source: Author's elaboration.

In the average data for the period 2005-2010, the high value score of the vector measure was 100 to Poland. Egypt was in the second rank with a score of 81.05 (see Appendix 34). Saudi was in the third rank with a score of 80.87. Qatar's position was in the rank of 4 with a score of 71.52. This was followed by Morocco, ranking 5 with a score of 57.99 in the average data for the period 2005-2010 Algeria was at the rank of 6 with a score of 56.52. Kuwait was at the rank of 7 with a score of 55.90. Tunisia was in the rank of 8 in the period 2005-2010 average data, with a score of 50.14, followed by Bahrain with a score of 48.52. The UAE was at ranked 10 with a score of 47.12 in the years 2005-2010 average. Oman was ranked 11 with a score of 46.89. Jordan was ranked 12 in the period 2005-2010 average with a score of 42.19. Lebanon was in the rank of 13 with a score of 40.33. Iraq was in the last rank with 14 and a score of 0. Figure 4-16 shows the FDI attractiveness scores composite vector measures for the period 2005-2010 average data.

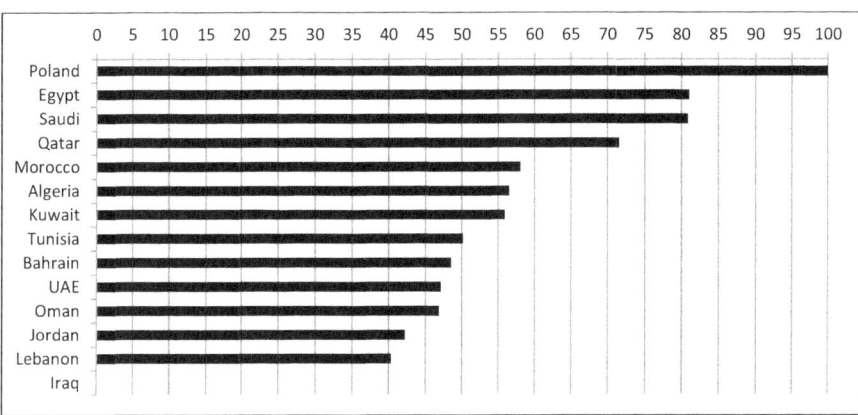

Figure 4-16. FDI attractiveness scores composite vector measures for the period 2005-2010 average data

Source: Author's elaboration.

The analyses of the FDI attractiveness score of key determinants for the average data in the period 2005-2010 for the Arab countries and Poland (see Figure 4-17) show that, in the key economic determinants, Poland, Qatar and Saudi are in the top three positions respectively. The last three positions went to Oman, the UAE and Iraq. In the key social determinants, the first three positions went to Egypt, Saudi and Poland. In the last three positions were Qatar, Lebanon and Bahrain. In the key political determinants the first three positions went to Qatar, the UAE and Oman. The last three positions went to Algeria, Lebanon and Iraq. These are natural results because these countries had almost the same positions throughout the period.

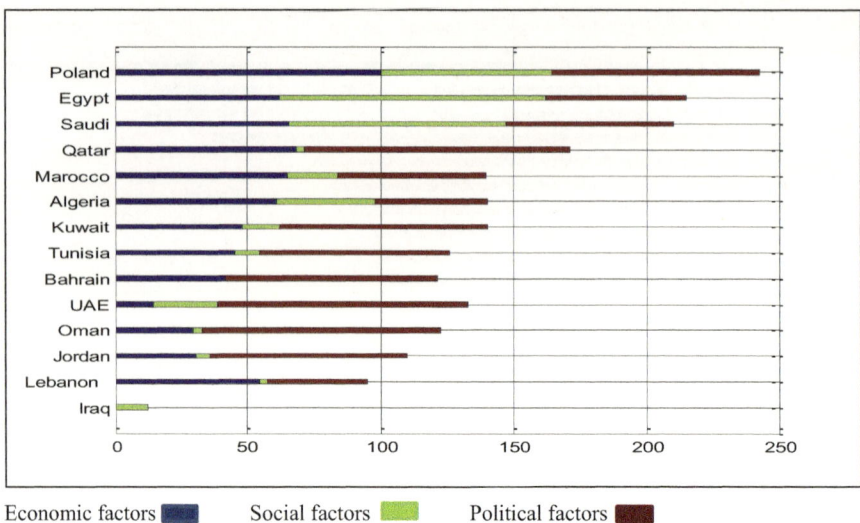

Economic factors ▬   Social factors ▬   Political factors ▬

Figure 4-17. FDI attractiveness score of key determinants for the period 2005-2010 average data

Source: Author's elaboration.

It is interesting to compare our ranking list with ranking of other comparative indicators. We have chosen a few indexes for the following reasons:

1. These indexes are available for almost all the countries being analysed in this research. The other indexes do not show all our countries.

2. Some indexes should be excluded because we have used them as input data in our research.

We have chosen the year 2009 for a comparison because almost all the data are available from almost all the indexes in this year (the last data available for the FDI potential index is 2009). Below we show four indexes to compare with our index. These are: the FDI potential index, the inward FDI performance index, the global competitiveness index and the doing business index. It should be noted here that we refer to all these indexes in chapters 2 and 3.

Table 4-2. Composite vector measure rank in comparison to other indexes of 2009

Country	Composite vector measure rank	FDI Potential Index rank	Inward FDI Performance Index rank	Global Competitiveness Index rank	Doing Business Index rank
Qatar	1	1	4	1	4
Poland	2	7	7	8	8
Saudi Arabia	3	4	3	3	1
Egypt	4	12	6	10	10
Algeria	5	11	10	12	13
Oman	6	6	8	7	6
Kuwait	7	5	13	5	5
UAE	8	2	11	2	3
Bahrain	9	3	12	4	2
Morocco	10	13	9	11	12
Jordan	11	8	2	9	9
Tunisia	12	9	5	6	7
Iraq	13	-	-	-	14
Lebanon	14	10	1	-	11

- We have arranged the ranking of the indexes according to the group of countries in this table, and not necessarily the ranks are the same as in the main sources
- There are no index values for Iraq in the FDI Potential Index for the period 2005-2010.

Source: Author's elaboration.

Table 4-2 shows there is instability between the ranks among the four indicators. This is something we take for granted, because the methods of calculation, the sample size and the variables used in the calculation process are different. Thus, the results are different, with a similarity in some of them. However, our ranking is closer to the FDI Potential Index in the cases of both Saudi Arabia and Kuwait. In addition, it is the same ranking in the cases of Qatar and Oman. Our composite vector measure is closer to the ranking of the Index FDI Performance in Morocco. There is the same ranking in both our index and the FDI Performance Index in the case of Saudi. The Global Competitiveness Index ranking is the same as our rank composite in the case of both Saudi and Qatar, while it is closer to our ranking index in the cases of Oman and Morocco.

The Doing Business Index ranking of Oman is the same as our ranking index, and the rankings of Iraq in both of the indexes are fairly close each other, and ranking of other countries are dissimilar. Thus, it is a sign that our results are not very far from the results of other studies.

The explanatory power of different index versions was tested by comparing them with the actual FDI activity in the particular countries. FDI inflows to a particular country are a sufficient indication of the country's attractiveness to foreign investors. We deflate foreign direct investment by GDP. The best result as measured by the Pearson correlation of the FDI/GDP was obtained for the index calculated using z-scores to standardise the data, equal weighting, and linear aggregation technique.

To gain further information about the quality of the results of our index, we benchmark our FDI index with the study of Groh (Groh & Wich, 2009). However, the scope of our FDI index does not include the same country sample and the same period, but we use the same criteria. The analyses show that our FDI index, through the correlation with FDI inward flows, is 0.62 for the period 2005-2010 (see Appendix 34). Compared with 0.54 in the index of Groh (Groh & Wich, 2009, p. 21) Groh's method is different from the method used by us and we received slightly better correlation between the index and the FDI inflow. We also benchmark our FDI index for the period 2005-2010 with both the Inward FDI Potential Index 2004-2006 and the Global Competitiveness Index 2008-2009. However, the benchmark indexes and our FDI index do not include the same sample study and period. The correlation for the Inward FDI Potential Index is 0.31, while for the Global Competitiveness Index it is 0.315 (Groh & Wich, 2009, p. 21). In both of the results we can see that our index gives a better correlation.

4.2. Analyses of Factors Influencing Investment Attractiveness in Arab Countries (in Comparison with Poland)

In this section we will analyse the factors affecting foreign direct investment attractiveness for each country, compared with Poland for the period 2005-2010 for each year separately, and the average data for the period 2005-2010. We will analyse economic factors, social factors and political factors.

Figure 4-18 shows that the economic factors for Algeria increased in the years 2005 and 2007. These factors were characterized by high volatility in these years and were almost unstable in other years. The social factors were unstable in the period 2005–2008 but started to increase in 2009 due to an increase in secondary education. The best score in the key social determinant was 46.44 in the year 2010 compared with Poland, which had 62.24 in the same year. The political factors started decreasing from the year 2007, due to a decrease in the political stability and rule of law factors.

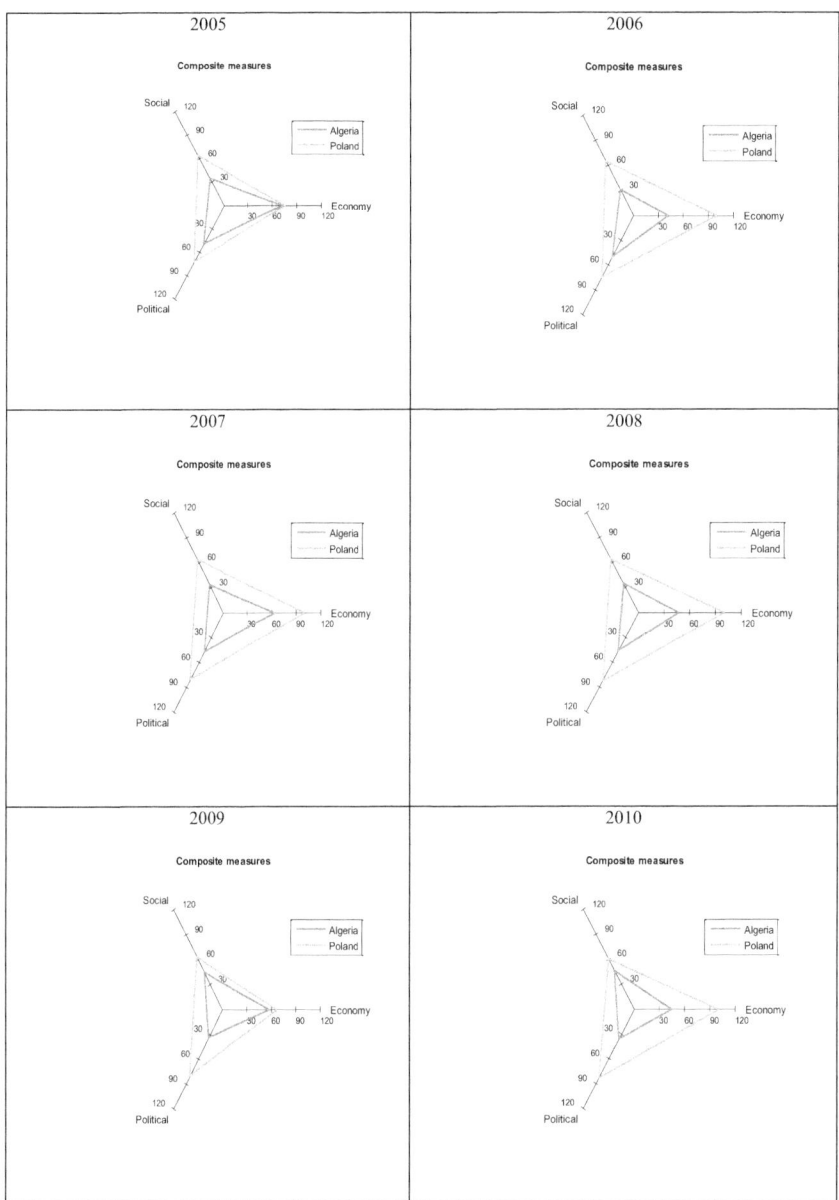

Figure 4-18. Comparison of composite vector measure of Algeria vs. Poland for the period 2005-2010

Source: Author's elaboration.

Figure 4-19 shows that Poland had a better position than Algeria in the period 2005-2010 average data. The figure shows that, in all the three dimensions, Poland had a higher rank and score than Algeria. It is due to the differences in all the input factors among them. The key economic determinant value for Algeria was 60.51, compared with Poland, which was 100. In the social factors, the score for Poland was 64.24, while Algeria's score was 37.30. In the political factors, Poland had a score of 78.80, while Algeria had a score of 42.57.

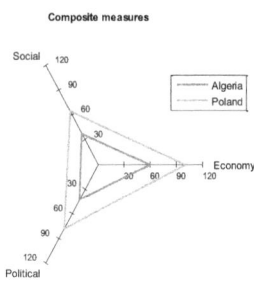

Figure 4-19. Comparison of composite vector measure of Algeria vs. Poland for the period 2005-2010 average data

Source: Author's elaboration.

Figure 4-20 shows the economic factors assessment was volatile during the period 2005-2010. The best value of economic factors score for Bahrain is in the year 2005 which was 64.29, compared to Poland which had 99.4. After 2005, the same economic factors - especially the GDP per capita and GDP per capita growth - started to decrease (see Appendix 2). The social factors assessment in Bahrain was a score zero throughout the period 2005-2010.

This was due to the size of this country compared with the others countries of this study. Thus the numbers for secondary education in Bahrain are among the lowest compared to other countries in this study. The political factors started to decrease from the year 2006, due to decreases in the rule of law and transparency factors. Bahrain had a better position than Poland in the period 2005-2007. This was due to the scores for both rule of law and transparency in Bahrain being better than in Poland.

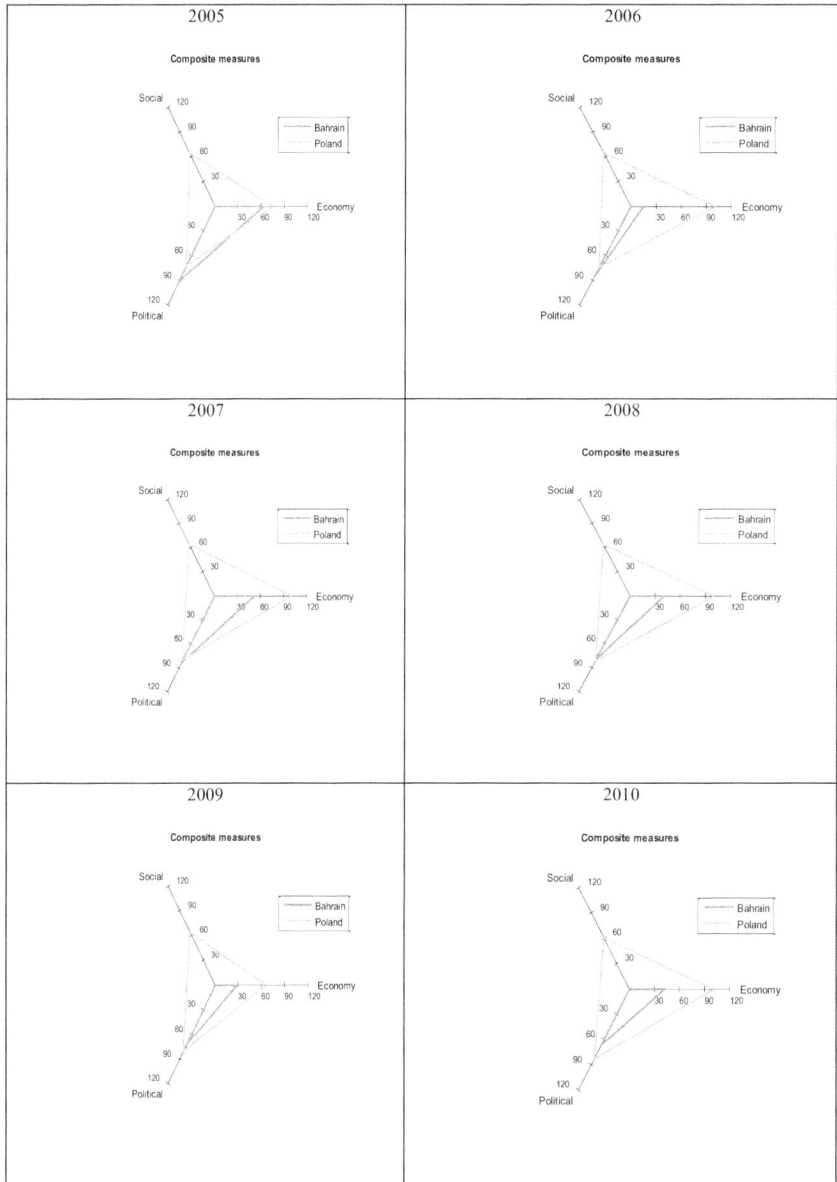

Figure 4-20. Comparison of composite vector measure of Bahrain vs. Poland for the period 2005-2010

Source: Author's elaboration.

Figure 4-21 shows that Poland had a better position than Bahrain in the period 2005-2010 average data in both the economic and social dimensions. This was due to the difference in all the input factors in these two dimensions between them. The key economic determinant value for Bahrain was 41.92, compared with Poland which was 100. In the social factors, the score for Poland was 64.24, while Bahrain scored zero, and this was because of demographic factors, as we noted previously. The political factors assessment shows that Bahrain had a score of 79.25 and was in a better position than Poland, which had a score of 78.80. This simple difference is due to bureaucracy in the time required to complete the import and export operations. While they range from 14-15 days in Bahrain, it is 17 days in Poland.

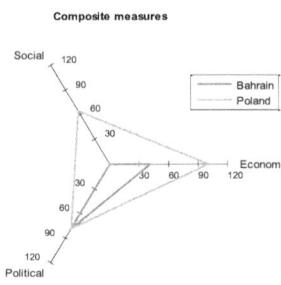

Figure 4-21. Comparison of composite vector measure of Bahrain vs. Poland for the period 2005-2010 average data

Source: Author's elaboration.

Figure 4-22 shows the score of key economic determinant in Poland was higher than in Egypt in the year 2005. This was due to the GDP growth difference between these countries in this year (see appendices 3, 14). The social factors assessment was stable and the score for Egypt was 100 in the whole period 2005-2010. This was the highest out of all the countries in our study. It can be noted here that lack of access to certain data can be the reason of this results. This was due to a demographic factor, which was the numbers in secondary education. The political factors decreased in the period 2005-2010, due to a decrease in the rule of law factor. In political factors the best position to Egypt of Poland is in the year 2005.

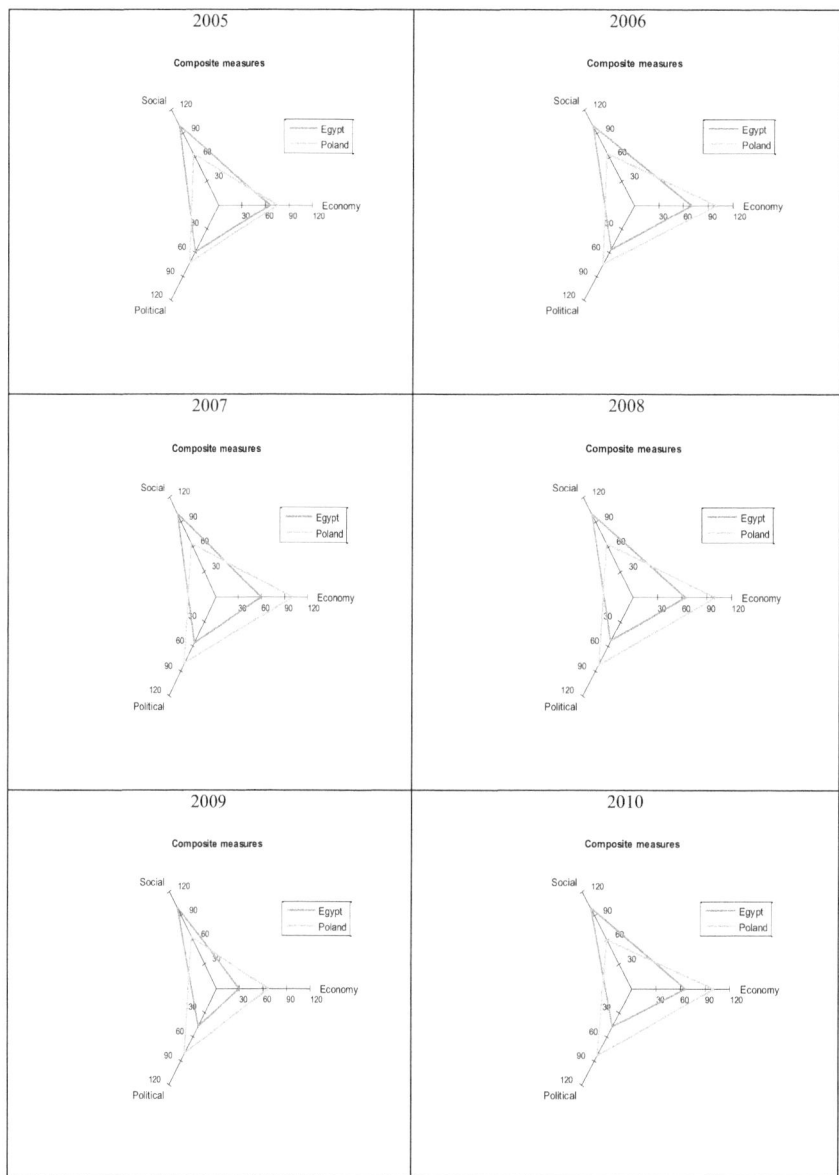

Figure 4-22. Comparison of composite vector measure of Egypt vs. Poland for the period 2005-2010

Source: Author's elaboration.

Figure 4-23 shows that Poland had a better position than Egypt in the period 2005-2010 average data in both the economic and the political dimension. This can be seen as a natural result due to the difference in the input values between these two dimensions. The key social determinant value for Egypt is 100 compared with Poland which was 62.24. This is because of the demographic factor, as we noted previously.

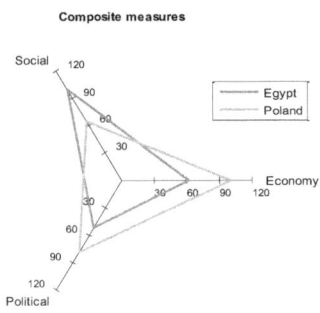

Figure 4-23. Comparison of composite vector measure of Egypt vs. Poland for the period 2005-2010 average data

Source: Author's elaboration.

Figure 4-24 shows the economic factors assessment is volatile during the period 2005-2010. Except for the years 2006 and 2009, the value of the economic factors score in the other years was zero. This is a natural result because Iraq was suffering as a result of difficult economic and political conditions; we have pointed at them and will be pointing at them in detail later in this chapter. The best value of economic factors score for Iraq is in the year 2009, which is 41.3 compared to Poland which had 100. This best position is due to the increase in GDP per capita and the decline in inflation compared with other years. The social factors in Iraq has increased in general, but is still far from the position of Poland. This is due to demographic reasons, and to the difficulties facing the electricity sector after the war to deal with the significant shortage of electric power suffered by the country. The political factors assessment score was zero over the period 2005-2010. This was because Iraq occupied the last place in the ratings of all political factors among the countries of our study for many years. This is a natural result because Iraq is in a state of instability.

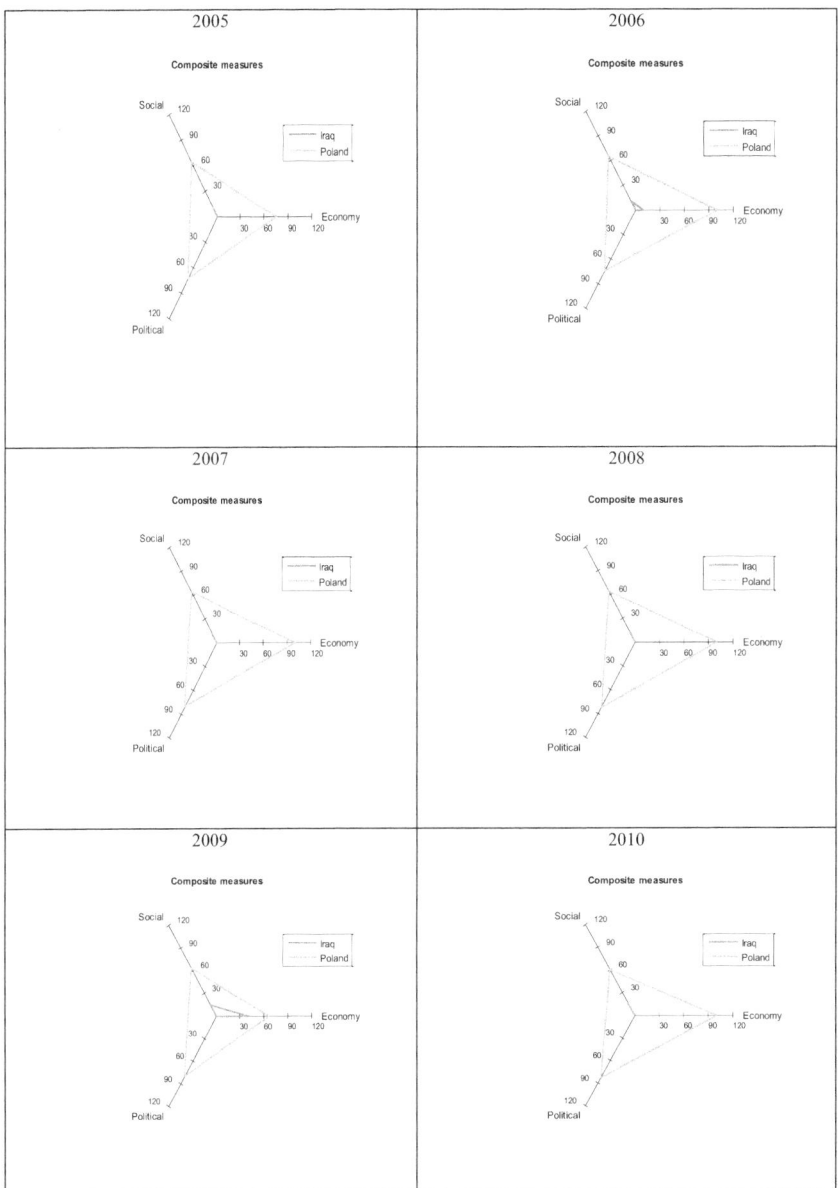

Figure 4-24. Comparison of composite vector measure of Iraq vs. Poland for the period 2005-2010

Source: Author's elaboration.

Figure 4-25 shows that Poland had a better position than Iraq in the period 2005-2010 average data in all the dimensions, due to the difference in all the input factors in these dimensions. The key economic and political determinants' values for Iraq were zero compared with Poland's, which were 100, 78.8. As for the social factors, the score for Poland was 64.24, while Iraq's score was 12.35.

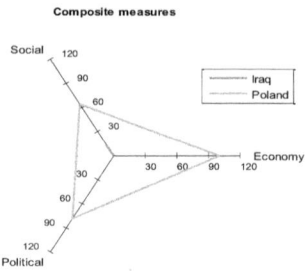

Figure 4-25. Comparison of composite vector measure of Iraq vs. Poland for the period 2005-2010 average data

Source: Author's elaboration.

Figure 4-26 shows that in the year 2005 the economic factors in Jordan level was better than in Poland. This was due to the GDP growth difference between them (see appendices 5, 14). In the period 2006-2010 the economic factors assessment refers to volatile results. The social factors assessment is almost stable over the whole the period 2005-2010. The political factors assessment was volatile in the period 2005-2010. In the years 2005 and 2006, the position of Jordan was better than Poland's, and this was because Jordan in these two years had a better score for transparency than Poland. From the year 2007 Jordan's score for the key political determinant start to decrease.

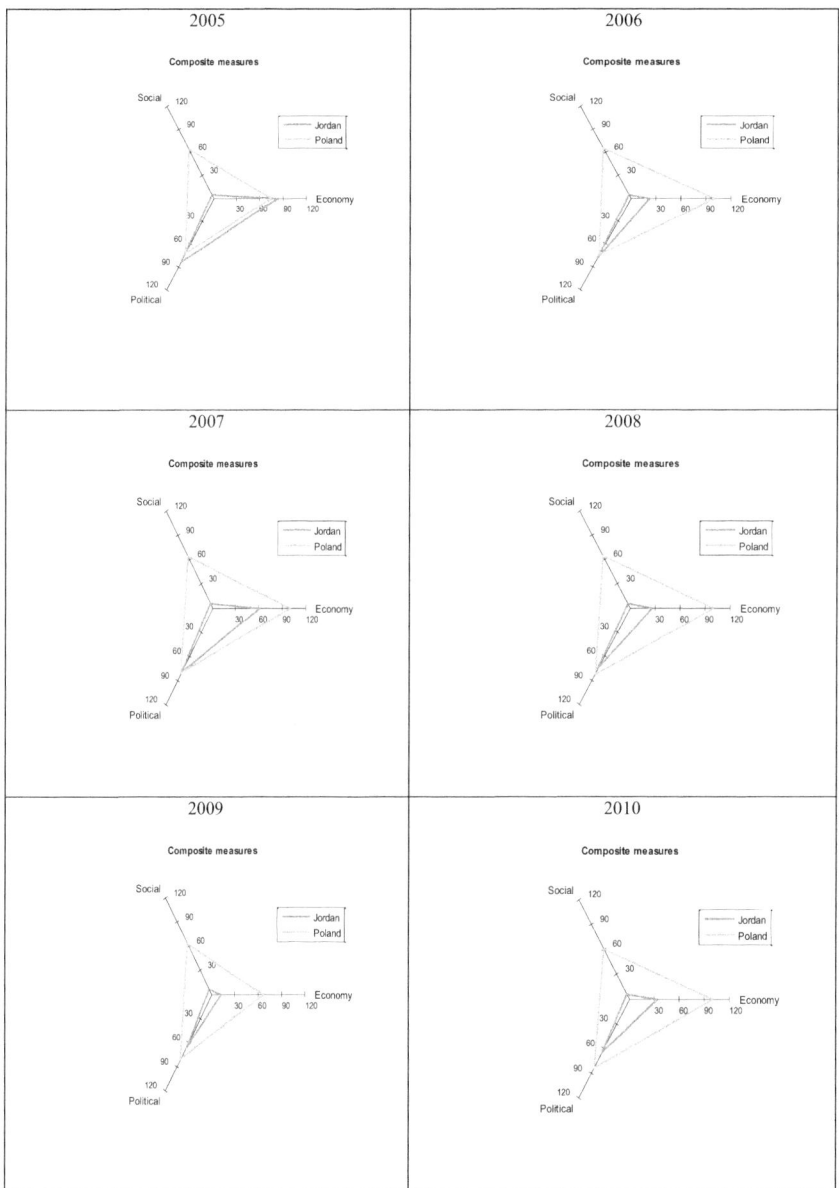

Figure 4-26. Comparison of composite vector measure of Jordan vs. Poland for the period 2005-2010

Source: Author's elaboration.

144

Figure 4-27 shows that Poland had a better position than Jordan in the period 2005-2010 average data in all dimensions. It could be a natural result due to the difference in the input values data between these dimensions. In the key political determinant, Jordan was closer to Poland compared with other determinants. It is because it had a good score for the rule of law and transparency, and in some years it had higher scores than Poland.

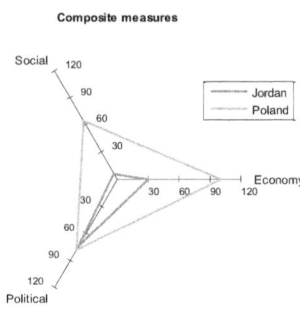

Figure 4-27. Comparison of composite vector measure of Jordan vs. Poland for the period 2005-2010 average data

Source: Author's elaboration.

Figure 4-28 shows that in the year 2005 the score of key economic determinant factors in Kuwait's was better than Poland's. This was due to the GDP growth difference between them (see appendices 6, 14). In the period 2006-2010 the economic factors assessment refers to volatile results. This was also due to the volatile GDP growth in this period. The social factors assessment is almost stable over the whole period of 2005-2010. The political factors assessment was volatile in the period 2005-2010. In the years 2006 and 2007, Kuwait's position was better than Poland's and this was because of a better score for Kuwait in the rule of law and transparency.

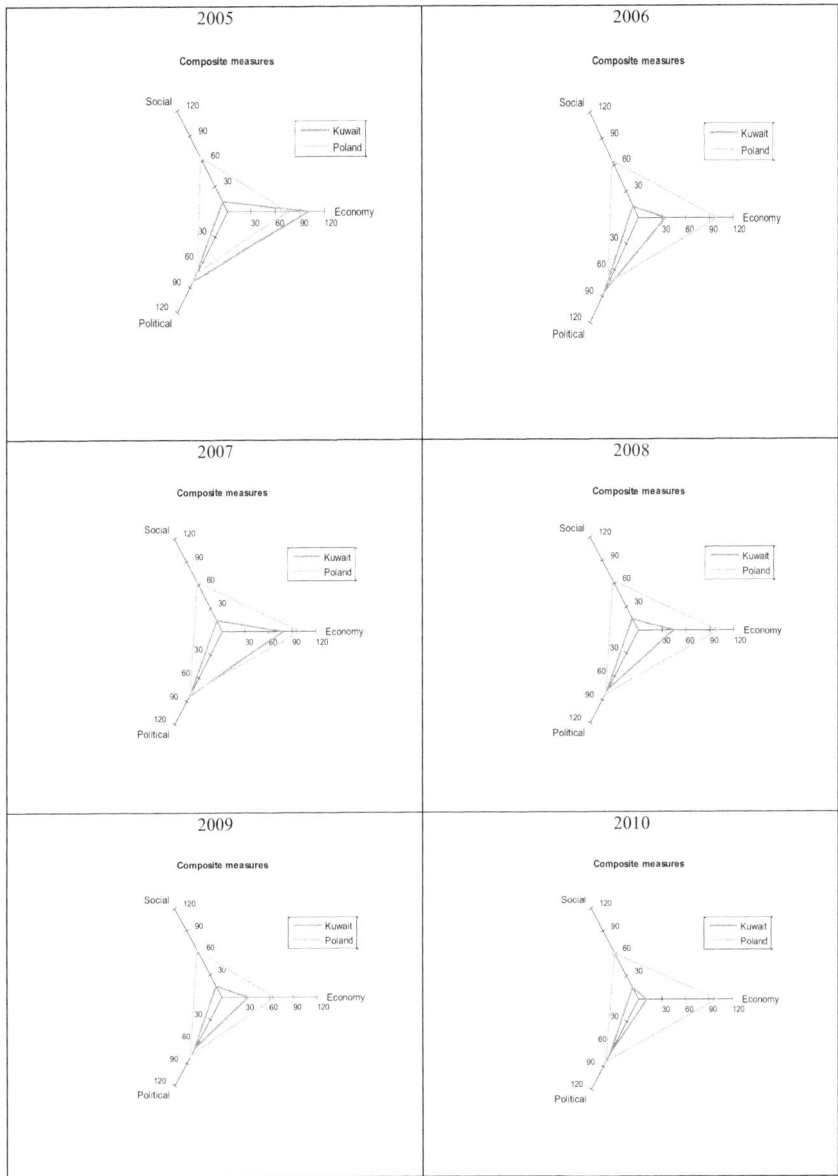

Figure 4-28. Comparison of composite vector measure of Kuwait vs. Poland for the period 2005-2010

Source: Author's elaboration.

Figure 4-29 shows that Poland had a better position than Kuwait in the period 2005-2010 average data in the all dimensions. In the key political determinants, Kuwait was closer to Poland compared with other determinants. This is because it had a good score for rule of law and transparency, and for the time to export.

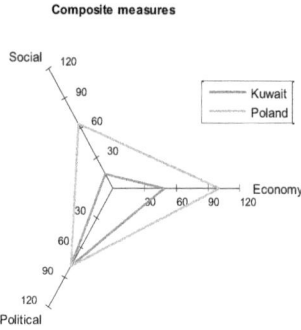

Figure 4-29. Comparison of composite vector measure of Kuwait vs. Poland for the period 2005-2010 average data

Source: Author's elaboration.

Figure 4-30 shows that the economic factors assessment for Lebanon was volatile in the period 2005-2010 average data. This is because of the volatility of the GDP growth and inflation in Lebanon compared with Poland (see appendices 7, 14). The social factors assessment was stable in the period 2005-2010. The situation of Lebanon is not so far from Iraq. Both of these countries have a position of instability. For that reason these two countries are often in last place in the standings of our index. The political factors assessment refers to a decrease during the period, due to a decrease in the rule of law and transparency factors.

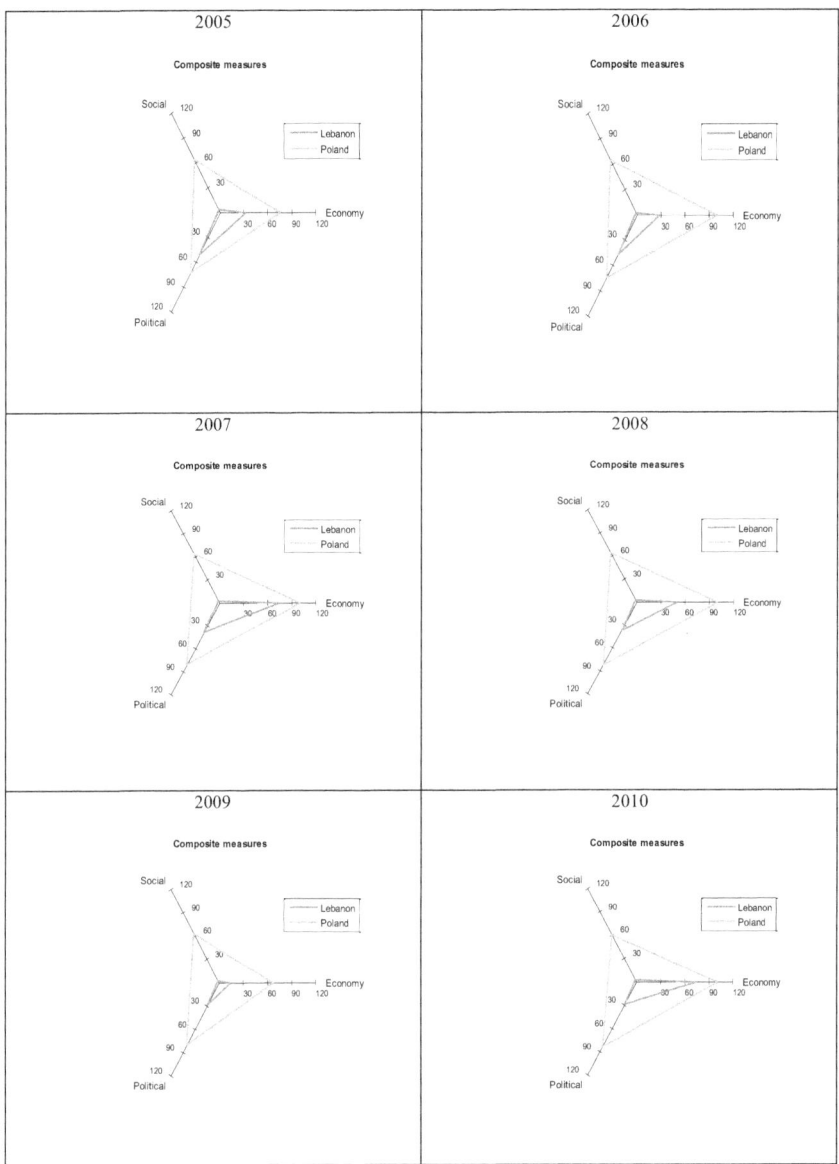

Figure 4-30. Comparison of composite vector measure of Lebanon vs. Poland for the period 2005-2010

Source: Author's elaboration.

Figure 4-31 shows that Poland had a better position than Lebanon in the period 2005-2010 average data. The figure shows that in all the three dimensions Poland had higher rank and score than Lebanon. This was due to the difference in all the input factors between them. Lebanon were closer to the position of Poland in key economic and political determinants than the social factors.

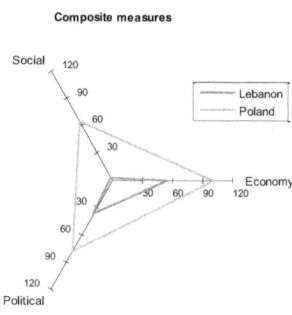

Figure 4-31. Comparison of composite vector measure of Lebanon vs. Poland for the period 2005-2010 average data

Source: Author's elaboration.

Figure 4-32 shows that the economic factors assessment for Morocco was volatile in the period 2005-2010. In the years 2006 and 2010, the of economic factors showed an increase due to a rise in the value of GDP growth in 2006 and due to the decline of inflation in 2010 (see Appendix 8). The social factors assessment was almost stable in the period 2005-2008, but started to increase from 2009 because of increased demographic factors and the increase achieved in the production of electrical power. The political factors assessment was almost stable and the best position for Morocco in the year 2010.

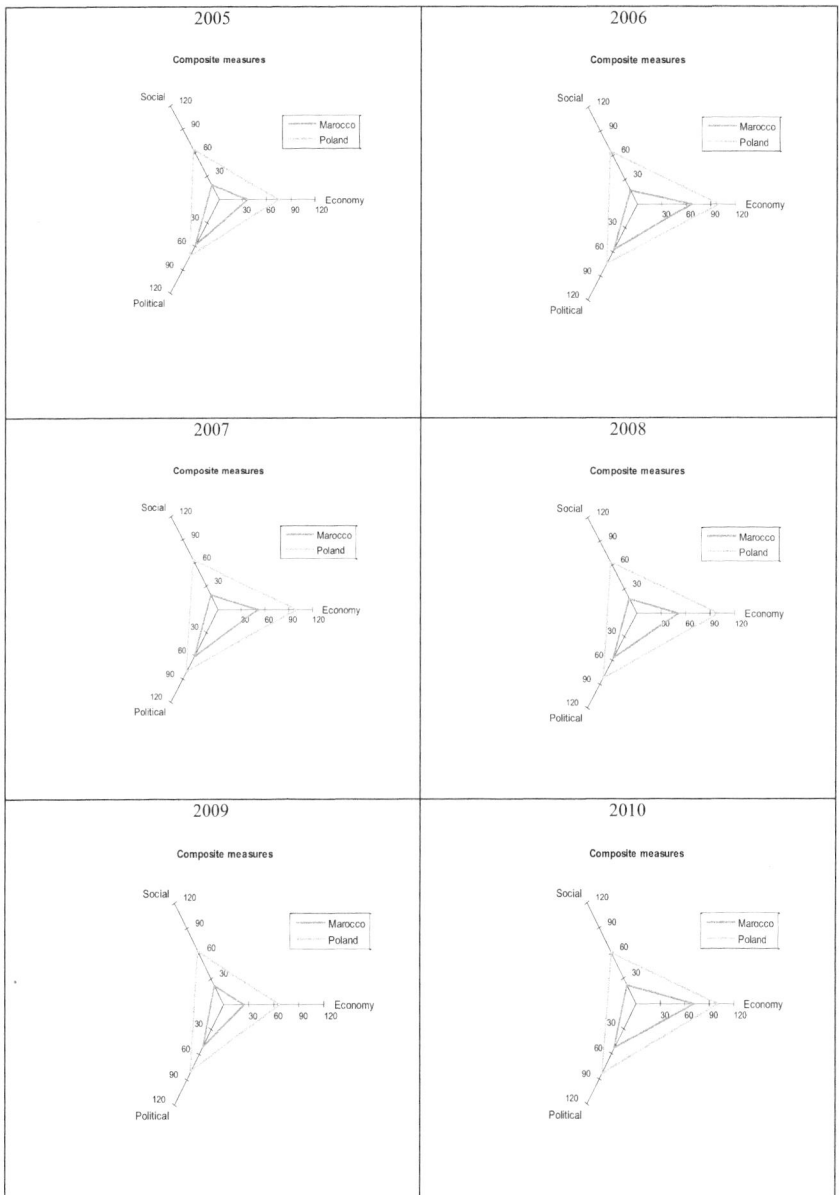

Figure 4-32. Comparison of composite vector measure of Morocco vs. Poland for the period 2005-2010

Source: Author's elaboration.

Figure 4-33 shows that Poland had a better position than Morocco in the period 2005-2010 average data. The figure shows that in all three dimensions Poland had a higher rank and score than Morocco. It is due to the differences in all the input factors among them. The key economic determinant value for Morocco was 65.05 compared with Poland, which was 100. In the social factors, the score for Poland was 64.24, while Morocco's score was 18.96. In the political factors, Poland had a score of 78.80, while Morocco's score was 55.48.

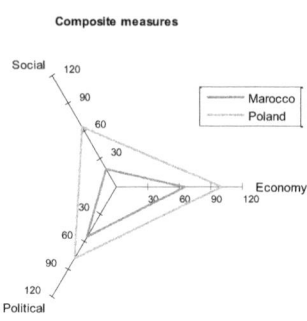

Figure 4-33. Comparison of composite vector measure of Morocco vs. Poland for the period 2005-2010 average data

Source: Author's elaboration.

Figure 4-34 shows that the economic factors assessment in Oman in the period 2005-2010 was volatile. This was due to the GDP growth, GDP growth per capita and the inflation values being volatile during the period. The best position to Oman of Poland in economic factors is in the year 2007. The social factors assessment was almost stable throughout the period 2005-2010. The political factors assessment was almost stable in the period 2005-2010. In the period 2005-2009, the position of Oman was better than Poland's, and this is because Oman in these years had a better score for political stability and transparency than Poland. In 2010, political stability, rule of law and transparency in Oman decreased, while they increased in Poland.

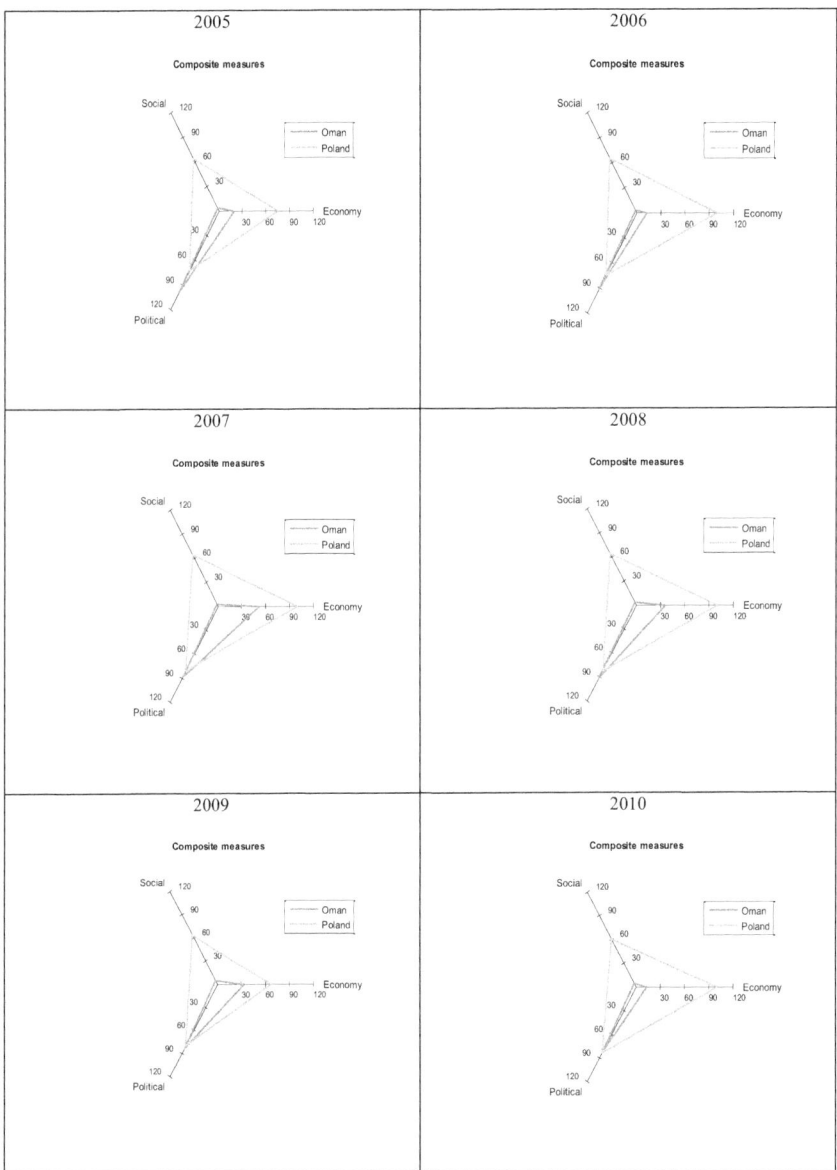

Figure 4-34. Comparison of composite vector measure of Oman vs. Poland for the period 2005-2010

Source: Author's elaboration.

Figure 4-35 shows that Poland had a better position than Oman in the period 2005-2010 average data in the economic and social dimensions. This could be a natural result due to the difference in the input values data between these dimensions. In the key political determinants, Oman was in a better position than Poland. This was because it had a good score for rule of law and transparency, and in some years it had a higher score than Poland.

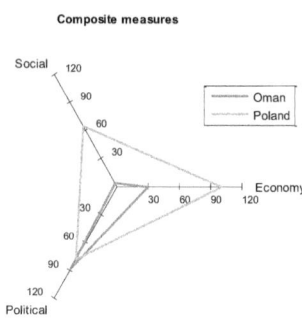

Figure 4-35. Comparison of composite vector measure of Oman vs. Poland for the period 2005-2010 average data

Source: Author's elaboration.

Figure 4-36 shows that in the year 2009 the score of key economic determinant factors in Qatar was better than in Poland. This was due to the GDP growth and inflation differences between them (see appendices 10, 14). In the other years the economic factors assessment refers to volatile results. This is also due to the volatility in most of the economic factors in this period. The social factors assessment was almost stable over the whole period 2005-2010. The political factors assessment shows that Qatar was in a better place than Poland in the period 2005-2010. This was because of a better score for Qatar in political stability, rule of law and transparency.

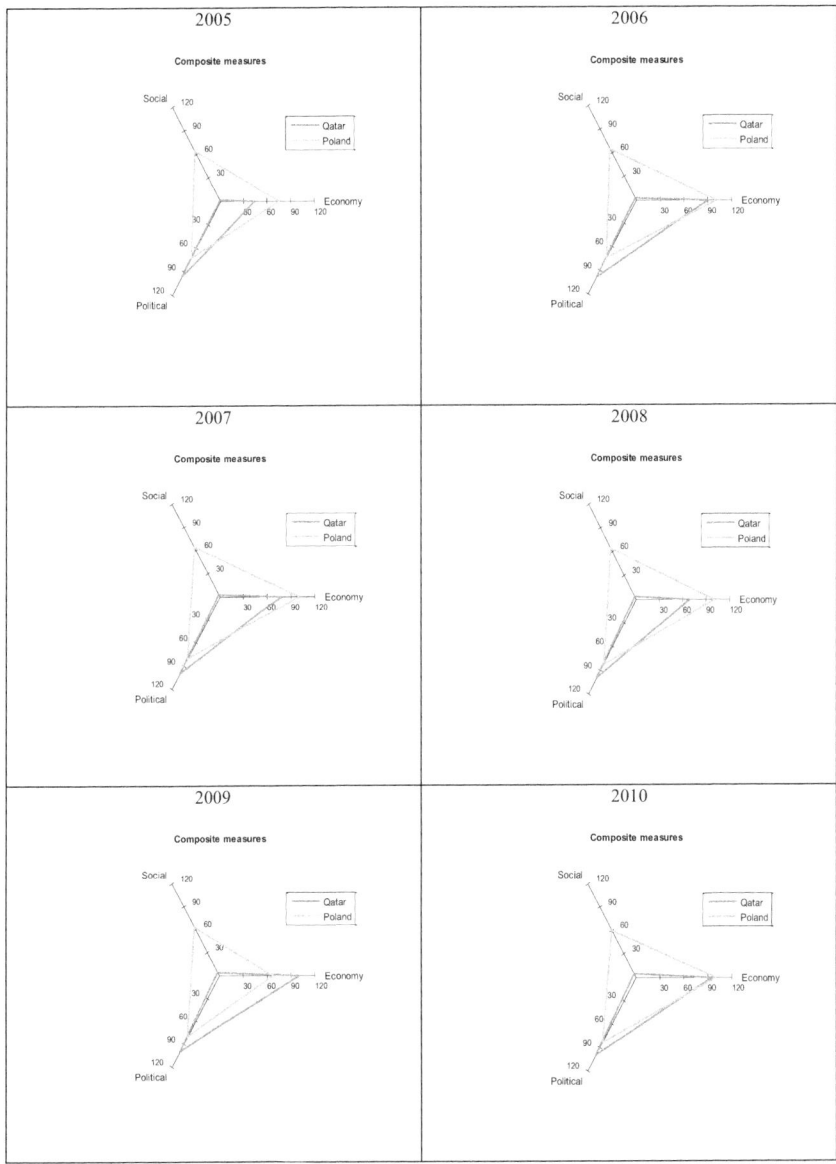

Figure 4-36. Comparison of composite vector measure of Qatar vs. Poland for the period 2005-2010

Source: Author's elaboration.

Figure 4-37 shows that Poland had a better position than Qatar in the period 2005-2010 average data in both the economic and social dimensions. In the key political determinants, Qatar was better than Poland. This is because it had a good score for political stability, rule of law and transparency during the period.

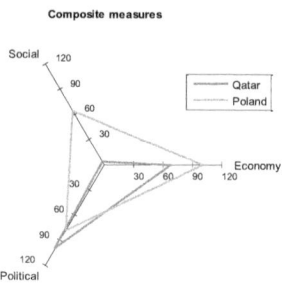

Figure 4-37. Comparison of composite vector measure of Qatar vs. Poland for the period 2005-2010 average data

Source: Author's elaboration.

Figure 4-38 shows the key determinants. From the economic factors assessment in Saudi it is clear how volatile the value score was in the period 2005-2010. This was due to the volatility in GDP growth, inflation and trade as a percentage of GDP. As we know, Saudi is one of the biggest producers of oil in the world and the volatility in the price of oil is reflected directly in GDP and trade. The year 2005 could be the only case of conformity to a large extent to the case of Poland from all the dimensions. We can say it is the proper situation, which is close to the case of Poland among all the countries in our study (see Figure 4-38). The score of key social determinant was stable and the score for Saudi was higher than for Poland in the whole period 2005-2010. This was due to the difference in electricity production, taking into account that Saudi has large reserves of natural resources that help produce electricity at good prices. The political factors was almost stable in the period 2005-2010. The best position of Saudi in relation to Poland in political factors was in the year 2005.

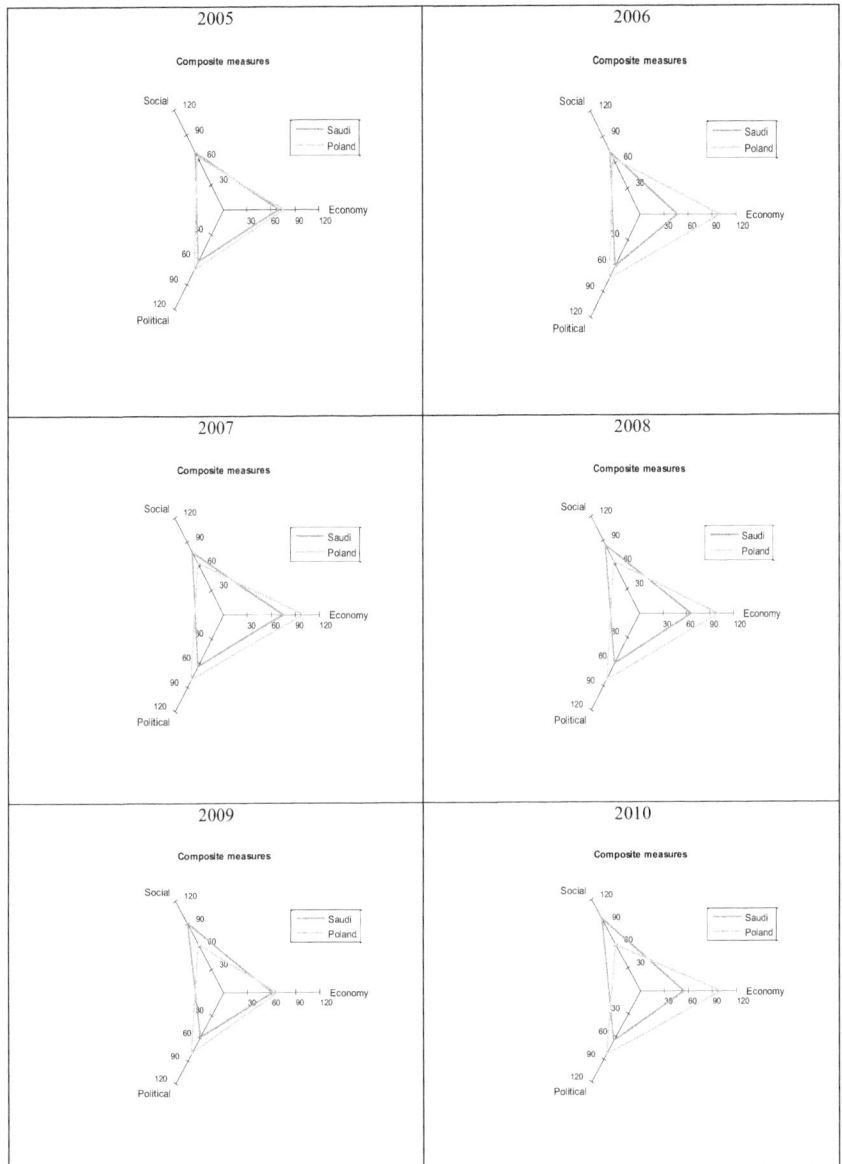

Figure 4-38. Comparison of composite vector measure of Saudi vs. Poland for the period 2005-2010

Source: Author's elaboration.

Figure 4-39 shows that Poland had a better position than Saudi in the period 2005-2010 average data in both the economic and political dimensions. This could be a natural result due to the difference in the input values between these two dimensions. The key social determinant value for Saudi was 82.09 compared with Poland which was 62.24. This was because of electricity production, as we noted previously.

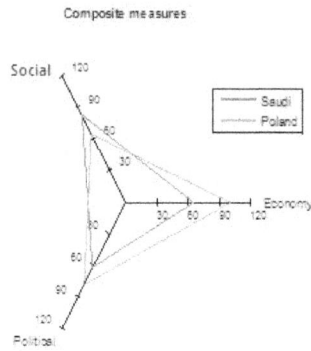

Figure 4-39. Comparison of composite vector measure of Saudi vs. Poland for the period 2005-2010 average data

Source: Author's elaboration.

Figure 4-40 shows that the economic factors assessment for Tunisia was volatile in the period 2005-2010. In the year 2007 the of economic factors showed an increase due to the rise in the value of GDP growth, trade as a percentage of GDP and owing to the decrease in inflation. In the year 2009, the economic factors showed a big drop due to a decrease in GDP growth and trade (see Appendix 12). We should bear in mind the effect of the global crisis in that year. The social factors assessment were almost stable in the period 2005-2010 and this dimension was far from the position of Poland as a result of increased demographic factors and the low production of electrical power. The political factors assessment was almost volatile. In the years 2005 and 2006, the position of Tunisia was higher than Poland due to a higher score on the transparency of Tunisia than for Poland in these two years. In the year 2007, Poland started to have a better position in this index as the position of Tunisia decreased in this dimension and both countries started be equal in this dimension. In the years 2008-2010, Poland's transparency score started to get higher than Tunisia's.

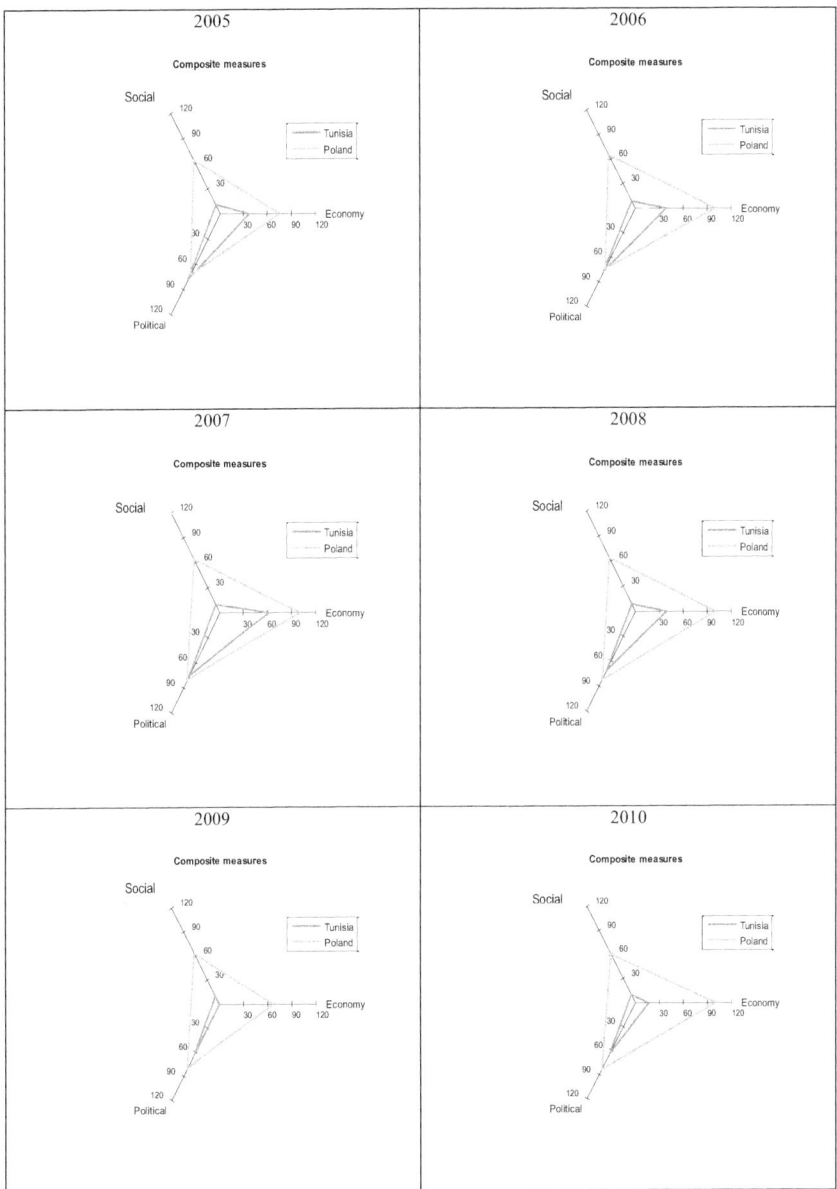

Figure 4-40. Comparison of composite vector measure of Tunisia vs. Poland for the period 2005-2010

Source: Author's elaboration.

Figure 4-41 shows that Poland had a better position than Tunisia's average data in the period 2005-2010. The figure shows that in all three dimensions Poland had a higher ranking and score than Tunisia. It is due to the differences between them in all the input factors. In the key economic determinants, the value for Tunisia was 45.08 compared with Poland, which was 100. In the social factors, the score for Poland was 64.24, while Tunisia's score was 9.25. In the political factors, Poland had a score of 78.80, while Tunisia's score was 71.25, and this is the closest dimension to Poland.

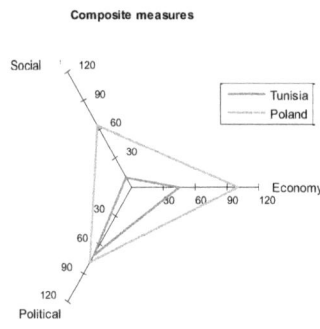

Figure 4-41. Comparison of composite vector measure of Tunisia vs. Poland for the period 2005-2010 average data

Source: Author's elaboration.

In Figure 4-42 the economic factors assessment in the UAE shows that the value score of economics factors was volatile during the period 2005-2010. This can be due to many reasons: the UAE is one of the largest producers of crude oil among the Arab countries. Therefore, the economic factors are a reflection of the high or low oil prices. The UAE saw an economic crisis in 2009. Our data in Appendix 13 shows negative growth in GDP per capita mixed and continuous for the period 2005-2010. The data in the same appendix also show a mixed and sometimes negative value for inflation during the same period. All these reasons and maybe more could be responsible for the lower score for economic

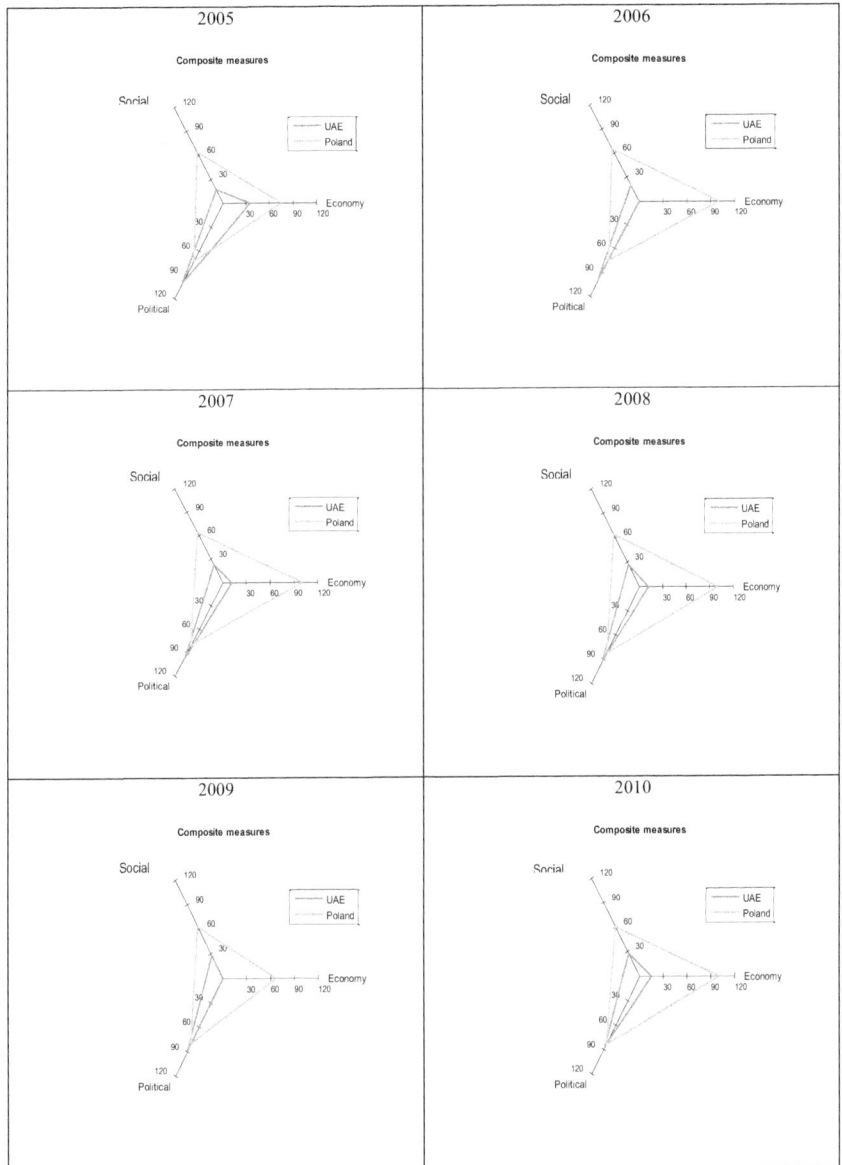

Figure 4-42. Comparison of composite vector measure of UAE vs. Poland for the period 2005-2010

Source: Author's elaboration.

factors in the UAE. The best position of the UAE compared to Poland was in the year 2005. The social factors assessment was almost stable over the whole period 2005-2010. This was due to demographic reasons. The political factors assessment shows that the UAE was in a better place than Poland in the period 2005-2010. This was because of a better score for the UAE in transparency, time to export and time to import.

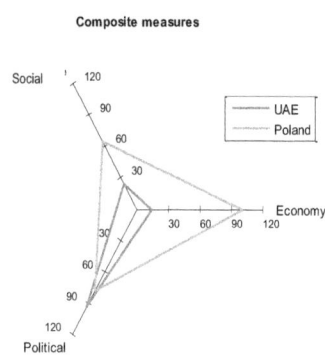

Figure 4-43. Comparison of composite vector measure of UAE vs. Poland for the period 2005-2010 average data

Source: Author's elaboration.

Figure 4-43 shows that Poland had a better position than the UAE in the period 2005-2010 average data in both the economic and social dimensions. In the key political determinants, the UAE was better than Poland, because it had a good score for political stability, the rule of law and transparency during the period.

The conclusion from our analyses is that Poland ranked 1 in the composite vector measure in the years 2006, 2007, 2008, 2010, and in the average data 2005-2010. Egypt and Qatar had a better position than Poland in the composite vector measure in 2005 and 2009 respectively. Egypt was better than Poland in the score for both economic and social factors in the year 2005. Egypt was in the top rank of social factors during the entire period. Qatar had a better score than Poland and all the Arab countries in political factors in the years 2007, 2008, 2009, 2010, and in the average data 2005-2010. The United Arab Emirates (UAE) had the first rank in political factors in the years 2005 and 2006. We can see from our analyses that factors such as GDP growth, GDP per capita, inflation, secondary education, political stability, the rule of law, transparency and time to export are the most important factors. It does not mean there is no significance to the rest of the factors in the process of attracting investment.

4.3. Changes in the Investment Attractiveness of Arab Countries and Poland in the period 2005-2010

In this section we shall analyse the of the changes in investment attractiveness in the Arab countries and Poland over the period 2005-2010 using the data of the year 2005 as a reference in these two ways: one outcome is calculated for each of the 6 years separately (see appendices 37-42); secondly, we have done a calculation for each factor as average data for all the period 2005-2010 for all the countries (see Table 4-8). In both ways, the year 2005 is a reference by using the procedures of vector measure, which are described in Chapter 2. It should be noted here again that only with the vector measure method can we make a dynamic analysis. Composite vector measures are calculated according to these procedures which we refer to in Chapter 2. In addition to that, the basic year for the analyses will be use the pattern of the year 2005. This is will be comparable and we will have the same measure point. It is mean that we will use the same pattern of the year 2005 to all the period.

Table 4-3.Composite Vector measure average data for the period 2005-2010 for the Arab countries and Poland

Series Name	Key drivers	Economic Key determinant	Social Key determinant	Political Key determinant
GDP growth (annual %)	E	0.10		
GDP per capita (constant 2005 US$)	E	0.06		
GDP per capita growth (annual %)	E	0.06		
Trade (% of GDP)	E	0.09		
Tax payments (number)	E	0.07		
Inflation, GDP deflator (annual %)	E	-0.10		
Imports of goods and services (% of GDP)	E	-0.09		
Urban population (% of total)	E	0.08		
Labour force, total	E	0.08		
Secondary education, general pupils	Q		0.58	
Electricity production (kWh)	Q		0.49	
Political Stability(-2.5 to 2.5)	P			0.18
Rule of Law (-2.5 to 2.5)	P			0.16
Transparency	P			0.31
Time to export(days)	P			-0.07
Time to import(days)	P			-0.12

Source: Author's elaboration

The results for the period 2005-2010 average with the year 2005 reference show that both GDP growth (annual percentage) and inflation are the most important factors among the key economic determinants. This proves our results from the previous sections. Among the key social determinants, secondary education was the most important factor. Of the key political determinants, transparency was the highest composite vector measure among the other factors (see Table 4-3). Below we will analyse the changes in composite vector measure and key determinant groups in the period 2005-2010, taking into account the year 2005 as a reference for each of the Arab countries and Poland separately, based on the results in appendices 37-42. As we refer to the procedure for calculating the results in this section according to the year 2005 as a reference, so we will not refer to this point again.

Figure 4-44 shows the unstable behaviour of trends in the key determinants of investment attractiveness in Algeria for the period 2005-2010. The value of the key economic determinants declined from the year 2005 to the year 2006. This can be attributed to the decline in the GDP growth rate of about -71 percent in 2006 compared with the year 2005. The key economic determinant is almost in a stable position in the period 2006-2008. In the year 2009, the value of the key economic determinants declined due to the decline of the inflation/GDP deflator by -170 percent compared with the year 2005. In the year 2010, the value of the key economic determinants declined. This could have been due to a rise in inflation to 16.1 percent, which is the same level as the year 2005.

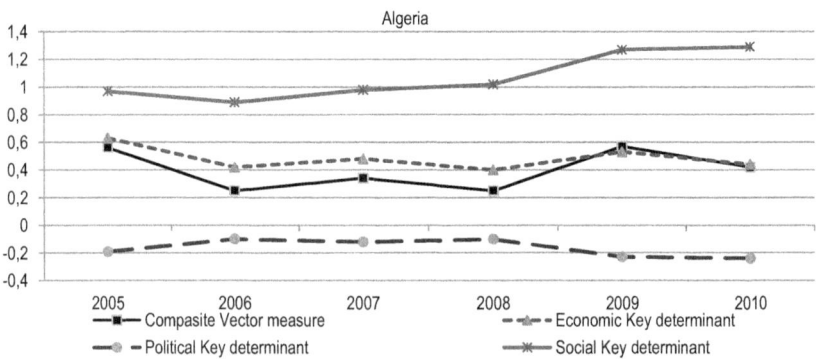

Figure 4-44. Change of Investment Attractiveness to Algeria in the period 2005-2010

Source: Author's elaboration.

The key social determinants were almost like a stable trend in the period 2005 to 2008. The value of the key social determinants was upward after 2008 due to the great demographic change in the number of students in secondary education. The number rose from about 3.5 million pupils in 2008, to about 4.1 million pupils in 2009, and to about 4.2 million pupils in 2010.

The key political determinants were almost as a stable trend in the period 2005 to 2008. After the year 2008, the key political determinants started to go downward due to a lowering of each of the factors - political stability, rule of law and transparency - in the years 2009 and 2010. The composite vector measure for Algeria was in the best position in the year 2009.

Figure 4-45 shows that the behaviour of the trend of the composite vector measure in Bahrain was downward in the period 2005-2010. The value of the key economic determinants declined from the year 2005 to the year 2006. This can be attributed to the decline in the GDP growth rate of about -4 percent in 2006 compared with the year 2005, and the rise in inflation of about 275 percent compared with the year 2005. In the period 2007-2010 the key economic determinants trend is almost stable. The key social determinant trend is stable in the period 2005 to 2010. The key political determinants trend is downward in the period 2005 to 2010. This could be due to a lowering of each of the factors - political stability, rule of law and transparency - in this period.

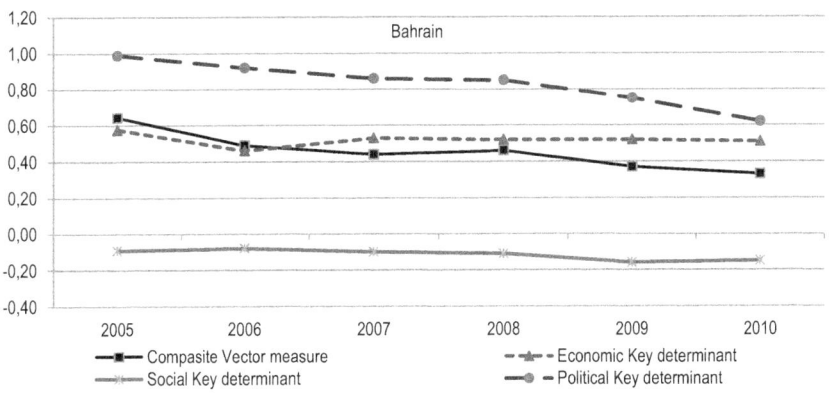

Figure 4-45. Change of Investment Attractiveness to Bahrain in the period 2005-2010

Source: Author's elaboration.

Figure 4-46 shows the stable behaviour of trends in the key determinants of investment attractiveness in Egypt in the period 2005-2010. The best position for Egypt in the composite vector measure was in the year 2008.

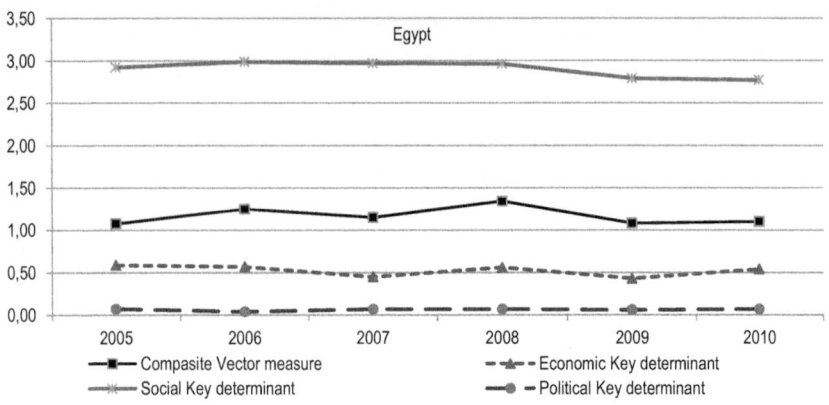

Figure 4-46. Change of Investment Attractiveness to Egypt in the period 2005-2010

Source: Author's elaboration.

Figure 4-47 shows the trend of composite vector measure in Iraq is upward in the period 2005-2010. The key economic determinant trend was downward from the year 2006 to the year 2008. This can be attributed to the decline in the GDP growth rate of about -68 percent in 2007 compared with the year 2005, and the decline in GDP per capita of about -159 percent in 2007 compared with the year 2005. The trend of the key economic determinants was upward from the year 2007 to the year 2009. This could be due especially to the decrease in inflation by about - 166 percent in the year 2009 compared with the year 2005. Also this was due to the rise in GDP growth per capita which amounted to 141 percent in 2008 and about 88 percent in 2009 compared with the year 2005. After the year 2009, the value of the key economic determinants declined and this could be due to the rise in inflation in 2010 compared with the year 2009. Both of the key social determinants and key political determinants in Iraq had a stable trend in the period 2005 to 2010.

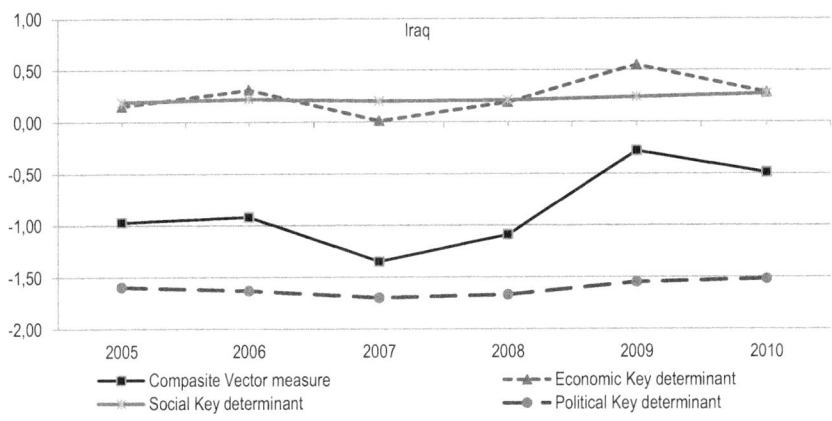

Figure 4-47.Change of Investment Attractiveness to Iraq in the period 2005-2010

Source: Author's elaboration.

Figure 4-48 shows the downward of trends of the composite vector measure, the key economic determinants and to some extent the key political determinants in Jordan in the period 2005-2010. The key economic determinant trend is downward from the year 2005 to the year 2006. This can be attributed to the rise in inflation of about 2 percent in the year 2005, to 10.7 percent in 2006. In the period 2006-2007, the behaviour of the trend is upward and this could be due to the decline in inflation from 435 percent more than 2005 in the year 2006 to about 155 percent in 2007, and due to the rise in GDP growth per capita by about 12 percent compared with 2005. From the year 2007 to 2010, the trend is downward and this could be attributed to the decline in GDP growth and the rise in inflation. The key social determinant is a stable trend in the period 2005 to 2010. The key political determinant trend is a decline in the period from 2005 to 2010. This could be due to a lowering of each of the factors - political stability and the rule of law - in this period.

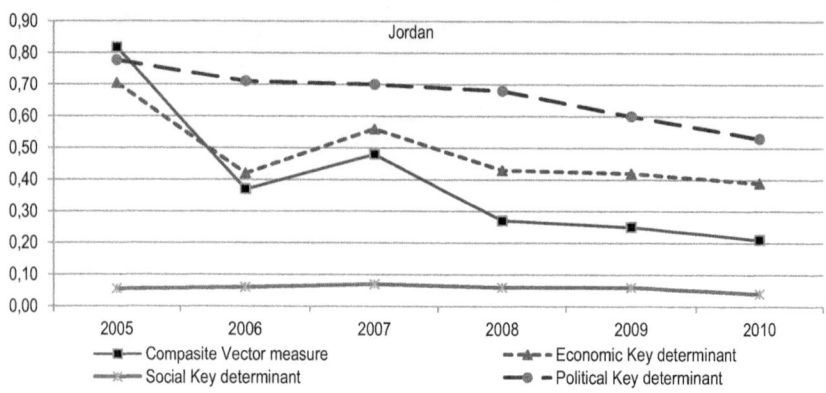

Figure 4-48. Change of Investment Attractiveness to Jordan in the period 2005-2010

Source: Author's elaboration.

Figure 4-49 shows the downward behaviour of the trends of the composite vector measure, the key economic determinants and, to some extent, the key political determinants in Kuwait in the period 2005-2010.

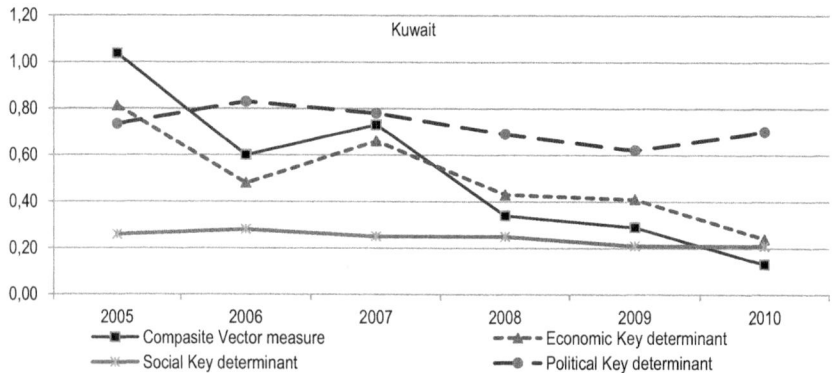

Figure 4-49. Change of Investment Attractiveness to Kuwait in the period 2005-2010

Source: Author's elaboration.

The key economic determinant trend is downward from the year 2005 to the year 2006. This can be attributed to the decline of GDP growth and GDP per capita growth of about -26 and -60 percent in the year 2006 respectively compared with the year 2005. In the period 2006-2007, the trend behaviour is upward and this could be due to the decline in inflation from 22.4 percent in 2005 to about 4.3 percent in 2007, and to the rise in the labour force by about 11 percent in 2007 of 2005. From the year 2007 to the year 2010, the behaviour of the trend is downward and this could be attributed to the decline in GDP growth, GDP per capita growth and a rise in inflation (see Appendix 6). The key social determinant values are almost stable in the period 2005 to 2010. The key political determinant trend is downward in the period 2005 to 2010. This could be due to the lowering of each of the factors - political stability and the rule of law - in this period.

Figure 4-50 shows the upward trends of the composite vector measure and the key economic determinants in Lebanon in the period 2005-2010. The key economic determinants trend is stable from the year 2005 to the year 2006.

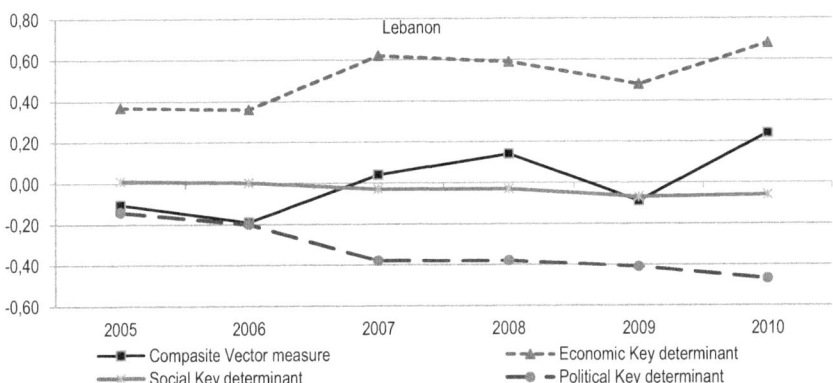

Figure 4-50. Change of Investment Attractiveness to Lebanon in the period 2005-2010

Source: Author's elaboration.

In the period 2006-2007 the key economic determinants trend is upward and this is could be due to a rise in the GDP growth of about 248 percent in 2007 comparing to the year 2005. The key economic determinant values were almost stable in the years 2007, and 2008. In the year 2009, the key economic determinants value declined and this could have been due to the rise in inflation which increased to 10.5 percent compared with -1.1 in the year 2005 (see Appendix 7). In 2010, the trend of key economic determinants upward and this could have been due to the decline in inflation to 0.2 percent.

The key social determinants trend is a stable in the period 2005 to 2010. The key political determinants trend is downward in the period 2005 to 2010. This could be due to the lowering of each of the factors - political stability, transparency and the rule of law - in this period.

Figure 4-51 shows the unstable trends of the composite vector measure and the key economic determinants in Morocco in the period 2005-2010. The key economic determinants trend is upward from the year 2005 to the year 2006. This could be due to the high growth in both GDP and GDP per capita which coincided with the inflation rates remaining unchanged. In the period 2006-2007, the trend is downward and this could be due to the decline in GDP growth of about -10 percent in 2007 comparing with the year 2005, the decline of GDP per capita of about -15 percent from 2005 and the rise in inflation of about 160 percent from 2005. In the year 2008, the trend of the key economic determinants is upward and this could be due to the rise in both GDP growth and GDP per capita. In 2009, the trend downward and this could be due to the decline in GDP growth; GDP per capita and trade as a percentage of GDP (see Appendix 8). The trend upward in 2010 and this is could have been due to the rise in trade as a percentage of GDP, and to the decline of inflation.

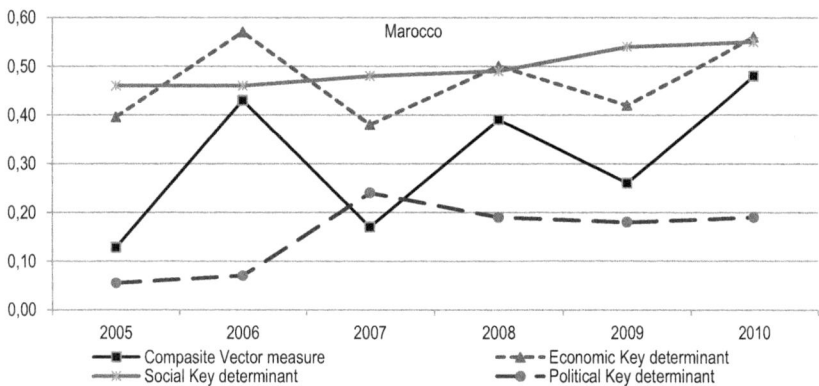

Figure 4-51. Change of Investment Attractiveness to Morocco in the period 2005-2010

Source: Author's elaboration.

The key social determinants trend stable in the period 2005 to 2010, and took upward to some extent in the last two years (2009-2010) and this could be attributed to a demographic reason: the increase in the number of students in secondary schools, in addition to the significant increase in the production of electricity. The key political determinants trend upward in the period 2005 to 2007. This could be due to the lowering of factors such as time of export and time of import in this period. In the period 2008-2010 the behaviour of the trend was almost stable.

Figure 4-52 shows the upward behaviour of the trends of the composite vector measure and the key economic determinants in Oman in the period 2005-2008. The trend is downward in the period 2009-2010. The values of the key economic determinants in the period 2005-2008 are upward and this could be due to the rise in GDP growth by about 220 percent in 2008 of the year 2005, and the rise in GDP per capita of about 638 percent in the 2008 comparing with 2005. From the years 2008-2010, the values of key economic determinants decline and this could be due to the decline of both GDP growth and GDP per capita, in spite of the decline of inflation by about -21.4 percent in 2009 comparing with 2005 (see Appendix 9). The key social determinant trend is stable in the period 2005 to 2010.

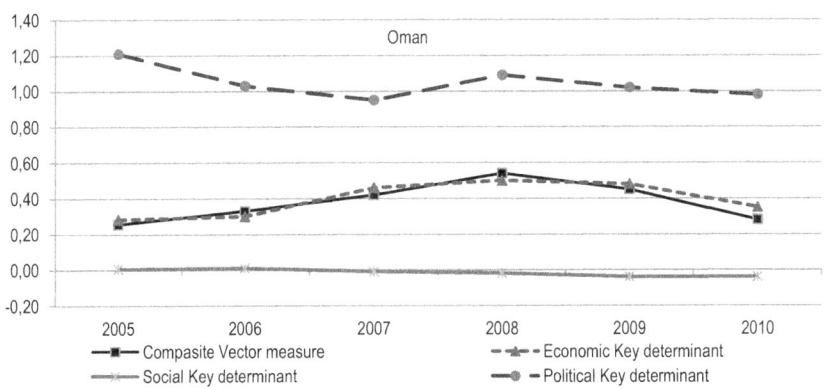

Figure 4-52. Change of Investment Attractiveness to Oman in the period 2005-2010

Source: Author's elaboration.

The key political determinants trend downward in the period 2005 to 2007. This could be due to the lowering of each of the factors - political stability, transparency and the rule of law - in this period. In 2008, the trend was a slight rise and this could be attributed to the rise in Morocco's position regarding the same factors above. The trend was downward in subsequent years due to the decline of the same factors.

Figure 4-53 shows the upward behaviour of the trend of the composite vector measure in Qatar in the periods 2005-2006 and 2007-2010. The key economic determinants trend is upward from the year 2005 to the year 2006. This can be attributed to the high growth in the GDP growth rate with about 249 percent in 2006 compared with the year 2005, and the rise in the GDP per capita from -5.7 percent in 2005 to 7.1 percent in 2006. The trend of the key economic determinants is downward from the year 2006 to the year 2008. This could be due especially to the decrease in the GDP growth and GDP per capita in this period (see Appendix 10). From the year 2008 to the year 2010, the key economic determinants trend is in an upward direction. This could be due to the sharp decrease in inflation from 22.9 percent in 2008 to -24.2 in 2009, and due to the rise in the labour force total of about 129, and 160 percent in the years 2009, and 2010 respectively comparing with the year 2005. The key political determinants trend is in an upward direction in the period 2005-2010. It is clear that Qatar was moving in the right direction to have a better position among the Arab countries with respect to political factors. We especially refer here to Qatar's score on transparency, which was 5.9 in the year 2005 and rose to 7.7 in the year 2010 (more details about this in Chapter 3). The key social determinants in Qatar values were almost stable in the period 2005 to 2010.

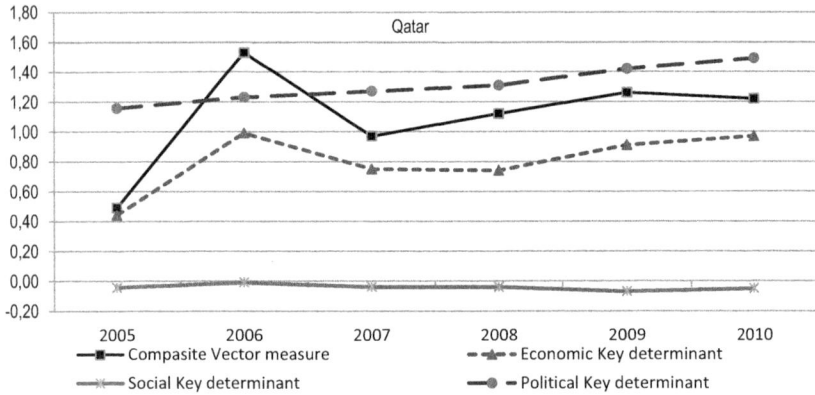

Figure 4-53. Change of Investment Attractiveness to Qatar in the period 2005-2010

Source: Author's elaboration.

Figure 4-54 shows the stability and to some extent upward trends of all the key determinants and composite vector measures in Saudi in the period 2005-2010. The key economic determinants trend is stable from the year 2005 to the year 2010. The key political determinants trend is in an upward direction in the period 2005-2010. It is clear that Saudi, like Qatar, in the correct way to have a better position among the Arab countries in consider of the political factors. We refer especially here to the score for Saudi on transparency, which was 3.4 in the year 2005 and rose to 4.7 in the year 2010, as well as the progress made by Saudi Arabia in shortening the time required for import and export procedures (see Appendix 11).

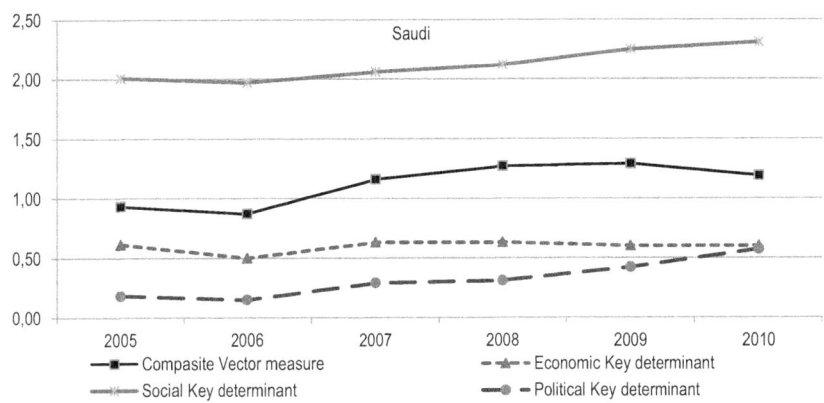

Figure 4-54. Change of Investment Attractiveness to Saudi in the period 2005-2010

Source: Author's elaboration.

The key social determinants scores in Saudi almost are a stable in the period 2005 to 2007. From the year 2007 to 2010 the trend starts upward direction and this is could be due to demographic reasons: the increase in the number of students in secondary schools and the increase in the production of electricity.

Figure 4-55 shows the instability trends of the composite vector measure, key economic determinants and to some extent the key political determinants in Tunisia in the period 2005-2010. The key economic determinants trend is upward from the year 2005 to the year 2007. This can be attributed to the rise in GDP growth and GDP per capita growth of about 63 and 86 percent in the year 2008 respectively compared with the year 2005, and the decline of inflation from 3.8 percent in 2005 to 2.6 percent in 2007. In the period 2007-2009, the behaviour of the trend, was downward and this could be due to the decline in GDP growth and GDP per capita growth. From the year 2009 to 2010, the behaviour of the trend was in a stable direction.

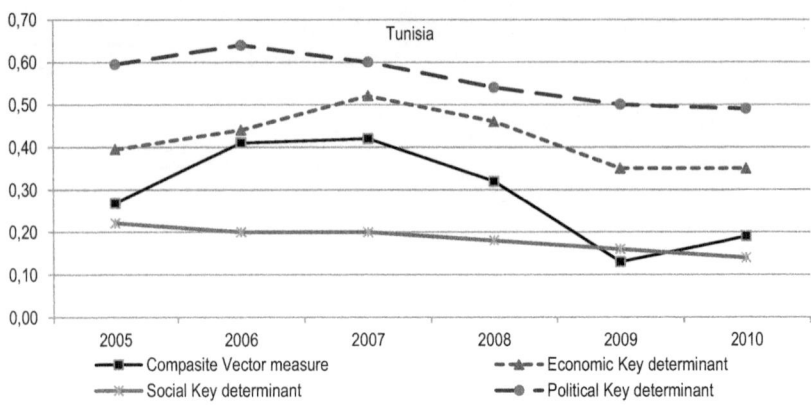

Figure 4-55. Change of Investment Attractiveness to Tunisia in the period 2005-2010

Source: Author's elaboration.

The key social determinant values were almost stable in the period 2005 to 2008. The trend in behaviour was downward after 2008 to 2010, and this was for a demographic reason: the declining numbers of students in secondary schools. Tunisia achieved growth in the period 2005-2006 in the factors of political stability and the rule of law. The key political determinant trend is downward in the period 2007 to 2010. This could be due to the lowering of each of the following factors in this period: political stability, the rule of law and transparency.

Figure 4-56 shows the unstable behaviour of the trends of the composite vector measure in the UAE in the period 2005-2010. The key economic determinant trend was stable from the year 2005 to the year 2006. This trend in behaviour declined from the year 2006 to 2007. This can be attributed to the decline of GDP growth by about -35 percent in the year 2007 compared with the year 2005, and the rise in the imports of goods and services as a percentage of GDP from 52 percent in 2005 to 64.4 percent in 2007. In the years 2007-2010, the trend behaviour was upward and this is could be due to the rise in GDP per capita growth and the decline of inflation over most of the period compared with 2005. The key social determinant trend was upward in the period 2005 to 2008. This could be due to a demographic reason: the rise in the numbers of students in secondary schools and an increase in electricity production. The UAE achieved growth in the period 2005-2006 in the factor of political stability. The key political determinants trend was almost a downward in the period 2006 to 2008. This could have been due to a lowering of the factor of transparency in this period. The impact of both of political stability and

173

transparency (see Appendix 13) is clear in the changes of the key political determinants trend in the period 2008-2010.

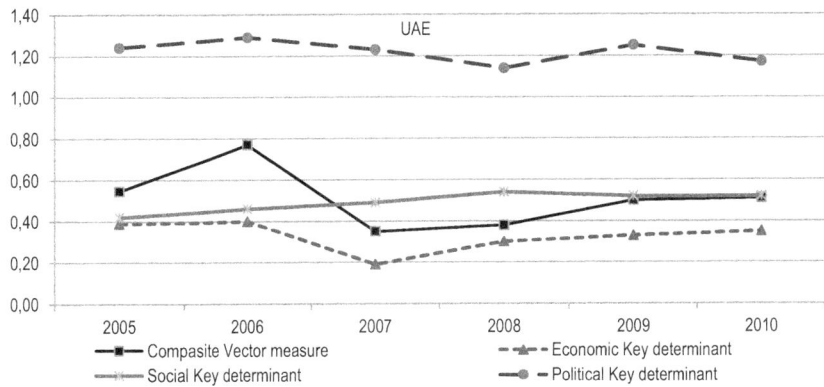

Figure 4-56. Change of Investment Attractiveness to UAE in the period 2005-2010

Source: Author's elaboration.

Figure 4-57 shows the unstable behaviour of the trends of the composite vector measure, the key economic determinants, in Poland in the period of 2005-2010.

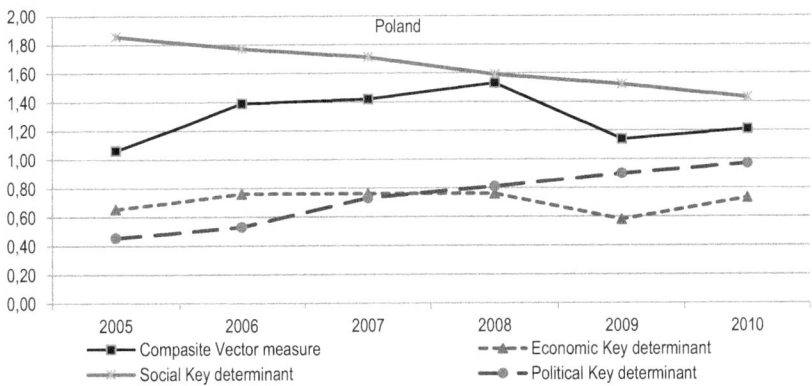

Figure 4-57. Change of Investment Attractiveness to Poland in the period 2005-2010

Source: Author's elaboration.

The key economic determinants trend was slightly upward from the year 2005 to the year 2006. This can be attributed to the rise in GDP growth and GDP per capita growth by about 72 and 70 percent in the year 2006 respectively compared with the year 2005, and due to the decline of inflation from 2.6 percent in 2005 to 1.5 percent in 2006. In the period 2006-2008, the key economic determinants trend was stable. From the year 2008 to 2009, the trend was downward. This is could be due to the rise in inflation to 3.6 percent in 2009 compared with 2.6 percent in 2005 (see Appendix 14). The key social determinants trend was almost a downward in the period 2005 to 2010. This was due to demographic reasons, namely the declining numbers of students in secondary schools. The key political determinants trend was almost a downward in the period 2005 to 2010. This could have been due to the rise in the factors of political stability, the rule of law and transparency in this period (see Appendix 14).

The conclusion from our analyses is that all the factors are important to the countries. Although some factors such as the GDP growth, inflation and transparency were the most important in some countries in some years, we can say that it is necessary for all countries to pay attention to all the variables. Anyway, the results were not so far from the results that we got in section 4.1. Thus we will suggest our propositions in section 4.4 according to the results which prove that some factors are more important in changes to investment attractiveness.

4.4. Propositions for Important Changes in Investment Attractiveness in Arab Countries

The propositions in this section are based on the results of Chapter 4 and the theoretical background. The proposals are aimed at increasing the attractiveness for foreign direct investment in Arab countries. The propositions will be presented for each Arab country separately.

Our main observations are that:

- the results showed that the factors GDP growth, and inflation/GDP deflator index are important economic factors for attracting investment,
- electricity production was the most important social factor for attracting investment,
- transparency was the most important political factor for attracting investment,
- in general, economic factors were the most important factors among the key determinants that attract investment. Thus, the Arab countries should use economic policies to improve these economic factors, and especially GDP growth and controlling inflation.

Below we shall analyse the results for each individual Arab country being investigated and propose changes in the key determinants of investment attractiveness. In general, we shall refer to the best position for each country in comparison with Poland, and we shall focus our analyses on the results for the year 2010.

- Algeria

Algeria had the highest rank in 2009 when it was ranked 5 and Poland was ranked 2. Generally, in all the key determinants Algeria has to improve some factors to be close to the position of Poland. In the year 2010, the rank of Algeria was 7, while Poland was 1. When we analysed the economic input data (appendices 1 and 14) we can see that in some factors, such as tax payments (number) and urban population (percentage of total), the level of factors in Algeria is the same or even higher than for Poland. The index of inflation/GDP deflator in Algeria is higher by about 1050% than the level achieved in Poland. Thus, here we propose to take action through fiscal and monetary policies aimed at controlling high levels of inflation. Other factors, such as GDP growth, GDP per capita (constant in 2005), GDP per capita growth (annual percent), trade (percentage of GDP) and labour force (total) had lower levels in Algeria than in Poland in the year 2010. Thus, here we propose to respond appropriately to improve the levels of these factors in order to achieve the level of Poland in 2010. The level of the economic factor (imports of goods and services (percentage of GDP) in Algeria was lower than in Poland in the year 2010, by about 28 percent. As this factor is a destimulant, thus the level of this factor for Algeria is better than for Poland. In the social factors Algeria's number of secondary education pupils is higher than in Poland by 208 percent. In electricity production Algeria achieves about 29 percent of Polish electricity production. Thus, we propose that Algeria increase its production of electric energy, since electricity is one of the elements that contribute to the increase of investment attractiveness. Especially as Algeria has large reserves of natural gas, it is possible to increase the production of electric energy based on its own resources. In the dimension of political factors (political stability, rule of law), Algeria was very far from the level of Poland in the year 2010. In the transparency factor, Algeria was ranked 105 in the year 2010 among the world's countries, with the score of 2.9 (see Table 3-10), while Poland's rank was 41 with the score of 5.3 (Transparency International). Thus, Algeria has to improve its level on the Transparency Corruption Index. Time to import in Algeria is higher than in Poland by about 35 percent, thus we propose that Algeria takes actions that contribute to reducing the time needed to complete the import procedure. In the other political factor, time to export, Algeria's level was the same as in Poland in the year 2010.

- Bahrain

The best ranking for Bahrain was 6, compared with 2 for Poland in the year 2005. The rank of Bahrain was 8 in the year 2010, while Poland was 1. Generally, in all the key determinants Bahrain has to improve some factors to come close to the position of Poland. In the year 2010, when we analysed the economic input data (appendices 2 and 14) we could see that in some factors, such as GDP growth, GDP per capita (constant 2005), trade (percentage of GDP) and urban population (percentage of total), the level of Bahrain was better than Poland. In other factors, such as the inflation/GDP deflator, Bahrain is higher by about 529 percent than the level achieved in Poland. Thus, here we propose that action be taken through fiscal and monetary policies aimed at curbing the high inflation situation. In other factors, such as GDP per capita growth (annual percentage), tax payments (number) and Labour force (total), the level of Bahrain was lower than that of Poland in the year 2010. Thus, here we propose an appropriate response to improve the levels of these factors to achieve the levels of Poland in 2010. The level of the economic factor (imports of goods and services (percentage of GDP)) in Bahrain was higher than in Poland in the year 2010, by about 17 percent. As this factor is a destimulant, the level of Bahrain is worse than that of Poland with regard to this factor. In the social factors, in Bahrain both the levels of secondary education pupils and electricity production are less than in Poland. Here we have to bear in mind the size of the economy in Bahrain, and the limited numbers of the population (see section 3.1). In the political factor political stability, Bahrain was very far from the level of Poland in the year 2010. In the other political factors (the rule of law and transparency) Bahrain was at a lower level than Poland in the year 2010. Therefore, Bahrain has to improve these factors in order to be at the same level as Poland or better. In other factors, like time to export and time to import, the level of Bahrain was better than the level of Poland in 2010.

- Egypt

The best ranking was 1 for Egypt in the year 2005, compared with the ranking of 2 for Poland in the same year. Egypt and Poland were in the same top group for four years. We can see through our results that the year 2005 was the best level for Egypt compared to Poland. However, in 2010 Egypt's ranking decreased to 4 compared with Poland's ranking of 1. Therefore, it is interesting here to analyse the changes in the input data in these two years. From appendices 3 and 14, it is clear that the factors GDP per capita (constant 2005), trade (as percentage of GDP), tax payments, rule of law and transparency in the year 2010 had decreased compared with Poland in the year 2005. At the same time, the inflation/ GDP deflator had increased to about 721 percent compared with Poland in the year 2010, while this was 238 percent in the year 2005. In our view, all these factors could be a reason for the fall in the ranking level of Egypt from 1 in the year 2005, to the rank of 4 in the year 2010. We propose here that the best level for Egypt was in the year 2005. Given the level of the year 2010, Egypt has to improve some of its economic and political factors to be on the same level as Poland.

• Iraq

As we mentioned in this section, Iraq has had an unstable economic and political situation for many years. This situation is proved by our results. The results show that the best ranking for Iraq was in the year 2009, when it was 13 among 14 countries. During the other years of our research, Iraq has been ranked 14 among our sample countries. With regard to the economic factors, the best score for Iraq was in the year 2009. As for social factors, Iraq was in the best position compared to Poland in the year 2010. This was due to the devastation of education and the electricity sector due to war conditions. In political factors, the results show that Iraq had the worst score among our sample study. The score for Iraq during the period 2005-2010 was 0 in every year. Again, we can attribute this to the special conditions in Iraq. Thus, our proposal here is to improve all the key determinant factors. It is important for Iraq for example to develop the agricultural sector because it has the benefit of large tracts of agriculture and labour-can be used to increase the proportion of the contribution of this sector to the gross domestic product. As well improve the non-oil sectors of the economy. As we saw in the year 2009, the changes of the scores for key economic determinants brought about a change in the ranking of Iraq.

• Jordan

The best ranking for Jordan was 5 in the year 2005, compared to Poland with a ranking of 2 in the same year. Generally, in all the key determinants Jordan has to improve some factors to be close to the position of Poland. For the year 2010, when we analyse the economic input data (appendices 5 and 14) we can see that in some factors, such as GDP growth, GDP per capita (constant 2005), GDP per capita growth (annual percentage), tax payments (number) and labour force (total) the level of Jordan is less than that of Poland. It is important here to bear in mind the small size of Jordan and the limited population (see section 3.1). In the other factors, such as trade (percentage of GDP), inflation/ GDP deflator, imports of goods and services (percentage of GDP), and urban population (percentage of total), the level of Jordan is high than that of Poland. Thus, here we propose to use the fiscal and monetary policies to control the high inflation situation, and we propose to respond appropriately to improve the levels of these factors to achieve the levels of Poland in 2010. With regard to the social factors, in Jordan both the levels of secondary education pupils and electricity production are less than in Poland. Here we have to bear in mind the size of Jordan's economy and the limited population (see section 3.1). With regard to the political factor of political stability, Jordan was very far from the level of Poland in the year 2010. In the other political factors (the rule of law and transparency), Jordan was on a lower level than Poland in the year 2010. Therefore, Jordan has to improve these factors. Regarding the factor of time to export, Jordan was about 82 percent of the level of Poland in 2010. For the factor of time to import, Jordan was higher than the level of Poland by about 6 percent. We propose that Jordan take actions that contribute to reducing the length of time needed to complete the import process.

- Kuwait

The best ranking for Kuwait was 3 out of our sample study in the year 2005, compared with a ranking of 2 to Poland in the same year. The ranking of Kuwait in the year 2010 was the worst position over the period 2005-2010. This could be due to the big change in the value of some factors. For example, the GDP growth (annual percentage) changed from 10.1 percent in the year 2005, to -2.4 percent in the year 2010. Also the GDP per capita growth (annual percentage) changed from 5.3 percent in the year 2005, to -7 percent in the year 2010. Generally, in all the key determinants Kuwait has to improve some factors to be close to the position of Poland. In the year 2010, when we analyse the economic input data (appendices 6 and 14) we can see that in some factors, such as GDP growth, GDP per capita growth (annual percentage), tax payments (number), and labour force (total) the level of Kuwait is less than that of Poland. It is important here to bear in mind the small size of Kuwait and its limited population (see section 3.1). In the other factors, such as GDP per capita (constant 2005), trade (as percentage of GDP), inflation/ GDP deflator, and urban population (percentage of total), Kuwait was higher than the level achieved in Poland, taking into consideration the stimulant and destimulant factors. Thus, here we propose that action be taken through fiscal and monetary policies aimed at curbing the high inflation situation, and we propose an appropriate response to improve the levels of these factors to achieve the levels of Poland in 2010. The factor of imports of goods and services (percentage of GDP) in Kuwait is less than the level of Poland in 2010. With regard to the social factors, in Kuwait both the level of secondary education pupils and electricity production are less than in Poland. We have to bear in mind the size of Kuwait, and the limited numbers in its population (see section 3.1). Of the political factors (rule of law, transparency and time to export), Kuwait was very close to the level of Poland in the year 2010. Regarding the political stability factor,

Kuwait was about 56 percent short of the level of Poland in the year 2010. Therefore, Kuwait has to improve these factors. Regarding the factor of time to import, Kuwait was on a higher level than Poland in 2010 by about 12 percent. We propose here that Kuwait takes action that contributes to reducing the length of time needed to complete the import process. Generally, when it comes to the political factors, Kuwait had a better score than Poland in the years 2005, 2006 and 2007.

- Lebanon

For many years, this country has had almost as unstable an economic and political situation as exists in Iraq. This situation is proved by our results. The results show that the best ranking for Lebanon was in the year 2010, which was 9 out of 14 countries. During the other years of our research, Lebanon was ranked 13 among our sample study, except it was ranked 14 in the year 2009. With regard to the economic factors, the best score for Lebanon was in the year 2007. When we analyse the economic input data (appendices 7 and 14), we can see that in some factors - such as GDP growth, GDP per capita growth (annual percentage), trade (percentage of GDP), and urban population (percentage of total), the level of Lebanon was better than that of Poland. The import of goods and services (percentage of GDP) in Lebanon was higher by about 43 percent than the level of Poland in the year 2010. When we take into account the fact that this factor is a destimulant, we propose that Lebanon take action through its trade policy to solve that. With regard to the other factors, such as GDP per capita (constant in 2005), tax payments (number) and labour force (percentage of total), Lebanon is far from the level of Poland in the year 2010. We propose to respond appropriately to improve the levels of these factors to achieve the levels of Poland in 2010. The inflation/ GDP deflator in Lebanon was less than in Poland by 86 percent in the year 2010. This could be one of the positive factors that help to attract investment, if there are other factors that help. As for the social factors, in Lebanon both the level of secondary education pupils and electricity production are less than in Poland. Here we have to take into account the size of Lebanon and its limited population (see section 3.1). As for the political factors (political stability, the rule of law and transparency), Lebanon was far from the level of Poland in the year 2010. This could be due to the unstable conditions, political and economic, which prevailed in Lebanon for many years. With regard to the factors of time to export and time to import, Lebanon was higher than the level of Poland in 2010 by about 47 percent and 94 percent respectively. We suggest that Lebanon take actions that contribute to reducing the length of time needed to complete these processes.

- Morocco

The best ranking for Morocco was 5 in both the years 2006 and 2010, which compares with Poland which ranked 1 in both years. From our results, we can see the unstable position of Morocco through the period 2005-2010. Generally, in all the key determinants Morocco has to improve some factors to be close to the position of Poland. In the year 2010, when we analysed the economic input data (appendices 8 and 14), we could see that in some factors - such as (GDP growth, GDP per capita (constant 2005), GDP per capita growth (annual percentage), trade (percentage of GDP), tax payments (number), urban population (percentage of total) and labour force (total) - the level of Morocco was less than that of Poland. It is important here to bear in mind the structure and the size of the Moroccan economy (see section 3.1). As for the other factors, such as inflation/ GDP deflator, and imports of goods and services (percentage of GDP), Morocco is at a better level than that achieved in Poland, taking into consideration the stimulant and destimulant factors. Regarding the social factors, Morocco's level of secondary education pupils was higher than Poland's by about 11 percent in the year 2010. However, electricity production was less than in Poland by about 85 percent. Here, as we mentioned before, we have to take into account the size of Morocco's economy (see section 3.1). As for the political factors (political stability and the rule of law), Morocco was very far from the level of Poland in the year 2010. In the transparency factor, Morocco was at a lower level than Poland in the year 2010. Therefore, Morocco has to improve these factors. For the factor of time to export, the level of Morocco was about 24 percent lower than the level of Poland in 2010. The time to import was the same in both Morocco and Poland in the year 2010.

- Oman

The best ranking of Oman was 6 in the years 2006, 2007 and 2009, compared to Poland with the ranking of 1 in the years 2006 and 2007, and the ranking of 2 in the year 2009. From our results, we can see the unstable position of Oman through the period 2005-2010. Generally, in all the key determinants Oman has to improve some factors to be close to the position of Poland. In the year 2010, when we analyse the economic input data (appendices 9 and 14), we can see that in some factors - such as GDP per capita growth (annual percentage), tax payments (number) and labour force (total) - the level of Oman was lower than that of Poland. It is important here to take into account the structure and the size of Oman's economy (see section 3.1). As for the other economic factors - such as GDP growth, GDP per capita (constant 2005), trade (percentage of GDP) in addition to urban population (percentage of total) - Oman is in better level achieved in Poland. The inflation/GDP deflator (annual percentage) in Oman was higher than in Poland by about 1000 percent in the year 2010. The imports of goods and services (percentage of GDP) in Oman was better than in Poland by about 25 percent if we take into account the destimulant factor. As for the social factors, both the level of the secondary education pupils and electricity production in Oman were less are than in Poland. Here we have to bear in mind the size of Oman, and the limited population (see section 3.1). Regarding the political factors (political stability and the rule of law), Oman was far from the level of Poland in the year 2010. Therefore, Oman has to improve these factors. With regard to the transparency factor, Oman was on the same level as Poland in the year 2010. On the factor of time to export, the level of Oman was about 41 percent lower than the level of Poland in 2010. The time to import in Oman was less than in Poland by about 47 percent in the year 2010. Thus, these are comparative advantages to Oman.

- Qatar

This country was ranked 1 in the year 2009, compared with Poland which was ranked 2 in the same year. The rank of Qatar in the year 2010 was 2 after Poland. Generally, in this year Qatar has to improve some economic key determinants, and in my opinion, it is not possible for it to make a big change in the social factors, especially in the secondary education, On the other hand, Qatar is one of the biggest countries when it comes to natural gas reserves in the world. Thus, this could be a comparative advantage for Qatar to have a high score in the key economic determinant. Also, the high scores Qatar achieved in the political factors throughout the period of 2005-2010 give it a comparative advantage to have a high rank of our composite vector measure. When we analyse the economic input data (appendices 10 and 14), we can see that in some factors - such as tax payments (number) and labour force (total) - the level of Qatar is less than that of Poland. The inflation/ GDP deflator in Qatar is higher than the level in Poland by about 586 percent. In the import of good and services (percentage of GDP), Qatar's level is better than that of Poland by about 45 percent. In the other economic factors, Qatar is better than Poland.

- Saudi Arabia

Saudi is one of the rich Arab countries that had a high rank in our composite vector measure during the period 2005-2010. This country was ranked 2 in the year 2007, compared with Poland which was ranked 1 in the same year. The rank of Saudi in the year 2010 was 3 after Poland and Qatar. When we analyse the economic input data (appendices 11 and 14) generally, in 2010 Saudi had to improve some economic key determinants, such as trade (percentage of GDP), tax payments (number), and labour force. The inflation/ GDP deflator in Saudi was higher than the level in Poland by about 921 percent. The import of goods and services (percentage of GDP), Saudi levels was better than the levels of Poland by about 24 percent. In the other economic factors, Saudi was also better than Poland. Saudi is one of the biggest countries involved in oil reserves and oil production in the world. Thus, this could be a comparative advantage for Saudi to have a high score in the key economic determinants. In the key social determinants, the level of Saudi was better than Poland in the year 2010. On the other hand, The political factors score in Saudi in the whole period 2005-2010 was "between" 59 and 60. This could be due to the lower level compared to Poland in the political stability, rule of law and transparency factors. Generally, the best position for Saudi in the key political determinant factors was in the year 2005 (Figure 4-38).

- Tunisia

The best ranking for Tunisia was 7 in the year 2006, compared to Poland with a ranking of 1 in the same year. From our results, we can see the position of Tunisia through the period 2005-2010 was in the same group. Generally, in all the key determinants Tunisia has to improve some factors to be close to the position of Poland. Nevertheless, the score on key political determinants for Tunisia was in a better position than Poland in both of the years 2005 and 2006 (Figure 4-40). In the year 2010, when we analysed the economic input data (appendices 12 and 14), we could see that in some factors - such as trade (percentage of GDP) and urban population (percentage of total) - Tunisia's level was better than that of Poland. In all other economic factors, the level of Poland was better than that of Tunisia. Therefore, Tunisia has to improve these factors. We can say that the best position regarding the key economic determinants of Tunisia compared with Poland was in the year 2007. In the social factors, both the levels of secondary education pupils and electricity production in Tunisia are less than in Poland. Regarding the political factors - political stability, rule of law, transparency and time to export - Tunisia was far from the level of Poland in the year 2010. Therefore, Tunisia has to improve these factors. The time to import was the same in both Tunisia and Poland in the year 2010.

- United Arab Emirate (UAE)

The United Arab Emirates (UAE) is one of the rich Arab countries and one of the biggest oil reserves and producers of oil in the Arab world. This country was ranked 6 in the year 2010, compared with Poland which was ranked 1 in the same year. This rank was the highest in the period 2005-2010. Generally, in the year 2010 the UAE has to improve some key economic determinants, such as GDP growth (annual percentage), GDP per capita growth (annual percentage), tax payments (number), and the labour force. The inflation/ GDP deflator in the UAE is higher than the level in Poland by about 679 percent. In the import of goods and services (percentage of GDP), the UAE's level is higher than the level of Poland by about 66 percent. With regard to the other economic factors, the UAE is better than Poland. Thus, the UAE has to use economic policy to improve the factors that are at a low level to make them the same level as Poland in the year 2010. In the key social determinants, the level of the UAE is lower than Poland's in the year 2010. In my opinion, it is not possible to make a big change in the social factors, at least not in the short term, especially in the secondary education, if we bear in mind the limited size of the population. In the political factors throughout the period of 2005-2010, the UAE's score was between 86 and 100, and in this whole period, the level of the UAE was better than the level of Poland. This could be due to the better level of factors (transparency, time to export and time to import) in UAE than the level of Poland throughout the period 2005-2010.

Conclusions and Future Research

By discussing the background of the problem, the objectives of the research study, and the data used to analysed, the researcher has established the methodology and has shown how to assess the investment attractiveness through the synthetic vector measure. Despite the lack of data available from Arab countries (one of the main obstacles faced by our research), the main hypothesis, i.e. the political factors have the major impact on investment attractiveness of Arab countries, have been verified negatively except for the year 2007. The results (see Appendix 36) shown that the economic key determinant is the most important factor among the other keys determinants factors in attracting investments in the Arab countries.

The research achieved all the goals through the results that have been reached, and the proposals that have been mentioned in section 4.3. The main goal assessing the investment attractiveness in Arab countries and comparing the results with Poland as a benchmark has been achieved. The sub goals identifying and analysing the factors that determine the investment attractiveness by defining the measure of the investment attractiveness, applying the measure to Arab countries, and proposed the changes that might improve the investment attractiveness to Arab countries have been achieved, and they have been referred to in details (see section 4.4). Our results show that there is a positive correlation between our vector measures and inflow of FDI. The analyses show that our FDI index, through the correlation with FDI inward flows, is 0.62 for the period 2005-2010 (see Appendix 34). Compared with 0.54 the correlation in the index of the study of Groh, 0.31 is the correlation for the Inward FDI Potential Index, and for the Global Competitiveness Index it is 0.31. In all the results, we can see that our index gives a better correlation. Besides, the research aims to improve the investment attractiveness of Arab countries (see section 4.4). The numbers of recommendations have been proposed for each Arab countries being researched.

In this dissertation, when we analysed the output from the composite synthetic measure, we conclude the following additional points:
1. In some Arab countries, there is no possibility for the social factors to grow significantly. These Arab countries have limited options to increase the social factors, because of the limited population and the size of the economy. When we analyses the data of some Arab countries, such as Bahrain, Jordan, Kuwait, Oman, Lebanon, Tunisia, and UAE, we observe this phenomenon.

2. Our results show that Arab countries were in a better position compared to Poland of the period 2005-2010 were only in the years 2005 and 2009. It can be attributed to the relative stability that followed the war in Iraq in 2003; instability that accompanied the economic crisis in 2008. If we know that, the period of the research is 2005–2010, then we can deduce that economic stability has a significant impact on the process of attracting foreign investment; some variables in some Arab countries were better than they are in Poland in some years. However, the years 2005 and 2007 were the best in investment attractiveness for most Arab countries for the reasons previously mentioned.

3. Some Arab countries have higher investment attractiveness than Poland. Besides, the results show that this applies to only some countries and in specific years. For example, Egypt has higher attractiveness than Poland in the year 2005. As well as Qatar has higher attractiveness than Poland in the year 2009.

4. According to the results, the important economic factors were (tax payment (number), Urban population, Labour force, GDP growth (annual percent), GDP per capita growth (annual percent), and the inflation/ GDP deflator.

5. In the case of the social factors, the results show that the number of secondary pupils was the most important factor for a five years and the average period. The electricity production was important in the year 2005.

6. Among the political factors, the results show that the transparency was the most important factor in each year and for the average for the five-year period. The political stability was the most importance factor only in the year 2010.

7. In economic key determinant, two Arab countries have a higher level than Poland. First, was Kuwait in the year 2005, and second was Qatar in the year 2009.

8. In social key determinant, Egypt has the high level than Poland in all the period of the study.

9. In political key determinant United Arab Emirates (UAE) has a high level than Poland in the years 2005, and 2006. Moreover, Qatar has a higher level than Poland in the period 2007-2010.

10. Iraq has suffered through several decades many wars, led to the destruction of infrastructure. Iraq also suffered from the economic blockade from 1990 until 2003. Consequently, in the input data do not reflect the social and economic reality. That is because not all data are available for some period then. Therefore, that should be hard to correlation.

Future Research: We must be noted that we tried to select more countries, but we could not find data that cover them. We suggest for the future studies is to add countries from the Middle East such as (Turkey, Iran, and another Arab countries that we could not include it in our study). Someone can extend the period to after 2010 or the period before 2005 if it is a possible to have a data and compare the stability and instability situation in Arab countries in attractive investment. Note that the Arab region suffers time to complete our study of the absence of political and economic stability since the beginning of the Arab Spring at the end of 2010. Moreover, we suggest for a future studies add another country for a comparison such as (South Korea, India, Russian, Brazil). Also use another method or other statistical methods can be a suggestion for the future studies. All these ideas and maybe another can be a guide for the policy maker to know the important factors affecting the attraction of foreign investment.

Polish summary

Streszczenie

Napływ inwestycji do krajów rozwijających się charakteryzuje się znacznym zróżnicowaniem w poszczególnych krajach. Ze względu na brak występowania rynków kapitałowych w niektórych krajach arabskich, w niniejszej pracy skupiono się na zagranicznych inwestycjach bezpośrednich, jako jednym z rodzajów inwestycji. Inwestycje, włączając zagraniczne inwestycje bezpośrednie (ZIB), dają siłę napędową do rozwoju gospodarczego w poszczególnych krajach. ZIB stanowią ważne źródło funduszy dla krajowych inwestycji, pobudzając tworzenie się kapitału w kraju przyjmującym. Współcześnie coraz większą uwagę, zarówno na poziomie krajowym jak i międzynarodowym, poświęca się kwestiom związanym z zagranicznymi inwestycjami bezpośrednimi. Według światowego raportu dotyczącego inwestycji, pomimo działań na rzecz otwarcia gospodarki wiele krajów rozwijających się, w tym krajów arabskich, zdołało przyciągnąć tylko niewielkie ilości ZIB.

Istnieje wiele czynników, które utrudniają napływ inwestycji zagranicznych do krajów arabskich. Atrakcyjność inwestycyjna jest zestawem cech i czynników, które pozwalają inwestorowi na ocenę i porównanie potencjału dowolnego kraju w stosunku do innych krajów. Istnieje wiele czynników ekonomicznych, społecznych i politycznych, które powodują wzrost poziomu zagranicznych inwestycji bezpośrednich. Potencjalny inwestor bierze te czynniki pod uwagę, przy wyborze kraju w celach inwestycyjnych i ocenia jego atrakcyjność w tym względzie. Termin atrakcyjność inwestycyjna oznacza zespół czynników, które przyczyniają się do zapewnienia odpowiedniego klimatu dla inwestycji. Termin klimat inwestycyjny oznacza warunki ekonomiczno-finansowe kraju, które oddziałują na osoby fizyczne lub firmy pragnące inwestować w danym kraju. Dobry klimat inwestycyjny jest zazwyczaj osiągany poprzez poprawę uwarunkowań inwestycyjnych. Problemem polityków w krajach arabskich jest identyfikacja czynników określających atrakcyjność inwestycyjną i ustalenie czynników, które wywierają na nią największy wpływ. W niniejszej pracy, starano się zidentyfikować najważniejsze czynniki wpływające na poziom inwestycji w krajach arabskich. Proces przyciągania inwestycji jest istotnym elementem konkurencyjności kraju. Warto w tym miejscu wspomnieć, że konkurencyjność oznacza zbiór instytucji, zasad działania i czynników określających poziom produktywności kraju*.

Istotnym w niniejszej pracy dla krajów arabskich jest opracowanie indeksu opisującego czynniki wpływające na atrakcyjność zagranicznych inwestycji bezpośrednich. Do obliczenia tego złożonego indeksu potrzebne są dane, które opisują czynniki wpływające na atrakcyjność inwestycji. Dane zostały dobrane z wielu źródeł jak np. UNCTA oraz Arab Investment and Export Credit Guarantee Corporation. W rezultacie indeks będzie pokazywał ranking wybranych krajów arabskich zgodnie z ich atrakcyjnością pod względem napływu ZIB a następnie zostanie porównany z Polską, stanowiącą dobrą bazę do porównań (szczegóły zostały wyjaśnione w Rozdziale 1). Dodatkowo, ze względu na budowę indeksu, istnieje możliwość przeprowadzenia i sprawdzenia szczegółowych informacji dotyczących atrakcyjności każdego kraju. Te analizy mogą zostać wykorzystane przez polityków do wyciągnięcia wniosków dotyczących uatrakcyjnienia kraju w taki sposób, aby powodowało to napływ ZIB.

Problem badawczy

Przez dziesięciolecia kraje arabskie starały się przyciągnąć inwestycje zagraniczne. Potrzeby związane z pozyskaniem większej ilości środków finansowych, w celu zaspokojenia rosnących potrzeb związanych z rozwojem infrastruktury, zmusiły te kraje do szukania zewnętrznych źródeł finansowania. W krajach arabskich istnieje również wyraźny brak inwestycji krajowych. Kraje arabskie dołożyły wielu starań w celu przyciągnięcia inwestycji zagranicznych, ale ich wielkość jest mniejsza niż planowano i oczekiwano. Dlatego ważne jest zrozumienie przyczyn takiej sytuacji.

Kraje arabskie mają wspólne cechy, takie jak język, religia, wspólna kultura i położenie. Jednakże te wspólne czynniki nie uniemożliwiają zróżnicowania tych krajów pod względem innych cech, takich jak struktura i rozmiar gospodarki, liczba ludności oraz wielkość i dostępność zasobów naturalnych, postęp gospodarczy a także wiele innych. Istnieje wiele opinii na temat tego, które czynniki są najważniejsze i mają największy udział w procesie przyciągania inwestycji. Badania teoretyczne wskazują, że najważniejszymi kwestiami, które determinują proces przyciągania inwestycji są motywy związane z inwestowaniem. Istnieje wiele motywów podejmowania inwestycji zagranicznych, takich jak poszukiwanie zasobów naturalnych, zwiększenie wydajności, rozwój rynków, taniej i niewykwalifikowanej lub średnio

---

* Produktywność jest powszechnie określana, jako stosunek wielkości produkcji do wielkości poniesionych nakładów (OECD,2001)

189

wykwalifikowanej siły roboczej, pozyskanie możliwości technologicznych, doświadczenia w dziedzinie zarządzania lub marketingu, umiejętności organizacyjnych. W pracy starano się znaleźć odpowiedź na pytanie, co powoduje przyciąganie inwestycji zagranicznych. Jeżeli motywy inwestycji zagranicznych w krajach arabskich są zróżnicowane między krajami, to powodem tego są różnice w strukturze i rozmiarze gospodarki. Wówczas, czynniki wpływające na proces przyciągania inwestycji zagranicznych w danym kraju nie są koniecznie takie same w innych krajach. Prowadzona jest analiza i badania czynników mających największy wpływ na proces przyciągania inwestycji zagranicznych w krajach arabskich. W wyniku tego przedstawione są praktyczne rozwiązania i rekomendacje pomagające decydentom w zwiększeniu atrakcyjności inwestycyjnej. Jest to możliwe przez wykorzystanie wiedzy na temat najważniejszych czynników wpływających na proces przyciągania inwestycji zagranicznych do ich krajów. Zostanie również przeprowadzone porównanie między krajami arabskimi a Polską, jako punktem odniesienia (benchmarkiem).

Cele pracy i hipoteza badawcza

Podstawowym celem niniejszej pracy jest dokonanie oceny atrakcyjności inwestycyjnej krajów arabskich. Cel podstawowy można dekomponować na pięć celów szczegółowych. Wówczas najważniejsze kwestie niniejszej pracy można przedstawić jako:

- Identyfikacja i analiza czynników określających atrakcyjność inwestycyjną;
- Budowa miary atrakcyjności inwestycyjnej;
- Zastosowanie miary do pomiaru atrakcyjności inwestycyjnej krajów arabskich;
- Propozycja zmian zmierzających do zwiększenia atrakcyjności inwestycyjnej krajów arabskich;
- Ocena atrakcyjności inwestycyjnej krajów arabskich i porównanie z Polską, jako benchmarkiem.

Główna **hipoteza** pracy zawiera się w stwierdzeniu, że największy wpływ na atrakcyjność inwestycyjną krajów arabskich mają czynniki polityczne. Rozprawa składa się z niżej przedstawionych czterech rozdziałów:

W rozdziale 1 w trzech podrozdziałach opisane zostały inwestycje oraz atrakcyjność zagranicznych inwestycji bezpośrednich. Rozdział zajmuje się inwestycjami i ich klasyfikacją, pojęciem inwestycji oraz teoriami dotyczącymi zagranicznych inwestycji bezpośrednich. Rozdział przedstawia również historię inwestycji zagranicznych na świecie. W tym rozdziale określono szczegółowo determinanty inwestycji zagranicznych jako jedną z barier inwestycyjnych;

W rozdziale 2 opisana została metodologia oceny atrakcyjności ZIB w trzech podrozdziałach. W tym rozdziale przeanalizowano wybrane indeksy oraz badania na temat atrakcyjności zagranicznych inwestycji bezpośrednich. Ponadto opisane zostały główne etapy budowy złożonych wskaźników oceny atrakcyjności inwestycyjnej. W tym rozdziale porównane zostały również metody stosowane do oceny atrakcyjności inwestycji;

W rozdziale 3 w trzech podrozdziałach przeanalizowano specyfikę inwestycji w krajach arabskich. W pierwszym podrozdziale został przeprowadzony krótki przegląd wybranych danych ekonomicznych i geograficznych dotyczących krajów arabskich oraz przedstawiony został przedmiot badania. W drugim podrozdziale przeanalizowano trendy ZIB w krajach arabskich. W trzecim podrozdziale, poprzez analizę wybranych wskaźników oceniony został klimat inwestycyjny panujący w krajach arabskich;

Rozdział 4 zawiera ocenę atrakcyjności inwestycyjnej krajów arabskich w czterech podrozdziałach. W pierwszym podrozdziale, za pomocą metod wektorowych oceniono analizę atrakcyjności krajów arabskich oraz Polski. Omówione zostały trzy etapy związane z budową złożonego indeksu zbudowanego na bazie syntetycznej miary wektorowej i przeprowadzono porównanie otrzymanych wyników z innymi indeksami. W drugim podrozdziale została przeprowadzona analiza czynników, które wpływają na atrakcyjności inwestycyjną krajów arabskich w porównaniu do Polski. W trzecim podrozdziale zostały zbadane zmiany atrakcyjności inwestycyjnej krajów arabskich i Polski. W ostatnim podrozdziale przedstawiono propozycje dla każdego z analizowanych krajów arabskich, które mogą pomóc zwiększyć napływ ZIB.

Spis treści rozprawy zaprezentowany jest poniżej.

Wstęp

1. Inwestycje i atrakcyjność zagranicznych inwestycji bezpośrednich

    1.1. Inwestycje i ich klasyfikacja

    1.2. Pojęcie, teorie i praktyka zagranicznych inwestycji bezpośrednich

        1.2.1. Teorie zagranicznych inwestycji bezpośrednich

        1.2.2. Zagraniczne inwestycje bezpośrednie w praktyce w różnych okresach
            historycznych

    1.3. Determinanty atrakcyjności inwestycyjnej

2. Metodyka badania atrakcyjności zagranicznych inwestycji bezpośrednich

    2.1. Przegląd metod oceny atrakcyjności zagranicznych inwestycji bezpośrednich

    2.2. Złożona miara atrakcyjności zagranicznych inwestycji bezpośrednich

    2.3. Zagregowane metody badania atrakcyjności inwestycyjnej

        2.3.1. Syntetyczna miara wektorowa

        2.3.2. Miara syntetyczna wykorzystująca metodę PCA

        2.3.3. Metoda Topsis

3. Specyfika inwestycji w krajach arabskich

    3.1. Kultura oraz geografia gospodarcza krajów arabskich

    3.2. Analiza trendów zagranicznych inwestycji bezpośrednich w krajach arabskich

        3.2.1. Zagraniczne inwestycje bezpośrednie w krajach arabskich

        3.2.2. Zagraniczne inwestycje bezpośrednie pomiędzy krajami arabskimi i ich analiza sektorowa

    3.3. Analiza wskaźników klimatu inwestycyjnego w krajach arabskich

4. Analiza empiryczna atrakcyjności inwestycyjnej krajów arabskich

    4.1. Badanie atrakcyjności inwestycyjnej krajów arabskich i Polski za pomocą metod wektorowych

    4.2. Analiza czynników wpływających na atrakcyjność inwestycyjną krajów arabskich w porównaniu z Polską

    4.3. Zmiany w atrakcyjności inwestycyjnej krajów arabskich i Polski w latach 2005-2010

    4.4. Propozycje istotnych zmian w kształtowaniu atrakcyjności inwestycyjnej krajów arabskich

Wnioski i przyszłe badania

Zakres pracy

Ze względu na ograniczenie w dostępie do danych dotyczących niektórych krajów, ograniczono liczbę analizowanych krajów arabskich jedynie do trzynastu, dla których istniały dane niezbędne do analizy. Na przykład w Sudanie nie ma danych dotyczących ZIB, w Państwie Palestyńskim brak jest danych na temat inflacji, w Komorach brak jest danych na temat PKB itd. W Somalii trwa wojna a sytuacja polityczno-gospodarcza jest niestabilna. W niektórych krajach arabskich istniejące dane nie są wiarygodne. Niniejsza praca jest pierwszym opracowaniem, które porównuje atrakcyjność inwestycyjną krajów arabskich Środkowego Wschodu i Afryki

Północnej z atrakcyjnością inwestycyjną Polski w latach 2005-2010. Przeprowadzono analizę baz danych zarówno Ministerstwa Szkolnictwa Wyższego i Badań Naukowych w Iraku, jak również różnego rodzaju baz danych dostępnych w Internecie i nie znaleziono prac na ten temat. Polska została wybrana, jako baza do porównań z niżej wymienionych powodów:

- Do porównań poszukiwano kraju, który jest dobrym wzorcem dla oceny atrakcyjności inwestycyjnej. Skoncentrowano się na Europie, ze względu na to, iż tutaj nastąpiło przejście z gospodarki centralnie planowanej do rynkowej, podobnie jak w niektórych krajach arabskich, które przeszły transformację z systemów scentralizowanych do rynkowych, jak na przykład Irak. Od czasów transformacji z systemu komunistycznego ponad 20 lat temu, Polska stała się najbardziej atrakcyjnym dla inwestycji zagranicznych państwem Europy Środkowej. Istnieją pewne wskazówki dotyczące napływu kapitału w niektórych krajach arabskich podobnie jak to miało miejsce w przypadku Polski w okresie komunizmu. Polska charakteryzuje się największą gospodarką w Europie Środkowej i była jedynym krajem środkowoeuropejskim, który odnotował wzrost gospodarczy, podczas gdy w innych krajach w okresie kryzysu finansowego w 2008 i 2009 roku nastąpił spadek. Polska posiada jedną z najmocniejszych giełd papierów wartościowych podczas, gdy rynki finansowe niektórych krajów arabskich charakteryzują się słabymi lub niefunkcjonującymi giełdami. Zatem Polska jest dobrym wzorcem dla krajów dążących do rozwoju rynków finansowych. Polska jest największym źródłem zasobów naturalnych w Europie, a niektóre kraje arabskie (jak Arabia Saudyjska, Irak, Katar) posiadają ogromny potencjał zasobów naturalnych, takich jak ropa naftowa i gaz oraz inne surowce mineralne (patrz Rozdział 3). Obecnie Polska może znajdować się na rozdrożu historii, w efekcie stając się jednym z wiodących krajów europejskich i wzorem dla gospodarek krajów arabskich;

- W pewnych kwestiach kraje arabskie są porównywalne z Polską. Społeczeństwo Polski jest społeczeństwem w dużej części religijnym podobnie jak w krajach arabskich. Przyjęcie do porównania innych krajów rozwijających się - jak Chiny, Indie itp. - mogłoby być błędne, ze względu na znaczną różnicę w rozmiarze ich gospodarki oraz liczby ludności w stosunku do poszczególnych krajów arabskich. Polska posiada również swoją własną, samodzielną walutę, podobnie jak w przypadku krajów arabskich.

Zamiarem było wybranie do analizy maksymalnie długiego okresu i taki wybór byłby najlepszy. Ale w przypadku krajów arabskich trudno wybrać jakiś stabilny okres. Wiele krajów arabskich jest niestabilnych ze względu na wojny, sankcje międzynarodowe, niepokoje polityczne i kryzys ekonomiczny. Dlatego w przeprowadzonej analizie skoncentrowano się na okresie 2005-2010. Przesłanki wyboru tego okresu analizy były następujące:

- W latach poprzedzających 2005 rok w regionie występował długi okres braku stabilizacji. Spowodowane to było wojną w Iraku i nałożeniem na Irak sankcji gospodarczych. Region arabski cierpiał z powodu sytuacji polityczno-ekonomicznej. Przed rokiem 2005 napływ ZIB, liczonych jako odsetek łącznych światowych ZIB był znikomy i nie przekraczał 3,4%. W 2005 roku ten odsetek wzrósł do 4,8% i osiągnął wartość maksymalną 7% w 2009 roku;

- Od początku 2011 roku, ze względu na tak zwaną Wiosnę Arabską albo rewolucje arabskie świat arabski doświadczał braku stabilizacji polityczno-ekonomicznej, która trwa aż do dzisiaj. Okres, który nastąpił po wydarzeniach Wiosny Arabskiej charakteryzuje się niewystarczającą ilością lub brakiem wiarygodnych danych pochodzących z wielu krajów arabskich.

Metody

Istnieje wiele czynników mających wpływ na przyciąganie ZIB. W niniejszej pracy zdecydowano się na analizę czynników, które można podzielić na trzy grupy: czynniki ekonomiczne, społeczne i polityczne. Poprzez wykorzystanie trzech grup otrzymano jasny obraz czynników wpływających na przyciągnięcie inwestycji. Zgodnie z literaturą przedmiotu, do której odwołano się szczegółowo w tabeli 1-9, do przeprowadzenia badania wybrano 16 możliwych czynników i 13 krajów arabskich.

Te dane posłużyły jako dane wejściowe do syntetycznej miary wektorowej w dwojaki sposób. W pierwszej metodzie, zwanej metodą miary wektorowej, wykorzystano wszystkie dane równocześnie, czyli 16 parametrów wejściowych. W drugiej metodzie, zwanej złożoną miarą wektorową, wykorzystano dane zgromadzone w trzech grupach: czynniki ekonomiczne, społeczne i polityczne. Aby ułatwić porównanie, po kolokacji każdej grupy pozostały tylko trzy parametry wejściowe. Te porównania ułatwiają wyciąganie właściwych wniosków odnośnie sposobów poprawy atrakcyjności inwestycyjnej kraju. Jakość indeksu została zmierzona za pomocą zależności pomiędzy faktycznym napływem ZIB i zaproponowanym indeksem atrakcyjności ZIB.

Ponieważ celem pracy jest także przeprowadzenie analizy dynamicznej (przyjęto rok 2005 jako punktu odniesienia dla pozostałych lat), zastosowano syntetyczną miarę wektorową. Nie ma możliwości przeprowadzenia podobnej analizy dynamicznej stosując inne metody. Dane wejściowe zostały pozyskane z różnych źródeł, takich jak Bank Światowy, Konferencja

Narodów Zjednoczonych do spraw Handlu i Rozwoju, Arabski Fundusz Walutowy, Arabskie Banki Centralne, Arabski Program Finansowania Handlu, Liga Arabska, Arabska Organizacja do spraw Rozwoju Przemysłu i Górnictwa, Związek Banków Arabskich, Rada Arabskiej Jedności Gospodarczej.

Wnioski i kierunki przyszłych badań

Omawiając tło problemu badawczego, przedstawiając cele pracy i dane wykorzystane w badaniu założono metodykę badań i wykorzystano metody oceny atrakcyjności inwestycyjnej oparte na zastosowaniu syntetycznej miary wektorowej. Mimo braku pełnych danych dotyczących krajów arabskich (jedna z głównych przeszkód napotkanych podczas badań), hipoteza główna, mówiąca, że czynniki polityczne mają duży wpływ na atrakcyjność inwestycyjną krajów arabskich została zweryfikowana negatywnie (za wyjątkiem roku 2007). Wyniki (patrz załącznik nr 36) pokazują, że determinanta ekonomiczna jest najważniejszą spośród innych kluczowych determinant atrakcyjności inwestycyjnej krajów arabskich.

Na podstawie otrzymanych wyników i propozycji, które zostały wymienione w podrozdziale 4.3 można stwierdzić, że główny cel pracy i cele pomocnicze zostały osiągnięte. Główny cel, który polegał na ocenie atrakcyjności inwestycyjnej krajów arabskich i porównanie wyników z Polską jako punktem odniesienia został osiągnięty. Cele szczegółowe polegające na analizie czynników wpływających na atrakcyjność inwestycyjną przez zdefiniowanie miary atrakcyjności inwestycyjnej dla krajów arabskich oraz wskazanie zmian, które mogą poprawić atrakcyjność inwestycyjną krajów arabskich, zostały osiągnięte i szczegółowo omówione (patrz podrozdział 4.4). Otrzymane wyniki pokazują, że istnieje dodatnia korelacja między miarami wektorowymi i napływem ZIB. Analizy pokazują, że korelacja napływu ZIB w latach 2005-2010 z wyliczonym w pracy indeksem ZIB wynosi 0,62 (patrz załącznik 34). Dla porównania korelacja indeksu będącego przedmiotem badań Groh'a wyniosła 0,54, a korelacja Światowego Indeksu Konkurencyjności z napływem ZIB wynosi tylko 0,31. We wszystkich porównywanych wynikach można zauważyć, że zaproponowany w pracy indeks charakteryzuje się lepszą korelacją. Ponadto badanie ma na celu zwiększenie atrakcyjności inwestycyjnej krajów arabskich (patrz podrozdział 4.4). Dla każdego kraju arabskiego zaproponowano zatem szereg rekomendacji wynikających z otrzymanych w pracy rezultatów badania.

W niniejszej pracy, na podstawie analizy danych wyjściowych ze złożonej miary syntetycznej, można sformułować dodatkowe stwierdzenia:

1. W niektórych krajach arabskich nie ma możliwości znacznego wzrostu czynników społecznych. Te kraje arabskie mają ograniczone możliwości zwiększenia czynników społecznych, ze względu na ograniczoną liczbę ludności i wielkość gospodarki. To zjawisko można zauważyć analizując dane pochodzące z takich krajów arabskich jak Bahrajn, Jordania, Kuwejt, Oman, Liban, Tunezja oraz Zjednoczone Emiraty Arabskie;

2. Przeprowadzone badania pokazują, że biorąc pod uwagę okres 2005-2010 niektóre kraje arabskie znajdowały się, w wybranych wymiarach analizy, w lepszym położeniu niż Polska, ale tylko w latach 2005 i 2009. Można to przypisać względnej stabilizacji, która nastąpiła po wojnie w Iraku w 2003 roku oraz brakowi stabilności, który towarzyszył kryzysowi gospodarczemu w 2008 roku. Jeżeli wiadomo, że okres badawczy obejmuje lata 2005-2010, można wydedukować, że stabilizacja polityczno-gospodarcza ma istotny wpływ na proces przyciągania kapitału zagranicznego. W wybranych latach część zmiennych w niektórych krajach arabskich charakteryzowały się lepszymi poziomami niż w Polsce. Jednakże, z wyżej wymienionych powodów lata 2005 i 2007 były także najlepsze pod względem atrakcyjności inwestycyjnej dla większości krajów arabskich;

3. Niektóre kraje arabskie charakteryzują się wyższą niż Polska atrakcyjnością inwestycyjną. Poza tym, wyniki pokazują, że dotyczy to tylko niektórych krajów i konkretnych lat. Na przykład Egipt charakteryzuje się wyższą od Polski atrakcyjnością w roku 2005. Również Katar pokazuje wyższą atrakcyjność niż Polska ale tylko w 2009 roku;

4. Na podstawie wyników, że ważnymi parametrami ekonomicznymi wpływającymi na atrakcyjność inwestycyjną były wzrost PKB (roczna wartość procentowa), wzrost PKB na mieszkańca (roczna wartość procentowa), płatności podatków (liczba tytułów podatkowych) oraz deflator inflacja/PKB;

5. W przypadku czynników społecznych, wyniki pokazują, że najważniejszym parametrem dla okresu pięcioletniego i wyników uśrednionych była wielkość wyprodukowanej energii elektrycznej. W 2005 r. istotna była liczba uczniów szkół średnich;

6. Wśród czynników politycznych, wyniki pokazują, że najważniejszym czynnikiem w każdym roku i średnio w ciągu całego okresu pięcioletniego była transparentność. Stabilizacja polityczna była najważniejszym czynnikiem w 2010 roku;

7. Pod względem kluczowych determinant dwa kraje arabskie charakteryzują się wyższym poziomem niż Polska. Pierwszy był Kuwejt w roku 2005, a drugi był Katar w roku 2009;

8. W zakresie kluczowej determinanty społecznej Egipt charakteryzował się wyższym poziomem niż Polska w całym okresie badawczym;

9. W odniesieniu do kluczowej determinanty politycznej wyższy od Polski poziom miały Zjednoczone Emiraty Arabskie w roku 2005 i 2006. Katar charakteryzował się wyższym niż Polska poziomem w latach 2007-2010;

10. Irak doświadczał przez wiele dziesięcioleci wojen, które doprowadziły do zniszczenia infrastruktury. Irak był również dotknięty blokadą gospodarczą trwającą od roku 1990 do 2003. W związku z tym dane wejściowe nie odzwierciedlają rzeczywistości społeczno-gospodarczej. Wynika to z tego, że nie wszystkie dane są dostępne dla pewnych okresów i dlatego są trudne do oceny i skorelowania z napływem ZIB.

Kierunki przyszłych badań. Należy zauważyć, że podjęto próbę uwzględnienia większej liczby krajów, ale nie można było pozyskać danych, z których można byłoby skorzystać. W przyszłych badaniach proponuje się uzupełnienie zbioru o kraje środkowego Wschodu (takie jak Turcja, Iran oraz inne kraje arabskie, których nie można było ująć w niniejszych badaniach). O ile będzie to możliwe, można rozszerzyć okres badawczy do okresu po roku 2010 lub przed 2005, aby otrzymać dane i porównać stabilną i niestabilną sytuację w krajach arabskich pod względem atrakcyjności inwestycyjnej. Należy zauważyć, że region arabski jest dotknięty brakiem stabilności politycznej i gospodarczej od początku Arabskiej Wiosny, czyli od końca 2010 roku. Ponadto proponuje się, aby w przyszłych badaniach do porównań włączyć inne kraje, takie jak Korea Południowa, Indie, Rosja i Brazylia. W przyszłych badaniach można zastosować również inne metody analizy. Wszystkie te i inne koncepcje mogą być dla polityków wskazówką do poznania ważnych czynników mających wpływ na atrakcyjność inwestycji zagranicznych.

LIST of FIGURES

LIST of TABLES

BIBLIOGRAPHY

A.T.Kearney Leading Global Management. (2014). *The A.T. Kearney Foreign Direct Investment Confidence Index Ready for Takeoff.* New York: A.T.Kearney Leading Global Management.

Abaza, H., Saab, N., & Zeitoon, B. (2011). *Report of the Arab Forum for Environment and Development (AFED).* Beirut: The Arab Forum for Environment and Development (AFED).

AfDB Group's Governance Strategic Framework. (2012, January). Morocco, Country Strategy Paper 2012-2016. *Working Paper.* Rabat, Morocco: The African Development Bank Portfolio in Morocco.

African Development Bank Group. (2012). Tunisia 2012. In A. D. Bank, *African Economic Outlook* (pp. 2-14). Paris: OECD Publishing.

Ahmed, H. F. (2010). *2010 Morocco Citrus Semi-annual.* Washington, D.C.: United States Department of Agriculture Foreign Agricultural Service.

Akrami, F. (2008). Foreign Direct Investment in Developing Countries: Impact on Distribution and Employment A Historical, Theoretical, and Empirical Study. *Thesis Doctor.* Switzerland: University of Fribourg.

Alasrag, H. (2005, December 01). Foreign Direct Investment Development Policies in the Arab Countries. *Working Paper No. 83.* Kuwait, Kuwait: The Industrial Bank of Kuwait.

Alavinasab, S. M. (2013). Determinants of Foreign Direct Investment in Iran. *International Journal of Academic Research in Business and Social Sciences* , 258-269.

Alfaro, L., & Charlton, A. (2007, October). Intra-Industry Foreign Direct Investment. *CEP Discussion Paper No. 825.* London, U.K: London School of Economics and Political Science.

Alfra', Ṭ. B. (2003). *The Arab World, its Components and its Problems.* Riyadh: Naif Arab University for Security Sciences.

Ali, A. A. (2001, August). Internal Sustainability and Economic Growth in the Arab States . *Working Paper.* Kuwait, Kuwait: UNESCO Encyclopedia of Life Support Systems (EOLSS).

Almokhtar, R. (2010). Strategy Competitive uUpgrade and Improve the Tunisian Industrial Sector for the Period 2007-2016. *Fourth International Forum on: Competition and Strategies of Industrial Enterprises Outside the Hydrocarbon Sector in the Arab Countries* (pp. 1-22). Chlef: The Faculty of Economic Sciences and Management Sciences at the University of Hassiba Ben Bu Ali Chlef-Algeria.

Alonso-Gamo, P., & Marston, D. (2010). *ALGERIA Staff Report for the 2010 Article IV Consultation.* Washington, D.C.: International Monetary Fund.

Alrawashdeh, R. (2013). The Competitiveness of Jordan Phosphate Mines Company (JPMC) Using Porter Five Forces Analysis. *International Journal of Economics and Finance*, 191-200.

Alʿtby, Ġ. B. (2010). *League of Arab States, the Resolution of the Arab Disputes.* Riyadh: Naif Arab University for Security Sciences.

Alzahrani, O. H., Badahdah, Y. S., Bamakrid, M. S., Alfayez, A. S., Alsaeedi, M. S., Mansouri, A. M., et al. (2013). The Diabetic Foot Research in Arabs' Countries. *Open Journal of Endocrine and Metabolic Diseases*, 157-165.

Alzhrany, S. B. (2004). Foreign Direct Investment and its Role in Economic Growth in Saudi Arabia. *Master's thesis.* Riyadh, Saudi Arabia: King Saud University.

Anand, A. (2006). Foreign Direct Investment India VIS-À-VIS China. *Delhi Business Review*, 43-58.

Arab Investment and Export Credit Guarantee Corporation. (2012-2013). *Investment Climate in Arab Countries.* Kuwait: Arab Investment and Export Credit Guarantee Corporation.

Arab Labor Organization. (2012). *Third Arab Report on Employment and Unemployment in Arab Countries.* Cairo: Arab Labor Organization.

Arab Labor Organization. (2014). *Arab Labor Organization.* Retrieved December 14, 2014, from Arab Labor Organization Population Statistical: http://www.alolabor.org/final/index.php?option=com_content&view=category&layout=blog&id=132&Itemid=85&lang=ar

Arab Monetary Fund. (2006). *Joint Arab Economic Report.* Abu Dhabi: Arab Monetary Fund.

Arab Monetary Fund. (2010). *Joint Arab Economic Report.* Abu Dhabi: Arab Monetary Fund.

Arab Monetary Fund. (2011). *Joint Arab Economic Report.* Abu Dhabi: Arab Monetary Fund.

Arab Monetary Fund. (2012). *Joint Arab Economic Report.* Abu Dhabi: Arab Monetary Fund.

Arab Monetary Fund. (2013). *Joint Arab Economic Report.* Abu Dhabi: Arab Monetary Fund.

Arab Organizations and Unions Administration - Economic Affairs. (2013, January). Arab Organizations. *Guide.* Cairo, Egypt: The Arab League.

Arslan, N., & Tathdil, H. (2012). Defining and Measuring Competitiveness: A Comparative Analysis of Turkey With 11 Potential Rivals. *International Journal of Basic & Applied Sciences*, 31-34.

Asiedu, E. (2002). On the Determinants of Foreign Direct Investment to Developing Countries: Is Africa Different? *World Development Journal*, 107-119.

Bahrain Economic Development Board. (2010). *Regional Pioneer Global Player-Annual Report 2010.* Manama: Bahrain Economic Development Board.

Bahrain Economic Development Board. (2013). *Kingdom of Bahrain Economic Yearbook.* Manama: Bahrain Economic Development Board.

Baig, M. B., & Al-Zaharani, K. H. (2012). Agricultural Extension in the Kingdom of Saudi Arabia: Difficult Present and Demanding Future. *Journal of Animal & Plant Sciences,* 239-246.

Bajo-Rubio, O., & Muñoz, M. M. (2000, November). Foreign Direct Investment and Trade: A Causality Analysis. *Working Paper.* Pamplona, Spain: Universidad Pública de Navarra.

Ballotta, M. (2004, 01). Factors, Actions and Policies to Determine the Investment Attractiveness of a Territorial System. *Working Paper.* Washington,D.C., U.S.A: The World Bank.

Bank Information Center. (2013, March). The World Bank Group and Tunisia A Country Study. *Study Paper.* Washington, D.C., U.S.A: Bank Information Center.

Bank Of Algeria. (n.d.). *Banque d'Algérie: Bank Of Algeria.* Retrieved June 11, 2014, from Banque d'Algérie: http://www.bank-of-algeria.dz/

Banque du Liban. (n.d.). *Banque du Liban.* Retrieved May 25, 2014, from Banque du Liban: http://www.bdl.gov.lb/

Barclay, L. A. (2002). *Foreign Direct Investment in Emerging Economies: Corporate Strategy and Investment behaviour in the Caribbean.* New York: Taylor & Francis Group.

Bayliss Associates Pty Limited. (n.d.). *CAAR - Department of Foreign Affairs and Trade.* Retrieved January 29, 2015, from http://www.dfat.gov.au/publications/caar_publications/business-guide-oman.pdf

ʿbd Alğfar, Ḥ. (2002). *The Foreign Direct Investment & International Tread Chains Example.* Baghdad: Byt Alḥkma.

ʿbd Almqṣwd, N. (2008). *Economic Effects of Foreign Investment.* Alexandria: Dar Alfkr Alğamʿy.

Beach, W. W., & Kane, T. (2008). *2008 Index of Economic Freedom Methodology: Measuring the 10 Economic Freedoms.* Washington, D.C.: The Heritage Foundation and Dow Jones & Company, Inc.

Bekhet, H. A., & Al-Smadi, R. W. (2015). Determinants of Jordanian Foreign Direct Investment Inflows: Bounds Testing Approach. *Economic Modelling,* 27-35.

Bergendahl, G. (1984). The Management of OPEC's Financial Surpluses. *Discussion Paper.* Oxford, U.K: Oxford Institute for Energy Studies.

Beyond, G. (2012). *Emst & Yong's 2012 attractiveness survey Middle East* . Qatar.

Blomström, M., & Kokko, A. (2002, August). FDI and Human Capital: A Research Agenda. *Working Paper No.195.* Paris, France: OECD Development Center.

Blyth, C. (2013). *American Business Cycles 1945–50.* London: British Library.

Bodie, Z., Kane, A., & Marcu, A. J. (2008). *Investment.* New York: McGraw- Hill Companies.

Bost, F. (2011, November). West African Challenges - Are Economic Free Zone Good for Development? *Working Paper No.4.* Paris, France: Sahel and West Africa Club Secretariat (SWAC/OECD).

Bova, F. (1995). American Direct Investment in the Italian Manufacturing Sector, 1900-1940. *Business and Economic History*, 218-230.

Brink, B. t. (2006, September). Indicators as Communication Tools: An Evolution Towards Composite Indicators. *Working Paper WPR2-2006-D3b.* Tilburg, Netherlands: ECNC – European Centre for Nature Conservation.

Brouthers, K. D., Brouthers, L. E., & Werner, S. (1996). Dunning's Eclectic Theory and the Smaller Firm: the Impact of Ownership and Locational Advantages on the Choice of Entry-modes in the Computer Software Industry. *International Business Review*, 377-394.

Burger, M., Ianchovichina, E., & Rijkers, B. (2013, December 01). Risky Business Political Instability and Greenfield Foreign Direct Investment in the Arab World. *Working Paper No. 6716.* Cairo, Egypt: The World Bank - The Middle East and North Africa Region.

Business Monitor International. (2010). *Algeria Oil & Gas Report Q4 2010.* London: Business Monitor International.

Callen, T. (2008). What Is Gross Domestic Product? *Finance & Development*, 48-49.

Carson, C. S. (2003, October 28). Foreign Direct Investment Trends and Statistics: A Summary. *Working Paper.* Washington, D.C., U.S.A: International Monetary Fund.

Castaings, W., Stefano, T., & Ari, L. (2008). The 2007 European e-Business Readiness Index. *OECD Statistics Working Paper JT00188147.* Directorate General Joint Research Centre and Directorate General for Enterprise and Industry.

Cederlöf, H., & Ålander, E. (2013). Does Corruption Matter for FDI Inflows? Experiences from Indonesia. . *Bachelors Thesis.* Stockholm, Sweden: Stockholm School of Economics.

Central Bank of Bahrain. (2010). *Economic Report.* Manama: Central Bank of Bahrain.

Central Bank of Bahrain. (n.d.). *Central Bank of Bahrain.* Retrieved July 25, 2014, from Central Bank of Bahrain: http://www.cbb.gov.bh/

Central Bank of Egypt. (n.d.). *Central Bank Of Egypt - Default.* Retrieved May 15, 2014, from Central Bank of Egypt: http://www.cbe.org.eg/English/

Central Bank of Kuwait. (n.d.). *Welcome to the Central Bank of Kuwait.* Retrieved July 28, 2014, from Central Bank of Kuwait: www.cbk.gov.kw/WWW/index.html

Central Bank of Oman. (2011). *Annual Report.* Muscat: Central Bank of Oman.

Central Department of Statistics and Information. (n.d.). *Central Department of Statistics and Information.* Retrieved July 29, 2014, from Central Department Of Statistics and Information: http://www.cdsi.gov.sa/english/

Central Intelligence Agency. (2014). *Egypt Background - CIA.* Retrieved December 16, 2014, from The World Factbook: https://www.cia.gov/library/publications/the-world-factbook/geos/print/country/countrypdf_eg.pdf

Central Intelligence Agency. (n.d.). *The World Factbook - CIA.* Retrieved May 26, 2014, from The World Factbook - CIA- Library: https://www.cia.gov/library/publications/the-world-factbook/

Central Statistical Organization. (n.d.). *Home.* Retrieved July 20, 2014, from Central Statistical Organization: http://www.cosit.gov.iq/en/

Çeviis, I., & Çamurdan, B. (2007). The Economic Determinants of Foreign Direct Investment in Developing Countries and Transition Economies. *The Pakistan Development Review*, 285-299.

Chaaban, Jad. (2010). Job Creation in the Arab Economies: Navigating Through Difficult Waters. *Research Paper Series.* New York, U.S.A: United Nations Development Programme.

Chang, H.-J. (2004). Regulation of Foreign Investment in Historical Perspective. *The European Journal of Development Research*, 687-715.

Checchi, D., De Simone, G., & Faini, R. (2007, May). Skilled Migration, FDI and Human Capital Investmen. *Discussion Paper No. 2795.* Bonn, Germany: Institute for the Study of Labor.

Chemingui, M. A., & Sánchez, M. V. (2011, October). Assessing Development Strategies to Achieve the MDGs in The Republic of Tunisia. *Country Study.* New York , U.S.A: United Nations Department for Social and Economic Affairs.

Chen, H., Chong, T. T., & She, Y. (2014, March 22). A Principal Component Approach to Measuring Investor Sentiment in China. *MPRA Paper No. 54150.* Munich, Germany: Munich Personal RePEc Archive.

Cheng, L. K., & Kwan, Y. k. (2000). What are the Determinants of the Location of Foreign Direct Investment? The Chinese Experience. *Journal of International Economics*, 380-400.

Claessens, S., & Kose, M. A. (2013). Financial Crises: Explanations, Types, and Implications. *Working Paper No. WP/13/28*. Washington, D.C., U.S.A: International Monetary Fund.

Collier, P., & Gunning, J. W. (1999). Explaining African Economic Performance. *Journal of Economic Literature*, 64-111.

Composite Indicators Research Group. (n.d.). *Composite Indicators Research Group (COIN)*. Retrieved June 21, 2012, from COIN: https://composite-indicators.jrc.ec.europa.eu

Contessi, S., & Pace, P. D. (2011, October). The (Non-)Resiliency of Foreign Direct Investment in the United States during the 2007-2009 Financial Crisis. *Working Paper No.2011-037B*. Louis, U.S.A: Federal Reserve Bank of St. Louis.

Cushman, D. O. (1988). Exchange-rate uncertainty and foreign direct investment in the United States. *Review of World Economics*, 322-336.

Dalsgaard, M. T. (2013, May). An Assessment of FDI Attractiveness A comparative study of emerging economies . *Bachelor Thesis*. Aarhus , Denmark: Aarhus University.

David, H. L. (2007, July 31). A Guide to Measures of Trade Openness and Policy. *Working Paper*. Indiana, U.S.A: Indiana University South Bend.

Denisia, V. (2010). Foreign Direct Investment Theories: An Overview of the Main FDI Theories. *European Journal of Interdisciplinary Studies*, 53-59.

Department of Economic and Social Affairs. (1973). *Multinational Corporations in World Development*. New York: United Nations.

Dodge, Y (2008). The concise encyclopedia of statistics, Springer Science & Business Media.

Dragon, S. (n.d.). *Snake Dragon Pomiędzy bodźcem a reakcją jest wolność wyboru*. Retrieved February 05, 2015, from https://snakedragon.wordpress.com/

Dubai Press Club. (2010). *Arab Media Outlook 2009-2013*. Dubai: Dubai Press Club.

Duce, M. (2004). Definitions of Foreign Direct Investment (FDI): A Methodological Note. *Foreign Direct Investment in the Financial Sector of Emerging Market Economies - Central Bank Papers Submitted by Working Group Members* (pp. 1-16). Basel: CGFS Publications .

Dunia Frontier Consultants. (2009). *Private Foreign Investment in Iraq*. Washington.

Dunning, J. H. (2001). The Eclectic (OLI) Paradigm of International Production: Past, Present and Future. *International Journal of the Economics of Business*, 173-190.

Economic and Social Commission for Western Asia. (n.d.). *Economic and Social Commission for Western Asia*. Retrieved July 22, 2014, from ESCWA Statistics Division (SD): http://www.escwa.un.org/divisions/main.asp?division=sd

Economic Research Department. (2013, October). Arab economy among the challenges of the new phase and obstacles rooted What are the pillars of the reform and prospects to 2015? *Working Paper*. Beirut, Lebanon: General Union of Chambers of Commerce, Industry and Agriculture for Arab Countries.

Economic Statistics and National Accounts Department. (2012). *Qatar Economic Statistics at a Glance*. Doha: Qatar Statistics Authority.

EIM Business & Policy Research. (2009). *EU SMEs and subcontracting*. Zoetermeer: EIM Business & Policy Research.

Eiras, A. I. (2003). *Ethics, Corruption, and Economic Freedom*. Washington, DC: Heritage Foundation.

Elaine Denny, Donnelly, K., McKay, R., Ponte, G., & Uetake, T. (2008, April). Sustainable Water Strategies for Jordan. *Working Paper*. Ann Arbor, Michigan, U.S.A: Gerald R. Ford School of Public Policy - University of Michigan.

Elbadawi, I. A. (2004, July). Reviving Growth in the Arab World. *Working Paper*. Washington, U.S.A: Forthcoming in Economic development and Cultural Change.

El-Erian, M. (2012). Iraq's National Investment Commissions. *Working Paper*. Washington, U.S.A.

El-Gindy, A.-G. .. (2011, June). *Ministry of Agriculture and Land Reclamation- Egypt*. Retrieved December 17, 2014, from Ministry of Agriculture and Land Reclamation- Egypt: www.iesc.org/.../egyptforward/.../Ag_El-GindyDr.Abdel-GhanyMohame..

El-Juhany, L. I. (2010). Degradation of Date Palm Trees and Date Production in Arab Countries: Causes and Potential Rehabilitation. *Australian Journal of Basic and Applied Sciences*, 3998-4010.

El-Seretty, S. M., & Shabbara, M. H. (2014). Inter-Arab Investments and Necessary Trends of the Senior Arab Investors in the Light of the Current Global Economic Situation. *World Applied Sciences Journal*, 1278-1287.

Energy Information Administration. (2011, March 23). *Iraq Energy Data, Statistics and Analysi*. Retrieved August 31, 2014, from http://www.iaccidatabase.com/PDF_files/Iraq%20Oil%20Data5965/Iraq%20Energy%20Data.pdf

Ernst & Young Global Limited. (2014). *EY's attractiveness survey Europe 2014 Back in the game*. Ernst & Young Global Limited.

European Commission - Directorate-General for Research and Innovation. (2011). *EuroMed-2030 Long term challenges for the Mediterranean area Report of an Expert Group*. Luxembourg: Publications Office of the European Union.

European Gas Advocacy Forum. (2011). *The Future Role of Natural Gas*. London: Xyntéo.

Fattouh, B., & El-Katiri, L. (2012). Energy and Arab Economic Development. *Research Paper Series*. Oxford, U.K: United Nations Development Programme.

Fayad, G., Raissi, M., Rasmussen, T., & Westelius, N. (2012). *Saudi Arabia: Selected Issues IMF Country Report No. 12/272.* Washington, D.C.: International Monetary Fund.

Federal Research Division. (2008, May). *Country Profile: Algeria.* Retrieved January 28, 2015, from Library of Congress – Federal Research Division: http://lcweb2.loc.gov/frd/cs/profiles/Algeria.pdf

Feldstein, M. S. (1995). The Effects of Outbound Foreign Direct Investment on the Domestic Capital Stock. *The Effects of Taxation on Multinational Corporations* (p. 46). Chicago: University of Chicago Press.

Foa, R., & Tanner, E. C. (2012). Methodology of the Indices of Social Development. *Working Paper*. Washington, D.C., U.S.A: The World Bank.

Foreign Investment Office of Dubai. (2012). Why Dubai? *Working Study*. Dubai, UAE: Dubai Department of Economic.

Franklin R, R. (1990). *International Trade & Investment Theory, Policy, Enterprise.* Ohio: Thomson South-Western .

Freudenberg, M. (2003, November 12). Composite Indicators of Country Performance A Critical Assessment. *OECD Science, Technology and Industry Working Papers*. Paris, France: OECD Publishing.

Fugazza, M., & Trentinin, C. (2014). Empirical Insights on Market Access and Foreign Direct Investment. *Study Series No.63*. Geneva, Switzerland : United Nations Publication.

Fulton, C., & Richard, N. (2011, December). *Mauritius Investment Promotion and Protection Agreements.* Retrieved December 12, 2014, from Conyers Dill & Pearman: http://www.conyersdill.com/publication-files/270_11_11_23_Mauritius_Investment_Promotion_and_Protection_Agreements.pdf

Gareib, B. (2012). Motivational Factors to Attract Foreign Direct Investment And Ways of its Evaluation: A Case Study of Algeria. *Al- Bahith Journal*, 99-110.

Gendrano, J. (2007). League of Arab States Greater Arab Free Trade Agreement. *Working Paper*. New Jersey, U.S.A: Institute for Domestic & International Affairs, Inc. (IDIA).

General of Agriculture& Livestock Research. (2011). *Agriculture & Livestock Research - Five-Year Research Strategy 2011-2015.* Muscat: Ministry of Agriculture (MoA).

Glese, A. S., Kahley, W., & Riefier, R. (1990). Foreign Direct Investment: Motivating Factors and Economic Impact. *Journal of Regional Analysis And Policy*, 105-127.

Görgen, M., Rudloff, B., Simons, J., Üllenberg, A., Väth, S., & Wimmer, L. (2009, December). Foreign Direct Investment (FDI) in Land in Developing Countries. *Working Paper.* Eschborn, Germany: Deutsche Gesellschaft für Technische Zusammenarbeit.

Groh, A. P., & Wich, M. (2009, November). A Composite Measure to Determine a Host Country's Attractivenss for Foreign Direct Investment. *Working Paper No.WP-833.* Barcelona, Spain: IESE Business School-University of Navarra.

Gwartney, J., Lawson, R., & Hall, J. (2013). *Economic Freedom of the World: 2013 Annual Report.* Toronto: The Fraser Institute.

Haas, R. D., & Horen, N. V. (2012, January). International shock transmission after the Lehman Brothers collapse – evidence from syndicated lending. *American Economic Review,* 231-237.

Hailu, Z. A. (2010). Demand Side Factors Affecting the Inflow of Foreign Direct Investment to African Countries: Does Capital Market Matter? *International Journal of Business and Management,* 104-116.

Hallward Driemeier, M. (2003, June). Do Bilateral Investments Treaties Attract FDI? Only a Bit... and They Could Bite. *Working Paper No.3121.* Washington.D.C, U.S.A: World Bank.

Haque, I. u. (1995). Technology and Competitiveness. In T. W. Bank, *Trade, Technology, and International Competitiveness.* New York: The World Bank.

Hardy, A., & Magnello, M. E. (2002). Statistical methods in epidemiology: Karl Pearson, Ronald Ross, Major Greenwood and Austin Bradford Hill, 1900–1945. *Sozial-und Präventivmedizin,* 80-89.

Hartmann, M., Khalil, S., Bernet, T., Ruhland, F., & Al Ghamdi, A. (2012). Organic Agriculture in Saudi Arabia. *Sector Study.* Riyadh, Saudi Arabia: Internationale Zusammenarbeit (Giz) GmbH- Office Riyadh.

Harvey, C. E., & Jon , P. P. (1990). International competition and industrial change: essays in the history of mining and metallurgy, 1800-1950. *Businesss History ,* 1-161.

Hasan, F. (2012). *Oman Economy.* Oman: Global Research Economy .

Hasen, B.-T., & Gianluigi, G. (2007). The Determinants of Foreign Direct Investment A Panel Data Study on AMU Countries. *Working Paper.* U.K: Liverpool Business School.

Hassan, K. (2003). FDI, Information Technology, and Economic Growth in The MENA Region. *Working Paper No.10th ERF.* New Orleans, U.S.A: University of New Orleans.

Hellwig, Z. (1968). Zastosowanie metody taksonomicznej do typologicznego podziału krajów ze względu na poziom ich rozwoju oraz zasoby i strukturę wykwalifikowanych kadr. *Przegląd statystyczny 4, 307-326.*

Heshmati, A., & Davis, R. (2007, December). The Determinants of Foreign Direct Investment Flows to the Federal Region of Kurdistan. *Working Paper No.32*. Bonn, Germany: Institute for the Study of Labor.

Hickman, B. G. (1992). *International Productivity and Competitiveness.* Oxford: Oxford University Press.

Hill, C. .. (1997). *International Business.* New York: McGraw– Hill.

Hollyer, J. R., Rosendorff, B. P., & Vreeland, J. R. (2011, March 11). Democracy and Transparency. *Working Paper*. New York, U.S.A: New York University.

House, C. (2013). *Global Food Insecurity and Implications for Saudi Arabia.* London: Chatham House.

Hristova, K. D. (2012, May). Does Economic Freedom Determine Economic Growth? *Thesis Bachelor of Arts with Honors A Discussion of the Heritage Foundation's Index of Economic Freedom.* South Hadley, Massachusetts, U.S.A: Mount Holyoke College.

Ḥšad, N. (2008). *Recent Trends in Global Investment and Arabi. General Union of Chambers of Commerce, Industry, and Agriculture for Arab Countries.* Beirut.

Ḥsawna, Q. M. (2010). *The Investments in Free Zone.* Amman: Dar Alfkr.

Humanicki, M., Kelm, R., & Olszewski, K. (2013). Foreign Direct Investment and Foreign Portfolio Investment in the Contemporary Globalized World: Should they be Still Treated Separately? *Working Paper No.167.* Warszawa, Poland: Narodowy Bank Polski.

Ibrahim, I., & Harrigan, F. (2012). Qatar's Economy: Past, Present and Future. *Qatar Foundation Academic Journal*, 1-24.

Independent Statistics & Analysis. (2014, July 24). Country Analysis Brief: Algeria. *Working Paper*. Washington, D.C., U.S.A: U.S. Energy Information Administration.

Inter-Agency Information and Analysis Unit. (2011, October). *Oil and Gas Factsheet.* Retrieved July 31, 2014, from IAU: http://iq.one.un.org/documents/327/Oil%20Factsheet%20-%20English.pdf

International Monetary Fund. (n.d.). *IMF eLibrary Data Home Page.* Retrieved December 16, 2014, from IMF eLibrary Data: http://elibrary-data.imf.org/DataReport.aspx?c=1449311&d=33060&e=161886

Iran Group on Exonyms. (2006, March 28). Historical, Geographical and Legal Validity of the Name : PERSIAN GULF. *Working Paper No. 61.* Vienna, Austria: United Nations.

Iraq, C. B. (2015). Statistics. Baghdad, Iraq.

Italian Multinational Oil and Gas Company. (2010). *World Oil and Gas Review.* Rome: Marchesi Grafiche Editoriali SpA.

Jahanshahloo, G. R., F, H. L., & Izadikhah, M. (2006). Extension of the TOPSIS method for decision-making problems with fuzzy data. *Applied Mathematics and Computation*, 1544-1551.

Japan the Institute of Energy Economics. (2011). *IRAQ. Country Report.* Tokyo: The Institute of Energy Economics, Japan.

Jaradat, H. (2010, October 31). Jordan's Economy Crisis, Challenges & Measures. *Working Paper*, 1-19. Dubai, UAE: 3rd Annual Meeting of Middle East and North African Senior Budget Officials (MENA-SBO) .

Jelili, R. B. (2013). Dhaman FDI Attractiveness Index What The Regional Results Reveal . *Opportunities and Challenges for FDI Attraction in MENA* (pp. 1-13). Muscat: The Arab Investment and Export Credit Guarantee Corporation.

Jickling, M. (2008, November 24). *Containing Financial Crisis.* Washington, D.C.: Congressional Research Service.

Johnson, A. (2005). Host Country Effects of Foreign Direct Investment , The Case of Developing and Transition Economies. *JIBS Dissertation Series No. 031.* Sweeden: Jönköping International Business School.

JRC Science Hub-European Commission. (2008). Handbook on Constructing Composite Indicators. *Methodology and User Guide.* Paris, France: OECD Publications.

Kabir, G., & Hasin, A. A. (2011). Comparative Analysis of AHP and Fuzzy AHP Models for Multicriteria Inventory Classification. *International Journal of Fuzzy Logic Systems (IJFLS)*, 1-16.

Kamal, P. (n.d.). *Education and Science.* Retrieved February 03, 2015, from hubpages: http://preetkamal.hubpages.com/hub/pks

Kamga Wafo, G. L. (1998). Political Risk and Foreign Direct Investment. *Licentiate thesis.* Konstanz, Germany: University of Konstanz.

Karimi, P., Molden, D., Notenbaert, A., & Peden, D. (2012). Nile Basin farming systems and productivity. In S. B. Awulachew, V. Smakhtin , D. Molden , & D. Peden, *The Nile River Basin Water, Agriculture, Governance and Livelihoods* (pp. 133-153). New York: Routledge .

Karunatilleka, E. (1999). The Asian Economic Crisis. *Research Paper No.99/14.* U.K: House of Commons Library.

Kasparian, R. (2011). *Economic Accounts of Lebanon 2010.* Beirut: Presidency of the Council of Ministers of Lebanon.

Kaufmann, D., & Kraay, A. (2007, November 28). Worldwide Governance Indicators vs. 'Afro-Pessimism': Lessons from an empirical perspective on governance in Africa countries.

Presentation at the Center for Global Development Seminar. Washington, D.C., U.S.A: The World Bank.

Kaufmann, D., & Vishwanath, T. (1999, September 06). Towards Transparency in Finance and Governance. *Working Paper*. Washington, D.C., U.S.A: The World Bank.

Kaufmann, D., Kraay, A., & Mastruzzi, M. (2010, September). The Worldwide Governance Indicators Methodology and Analytical Issues. *Working Paper No.5430*. USA: The World Bank.

Kawash, A. (2010). *Determinants of Foreign Direct Investment the Case of Jordan*. Saarbrücken: Lambert Academic Publishing.

Kehal, H. (2004). *Foreign Investment in Developing Countries*. New York: Palgrave Macmillan Ltd.

Khasawneh, M. Q. (2010). *Investment in Free Zones*. Amman : Dar Al Fkar.

Kindleberger, C. P. (2006). *A Financial History of Western Europe (Economic History)*. New York: Oxford University Press.

Kokkinou, A., & Psycharis, I. (2004, September). Foreign Direct Investment, Region Incentives and Regional Attractiveness in Greece. *Discussion Paper Series No.10*. Volos, Greece: University of Thessaly.

Krugman, P. (1998). What's new about the new Economic Geography? *Oxford Review of Economic policy*, 7-17.

Kuwait Investment Authority. (n.d.). *Kuwait Investment Authority*. Retrieved May 21, 2014, from Kuwait Investment Authority: http://www.swfinstitute.org/fund/kuwait.php

L.S.Walsh. (1983). *International Marketing*. London: MacDonald and Evans.

Lachgar, M. L. (2011). A Quick Look on the Steel Industry in the Arab World. *The Seventieth Session of the Steel Industry Committee in the Organization for Economic Cooperation and Development (OECD)* (pp. 1-11). Paris: Arab Iron and Steel Union.

Lambsdorff, J. G. (2007). *The Institutional Economics of Corruption and Reform*. Cambridge : Cambridge University Press.

Layachi, A. (2013, November 01). The Changing Geopolitics of Natural Gas: The Case of Algeria . *Working Paper*. Houston, U.S.A: Rice University's Baker Institute Center for Energy Studies.

Lim, E.-G. (2001, November 01). Determinants Of, And the Relation Between, Foreign Direct Investment and Growth: ASummary of the Recent Literature. *IMF Working Paper WP/01/175*. Washington,D.C., U.S.A: International Monetary Fund.

Limam, I. (1998, January). A Socio- Economic Taxonomy of Arab Countries. *Working Paper.* Kuwait, Kuwait: Arab Planning Institute.

Lintunen, J. (2011). Motives and Location Factors of Chinese Outward Foreign Direct Investments in a Small Develop Economy. *Master Thesis.* Finland: Aalto University School of Economics.

Lipsey, R. E. (2001). Foreign Direct Investment and the Operations of Multinational Firms: Concepts, History, and Data. *Working Paper No. 8665.* New York, U.S.A: National Bureau of Economic Research.

Lipsey, R. E., Feenstra, R. C., Hahn, C. H., & Hatsopoulos, G. N. (1999). The Role of Foreign Direct Investment in International Capital. In M. Feldstein, *International Capital Flows* (pp. 307-362). Chicago: University of Chicago Press.

Lipsey, Robert E. (1993). Foreign Direct Investment in the United States: Changes over Three Decades. In Kenneth A. Froot, *Foreign Direct Investment* (pp. 113 - 172). Chicago: University of Chicago Press.

LLP, L. &. (2011). *Doing Business in the United Arab Emirates Report.* New York: Latham & Watkins LLP.

Lucani, P., & Saade, M. (2012). *Iraq, Agriculture Sector Note.* Rome: FAO/World Bank.

Macharis , C., Springael , J., Brucker , K. D., & Verbeke , A. (2004). PROMETHEE and AHP: The design of operational synergies in multicriteria analysis. Strengthening PROMETHEE with ideas of AHP. *European Journal of Operational Research ,* 307-317.

Malik, M. (2008, November 3-4). Recent Developments in the Definition of Investment in International Investment Agreements. *Working Paper to Second Annual Forum of Developing Country Investment Negotiators.* Marrakech, Morocco: International Institute for Sustainable Development.

Mann, H. (2008, February). *Agreements, Business and Human Rights: Key Issues and Opportunities.* Winnipeg: International Institute for Sustainable Development.

Manuel, T., Arruda, C., Guriev , S., Azour, J., Labelle, H., en Bai, C., et al. (2013). *Independent Panel Review of the Doing Business Report.* Washington, D.C.: The World Bank.

Mardia, J., T, K., & Bibby, J. M. (1979). *Multivariate Analysis.* London: Academic Press.

Maurseth, P. B. (2009, February 16). Governance Indicators: A guided Tour. *NUPI Working Paper No.754.* Oslo, Norway: Norwegian Institute of International Afairs.

Maystadt, J.-F., Trinh Tan, J. F., & Breisinger, C. (2012, July). Does Food Security Matter for Transition in Arab Countries? *IFPRI Discussion Paper No.01196.* Washington, D.C., U.S.A: The International Food Policy Research Institute.

McKibbin, W. J., & Stoeckel, A. (2009, November). The Global Financial Crisis: Causes and Consequences. *Working Paper*. Australia: The Lowy Institute for International Policy.

Michalos, A. C., Andrew, S., & Nazeem , M. (n.d.). *An approach to the canadian index of wellbeing*. Retrieved February 14, 2015, from http://creativecity.ca/cecc/downloads/indicators-2006/Michalos-Sharpe-Muhajarine-Approach-CdnIndex-Wellbeing.pdf

Michela, N., Giovannini, E., Hoffman, A., Tarantola, S., Saltelli, A., & Saisana, M. (2005, August 09). Handbook on constructing composite indicators. *OECD Statistics Working Paper*. OECD.

Miller, T., Kim, A. B., & Holmes, K. R. (2014). *2014 Index of Economic Freedom Promoting Economic Opportunity and Prosperity.* Washington, D.C.: The Heritage Foundation and Dow Jones & Company, Inc.

Ming, L. (2010). Study on Management of Construction Joint Venture. *Management and Service Science (MASS), 2010 International Conference on* (pp. 1-4). Wuhan: Institute of Electrical and Electronics Engineers.

Ministry Of Agriculture And Fisheries . (2012). *Oman Salinity Strategy.* Muscat: Ministry Of Agriculture And Fisheries.

Mirkin, B. (2010). Population Levels, Trends and Policies in the Arab Region:Challenges and Opportunities. *Research Paper Series*. New York, U.S.A: United Nations Development Programme.

Mishkin, F. S. (2010, December). Over The Cliff: From the Subprime to the Global Financial Crisis. *NBER Working Paper No.16609*. Cambridge, U.K: National Bureau of Economic Research.

Mishra, S. K. (2007, June 1). *A comparative study of various inclusive indices and the index constructed by the principal components analysis.* Retrieved February 14, 2015, from SSRN: http://papers.ssrn.com/sol3/papers.cfm?abstract_id=990831

Mitchell, R. B. (1998). Sources of Transparency: Information Systems in International Regimes. *International Studies Quarterly* , 109-130.

Mndwr,. (2010). *Determinants of Foreign Direct Investment in The Light of the Current International Economic.* Alexandria: Dar Alt ͺ lym Alğam ͺ y.

Mobbs, P. M. (2012). *2010 Minerals Yearbook.* New York: U.S. Geological Survey.

Mohammed, F. A., Hazem A, A., & Ayman M, M. (2013). Integrated Fuzzy (GMM) -TOPSIS Model for Best Design Concept and Material Selection Process. *International Journal of Innovative Research in Science Engineering and Technology*, 6464-6486.

Moore, D., Galli, A., & Wackernagel, M. (2012). *Arab Atlas of Footprint and Biocapacity.* Oakland: Global Footprint Network.

Moreira, S. B. (2009). The Determinants of Foreign Direct Investment,What is the Evidence for Africa? *W Journal Universidade Federal De Santa Catarina*, 83-104.

Mottaleb, K. A., & Kalirajan, K. (2010). Determinants of Foreign Direct Investment in Developing Countries: A Comparative Analysis. *ASARC Working Paper No.2010/13* . Canberra, Australia: The Australia South Asia Research Centre.

Mottu, E., & Nakhle, N. (2010, July). Lebanon: Real GDP Growth Analysis. *Presentation*. Beirut, Lebanon: IMF Resident Representative Office in Lebanon.

Moukahal, W. (2011). The Banking Industry in the UAE. *A Middle East Point of View*, 16-19.

Msaadawi, J. (2008). Conduct of Foreign Direct Investment, with a Reference to the Cases of Some Arab Countries Risk. *Economic Research and Administrative*, 161-195.

National Competitiveness Center. (2010). *Annual Report of FDI Into Saudi Arabia.* Riyadh: Saudi Arabian General Investment Authority (SAGIA).

Naudé, W. (2009). The Financial Crisis of 2008 and the Developing Countries. *Discussion Paper No.2009/01*. Helsinki, Finland: United Nations University.

Nermend, K. (2006). A synthetic measure of sea environment pollution. *Polish Journal of Environmental Studies*, 127-129.

Nermend, K. (2007). Taxonomic Vector Measure of Region Development . *Polish Journal of Environmental Studies*, 195-198.

Nermend, K. (2009). *Vector Calculus in Regional Development Analysis: Comparative Regional Analysis Using the Example of Poland.* Berlin: A Springer Company.

Newman, H. R. (2012). The Mineral Industries of Morocco and Western Sahara. In U. G. Survey, *2010 Minerals Yearbook* (pp. 30.1-30.9). New York: U.S. Geological Survey.

Nielsen, L. (2011, February). Classifications of Countries Based on Their Level of Development: How it is Done and How it Could be Done. *Working Paper No.WP/11/31*. New York, U.S.A: International Monetary Fund.

Nizielska, A. (2012). The Criteria, Instruments, and Determinants of Investment Attractiveness of Silesia-Experts' Opinions. Journal of Economics & Management, 53-70.

Notta, O., Vlachvei, A., & Samathrakis, V. (2010). Competitiveness–The Case of Greek Food Manufacturing Firms. *International Journal of Arts and Sciences*, 211-225.

Nyarko, Y. (2010, February). The United Arab Emirates Some Lessons in Economic Development. *Working Paper No.2010/11*. Helsinki, Finland: United Nations University -World Institute for Development Economics Research.

OAPEC. (n.d.). *Welcome to OAPEC.* Retrieved September 30, 2014, from Organization of Arab Petroleum Exporting Countries: http://oapec.mawaqaademo.com/Home/DataBank

OECD. (2001). Measuring Productivity. *OECD Manual*. Paris, France: ORGANISATION FOR ECONOMIC CO-OPERATION AND DEVELOPMENT.

OECD. (n.d.). *Glossary of Statistica Terms*. Retrieved December 06, 2014, from Gross domestic product (GDP) deflator - OECD.Stat: http://stats.oecd.org/glossary/detail.asp?ID=4342

OECD. (n.d.). *Member countries - OECD*. Retrieved December 28, 2014, from OECD: http://www.oecd.org/about/membersandpartners/list-oecd-member-countries.htm

OPEC. (2011). *Annual Statistical Bulletin.* Vienna: Organization of the Petroleum Exporting Countries.

OpenOil. (n.d.). *Iraq Oil Almanac v 0.9*. Retrieved May 12, 2014, from OpenOil: http://wiki.openoil.net/index.php?title=Iraq

OpenOil. (n.d.). *OpenOil*. Retrieved May 16, 2014, from Iraq Oil Almanac v 0.9: http://wiki.openoil.net/index.php?title=Iraq

Organisation for Economic Co-operation and Development. (1996, April 19). *Definition of Taxes (Note by the Chairman) - OECD.* Retrieved January 23, 2015, from http://www1.oecd.org/daf/mai/pdf/eg2/eg2963e.pdf

Organization for Economic Co-operation and Development. (2008, March 17). Definition of Investor and Investment in International Investment Agreements. In OECD, *International Investment Law: Understanding Concepts and Tracking Innovations* (pp. 7-100). Paris, France: OECD Publishing.

Özalp, O. N. (2011). Where is the Middle East? The Definition and Classification Problem of the Middle East as a Regional Subsystem in International Relations . *Turkish Journal of Politics*, 5-21.

Panizza, U. (2008, March). Domestic and External Public Debt in Developing Countries. *Working Paper No.188*. Geneva, Switzerland: UNCTAD.

Patterson, B., & Lygnerud, K. (1999, December). The Determination of Interest Rates. *Working Paper No.116*. Luxembourg , Luxembourg : European Parliament.

Pilarska, C., & Wałęga, G. (2014). Determinants of FDI Inflows to Poland, Czech Republic, and Hungary in Context of Integration into European Union. *The 8th International Days of Statistics and Economics*, 1167-1177.

Pinfari, M. (2009, March). Nothing but Failure? The Arab League and the Gulf Cooperation Council as Mediators in Middle Eastern Conflicts. *Working Paper No.45*. London, U.K: Destin Development Studies Institute.

Piteli, E. E. (2009). Foreign Direct Investment in Developed Economies: A Comparison between European and non – European Countries. *Working Paper No.44*. Cambridge, U.K: University of Cambridge.

Planning and Decision Support Department. (2012). *Annual Economic Report*. Abu Dhabi: Ministry of Economy.

Porter, M. E. (2005). Building the Microeconomic Foundations of Prosperity: Findings from the World. In W. E. Forum, *The Global Competitiveness Report 2005-2006*. (pp. 29-56). Basingstoke: World Economic Forum.

Protsenko, A. (2003, February 11). Vertical and Horizontal Foreign Direct Investments in Transition Countries. *PhD Thesis*. M¨unchen, Germany: an der Ludwig-Maximilians-Universit¨at.

Puschmann, P., & Matthijs, K. (2012). The Janus Face of the Demographic Transition in the Arab World. *Working Paper No.WOG/HD/2012-4*. Leuven, Belgium: Centrum voor Sociologisch Onderzoek (CeSO).

Qasm, Ḥ. (1987). *The Politics of International Economic Relations*. Amman: Center Jordan Book.

Qatar Investment Fund. (2011). *Qatar Investment Fund plc*. Isle of Man: Qatar Investment Fund.

Qatar Statistics Authority. (2009). *Foreign Investment Survey in Qatar 2009*. Doha: Qatar Statistics Authority.

Quibria, M. G. (2014, March). Governance and Developing Asia: Concepts, Measurements, Determinants, and Paradoxes. *ADB Economics Working Paper Series No.388*. Manila, Philippine: Asian Development Bank.

R.Weeks, J., Getis, A., Hill, A. G., Gadalla, M. S., & Rashed, T. (2004, March). The Fertility Transition in Egypt: Intraurban Patterns in Cairo. *Association of American Geographers*, pp. 74-93.

Robinson, R. D. (1967). *International Management*. New York: Holt, Rinehart and Winston.

Robinson, S., & Gehlhar, C. (1995, January). Land, Water, and Agriculture in Egypt: The Economywide Impact of Policy Reform. *Discussion Paper No.1*. Washington, D.C., U.S.A: International Food Policy Research Institute.

Rodriguez, C. A. (2000, February 14). On the Degree of Openness of an Open Economy. *Working Paper*. Buenos Aires, Argentina: Universidad del CEMA.

Root, F. R. (1998). *Entry Strategies for International Markets*. New Jersey: Jossey Bass Wiley.

Rugman, A. M., & Verbeke, A. (2007). Internalization Theory and its Impact on the Field of International Business. In J. J. Boddewyn, *International Business Scholarship: AIB Fellows on the First 50 years and Beyond* (pp. 155-174). West Yorkshire: Emerald Group Publishing Limited.

S.C.Deshmukh. (2013). Preference Ranking Organization Method Of Enrichment Evaluation (Promethee). *International Journal of Engineering Science Invention*, 28-34.

Safi, A. E.-A. (2012, April). Foreign Direct Investment in the Arab world: an Analysis of Flows and an Evaluation of Country Specific Business Environment. *Master's Thesis*. Trento, Italy: University of Trento.

Şahin, S., & Şener, Ö. (2006). *Assessment of Foreign Direct Investment Attractiveness: an AHP Approach.* Retrieved February 11, 2015, from Assessment of Foreign Direct Investment Attractiveness:: http://www.issm.cnr.it/convegni/IW/abstract/Sahin%20Sener.pdf

Said, M. A., & Shelaby, A. A.-A. (2014). Potentials of Egypt Agricultural Bilateral Trade With the Arab Countries: Gravity Model Evidence. *International Journal of Food and Agricultural Economics*, 133-144.

Salacuse, J. W. (2013). *The Three Laws of International Investment: National, Contractual, and International Frameworks for Foreign Capital.* Oxford: Oxford University Press.

Saltelli, A., Nardo, M., Saisana, M., & Tarantola, S. (2005). Composite Indicators - The Controversy and the Way Forward. In OECD, *Statistics, Knowledge and Policy Key Indicators to Inform Decision Making: Key Indicators to Inform Decision Making* (pp. 359-372). Palermor: OECD.

Saltelli, Andrea; Annoni, Paola ; Tarantola, Stefano. (2008). Innovation and Innovation and Competitiveness Indicators. *Handbook on Constructing Composite Indicators: Methodology and User Guide.* OECD-JRC European Commission- Joint Research Centre.

Saudi British Bank. (2010). *Doing business in Saudi Arabia.* Riyadh: PricewaterhouseCoopers International Limited.

Schnittker, J., & Ahmed, T. (2012). *Iraq Grain and Feed Annual.* Washington, D.C.: United States Department of Agriculture Foreign Agricultural Service.

Sekkat, K., & Ange, M. (2004, September). Trade, and Foreign Exchange Liberalization Investment Climate and FDI in the MENA Countries. *Working Paper Series No.39.* U.S.A: The World Bank.

Singh, D., & Rahim, L. (2012). United Arab Emirates. In S. Robinson, *The Mergers & Acquisitions Review* (pp. 664-674). Dubai: Law Business Research Ltd.

Škuflić, L., Rkman, P., & Šokčević, S. (2013). Evaluation of the FDI Attractiveness of the European. Countries using PROMETHEE Method. *Croatian Operational Research Review*, 258-269.

Smith, B. (2011, November 15). The Arab uprisings. *Research Paper No.11/73.* London, U.K: House of Commons Library.

Soumia, Z., & Abderrezzak, B. (2013). The Determinants of Foreign Direct Investment and Their Impact on Growth: Panel Data Analysis for AMU Countries. *International Journal of Innovation and Applied Studies*, 300-313.

Speakman, J. (2003, October). Joint Iraqi Needs Assessment, The Investments Climate. *Working paper*. U.S.A: World Bank.

Šryf, M. (2003). Performance in International Construction Joint Ventures: Modeling Perspective. *Journal of Construction Engineering and Management*, 619-626.

Sulstarova, A. (n.d.). *FDI performance and potential rankings*. Retrieved March 03, 2015, from FDI performance and potential rankings - OECD: http://www.oecd.org/investment/globalforum/44246319.pdf

Sundaram, J. K., Schwank, O., & Arnim, R. v. (2011, February). Globalization and development in sub-Saharan Africa. *DESA Working Paper No.102*. New York, U.S.A: United Nations Department of Economic and Social Affairs.

Taib, M. (2011). The Mineral Industry of Qatar. In U. G. Survey, *USGS Minerals Yearbook 2009* (pp. 53.1-53.6). New York: U.S. Geological Survey.

Taib, M. (2012a). The Mineral Industry of Egypt. In U. G. Survey, *USGS Minerals Yearbook 2010* (pp. 13.1-13.12). New York: U.S. Geological Survey.

Taib, M. (2012b). The Mineral Industry of Qatar. In U. G. Survey, *USGS Minerals Yearbook 2010* (pp. 53.1-53.7). New York: U.S. Geological Survey.

Taib, M. (2012c, August). The Mineral Industry of the United Arab Emirates. In S. U. Geological, *2010 Minerals Yearbook* (pp. 57.1-57.9). New York: U.S. Geological Survey.

Tata, J. C., & Marston, D. (2010). *United Arab Emirates: 2009 Article IV Consultation—Staff Report; Public Information*. Washington, D.C.: International Monetary Fund.

Taylor, A. M., & Wilson, J. L. (2011). International trade and finance: Complementaries in the United Kingdom 1870–1913 and the United States 1920–1930. *Journal of International Money and Finance*, 268-288.

Taylor, M. P., & Sarno, L. (1997). Capital Flows to Developing Countries: Long- and Short-Term Determinants. *The World Bank Economic Review*, 451-470.

Technology Integration Division. (2012). *Oman in Perspective An Orientation Guide*. California: Defense Language Institute Foreign Language Center.

The Arab Fund for Economic and Social Development. (2010). An Overview of Agricultural Development and Food Security in Arab Countries. *Joint Technical Meeting* (pp. 1-64). Vienna: The Arab Coordination Group Institutions.

The Arab Investment and Export Credit Guarantee Corporation. (2005). *Investment Climate in Arab Countries*. Kuwait: The Arab Investment and Export Credit Guarantee Corporation.

The Arab Investment and Export Credit Guarantee Corporation. (2006). *Investment Climate in Arab Countries*. Kuwait: The Arab Investment and Export Credit Guarantee Corporation.

The Arab Investment and Export Credit Guarantee Corporation. (2007). *Investment Climate in Arab Countries*. Kuwait: The Arab Investment and Export Credit Guarantee Corporation.

The Arab Investment and Export Credit Guarantee Corporation. (2008). *Investment Climate in Arab Countries*. Kuwait: The Arab Investment and Export Credit Guarantee Corporation.

The Arab Investment and Export Credit Guarantee Corporation. (2009). *Investment Climate in Arab Countries*. Kuwait: The Arab Investment and Export Credit Guarantee Corporation.

The Arab Investment and Export Credit Guarantee Corporation. (2010). *Investment Climate in Arab Countries*. Kuwait: The Arab Investment and Export Credit Guarantee Corporation.

The Arab Investment and Export Credit Guarantee Corporation. (2011). *Investment Climate in Arab Countries*. Kuwait: The Arab Investment and Export Credit Guarantee Corporation.

The Arab Investment & Export Credit Guarantee Corporation. (2013, January-March). *DHAMAN Investment Attractivness Index. Quarterly Bulletin*. Riyadh, Kingdom of Saudi Arabia: The Arab Investment and Export Credit Guarantee Corporation.

The Internet Center for Corruption Research. (n.d.). *The Internet Center for Corruption Research*. Retrieved February 05, 2015, from Internet Center for Corruption Research: http://www.icgg.org/corruption.cpi_2004_faq.html

The World Bank. (1979). Development in Primary Producing Countries. In T. W. Bank, *World Development Report* (pp. 99-109). New York: Oxford University Press.

The World Bank. (1997). *Private Capital Flows to Developing Countries: The Road to Financial*. Oxford: Oxford University Press.

The World Bank. (2006). *Doing Business in 2006 Greating Jobs*. Washington, D.C.: A Copublication of the World Bank and the International Finance Corporation.

The World Bank. (2007). *Doing Business*. Washington, D.C.: A Copublication of the World Bank and the International Finance Corporation.

The World Bank. (2008). *Doing Business 2009*. Washington, D.C.: A Copublication of the World Bank, the International Finance Corporation, and Palgrave Macmillan.

The World Bank. (2009). *Doing Business 2010 Reforming Through Difficult Times*. Washington, D.C.: A Copublication of the World Bank, and Palgrave Macmillan.

The World Bank. (2010). *Doing Business 2011 Making a Difference for Entrepreneurs*. Washington, D.C.: A Copublication of The World Bank and the International Finance Corporation.

The World Bank. (2011, July 01). *Gross national income per capita 2010, Atlas method and PPP*. Retrieved December 31, 2014, from Gross national income per capita 2010, Atlas method and: http://siteresources.worldbank.org/DATASTATISTICS/Resources/GNIPC.pdf

The World Bank Group. (n.d.). *Worldwide Governance Indicators*. Retrieved July 18, 2013, from Worldwide Governance Indicators: http://info.worldbank.org/governance/wgi/index.aspx#reports

The World Bank. (n.d.). *The World Bank: Data*. Retrieved June 12, 2012, from Data: www.data.worldbank.org/country

The World Economic Forum. (2007-2008). *World Economic Forum*. Geneva: The World Economic Forum.

The World Economic Forum. (2010). *Global Enabling Trade Report*. Paris: World Economic Forum.

The World Economic Forum. (2011). *The Arab World Competitiveness Report 2011-2012*. Geneva: The World Economic Forum and the Organisation for Economic Co-operation and Development (OECD).

The World Economic Forum. (2012). *Global Enabling Trade Report*. Geneva: World Economic Forum.

The World Economic Forum. (n.d.). *World Economic Forum*. Retrieved March 18, 2015, from The Global Competitiveness Report | World Econom: http://www.weforum.org/reports

Thomas, M. (2010). What Do the Worldwide Governance Indicators Measure? *European Journal of Development Research*, 31-54.

Thompson, T., & Shah, A. (2005, March). Transparency International's Corruption Perceptions Index: Whose Perceptions Are They Anyway? *Discussion Paper*. Washington, D.C., U.S.A: The World Bank.

Toone, J. E. (2011). Foreign Direct Investment in Iraq: Reassessing the Legal Framework. *Digital Commons Network*, 4-18.

Transparency International. (n.d.). *Transparency International - Country Profiles*. Retrieved May 15, 2013, from Transparency International: www.transparency.org/country

Transparency International UK's Defence and Security Programme. (n.d.). *Methodology-Government Defence Anti-Corruption*. Retrieved January 03, 2015, from Transparency International Defence & Security Programme Government Defence Anti-corruption Index–Methodology (Long): http://government.defenceindex.org/sites/default/files/documents/GI-methodology-long.pdf

Trends, R. (n.d.). *Recent Trends in The Globalization of Business - Institute*. Retrieved January 25, 2015, from http://www.piie.com/publications/chapters_preview/54/2iie1117.pdf

Twomey, M. J. (1998, June). Patterns of Foreign Investment in the Third World in the Twentieth Century. *Working Paper*. Dearborn, Michigan, U.S.A: University of Michigan .

U.S. Energy Information Administration. (n.d.). *U.S. Energy Information Administration (EIA)*. Retrieved June 15, 2014, from U.S. Energy Information Administration: http://www.eia.gov/

UNCTAD. (1991). *World Investment Report.* Geneva: UNCTAD.

UNCTAD. (1994). *World Investment Report.* NewYork and Geneva: UNCTAD.

UNCTAD. (1995). *World Investment Report.* New York and Geneva: UNCTAD.

UNCTAD. (1998). *World Investment Report.* New York and Geneva: United Nations.

UNCTAD. (2001). *World Investment Report.* New York and Geneva: United Nations.

UNCTAD. (2002). *World Investment Report.* New York and Geneva: United Nations.

UNCTAD. (2003). *World Investment Report.* New York and Geneva: United Nations.

UNCTAD. (2004a). State Contracts. *UNCTAD Series on Issues in International Investment Agreements*. Geneva, Switzerland: United Nations.

UNCTAD. (2004b). *World Investment Report.* New York and Geneva: United Nations.

UNCTAD. (2005a). *World Investment Report.* New York and Geneva: United Nations.

UNCTAD. (2005b). *Investment Compass User's Guide.* New York: United Nations.

UNCTAD. (2006). *World Investment Report.* New York and Geneva: United Nations.

UNCTAD. (2007). *World Investment Report.* New York and Geneva: United Nations.

UNCTAD. (2008a, October). Identifying Core Elements in Investment Agreements in the APEC Region. *Working Paper.* Geneva, Switzerland: United Nations.

UNCTAD. (2008b). *World Investment Report.* New York and Geneva: UNCTAD.

UNCTAD. (2009a). The Role of International Investment Agreements in Attracting Foreign Direct Investment to Developing Countries. *United Nations Conference on Trade and Development* (pp. 1-145). Geneva: United Nations.

UNCTAD. (2009b). *World Investment Report.* New York and Geneva: United Nations.

UNCTAD. (2011a). Scope and Definition. *UNCTAD Series on Issues in International Investment Agreements II*. Geneva, Switzerland: United Nations.

UNCTAD. (2011b). *World Investment Report.* New York and Geneva: UNCTAD.

UNCTAD. (2012). *World Investment Report.* New York and Geneva: UNCTAD.

UNCTAD. (2015). *UNCTAD.* Retrieved May 02, 2015, from unctad.org | Home: http://unctad.org/en/Pages/Home.aspx

UNCTAD. (n.d.). *unctad.org | Statistics.* Retrieved December 13, 2014, from UNCTADSTAT: http://unctadstat.unctad.org/wds/ReportFolders/reportFolders.aspx

UNCTAD,b. (n.d.). *United Nations Conference on Trade and Development/ unctad.* Retrieved December 29, 2014, from unctad.org | Global FDI Flows Continue to Fall: http://unctad.org/en/pages/PressReleaseArchive.aspx?ReferenceDocId=4022

United Nations Centre on Transnational Corporations. (1992). *World Investment Report.* NewYork: United Nations.

United Nations Development Assistance Framework. (2010). *Annex III: UNDAF Outcomes, Indicators, and Outputs.* Belgrade: United Nations Development Assistance Framework (UNDAF),.

United Nations Development Programme. (1994). *Human Development Report.* New York: Oxford University Press.

United Nations Development Programme. (1997). *Human Development Report.* New York: Oxford University Press.

United Nations Development Programme. (2011). *Arab Development Challenges.* Cairo: United Nations Development Programme.

United Nations Population Division. (n.d.). *POPIN >> Data.* Retrieved May 22, 2014, from United Nations Population Information Network: http://www.un.org/en/development/desa/population/

United States Commercial Service. (2012). *Doing Business in Iraq:2012 Country Commercial Guide for U.S. Companies.* Washington, D.C.: U.S.& Foreign Commercial Service and U.S. Department of State.

Verner, D., & Breisinger, C. (2013). Economics of Climate Change in the Arab World Case Studies from the Syrian Arab Republic, Tunisia, and the Republic of Yemen. *World Bank Study.* Washington, D.C., U.S.A: International Bank for Reconstruction and Development / The World Bank.

Wall Street Journal. (n.d.). *Index of Economic Freedom - Heritage Foundation.* Retrieved June 20, 2012, from Index of Economic Freedom: www.heritage.org/index/

Walsborn, R. (2008). *Date Sector Repor and Value Chain Development Program.* California: Agland Investment Services, Inc.

Walter, A. (2000, January). British Investment Treaties in South Asia: Current Status and Future Trends. *Report Prepared for the International Development Center of Japan.* London, U.K: London School of Economics.

Wenke, L., & Jingfeng, Z. (2005, May). New Approach to Evaluate the Location Factors Affecting, FDI's Operations: A case of the NETD. *Master Dissertation.* Sweden: Kristianstad University.

Wheeler, D., & Mody, A. (1992). International Investment Location Decisions : The Case of U.S. Firms. *Journal of International Economics*, 57-76.

Winder, G. M. (2006). Webs of Enterprise 1850-1914: Applying a Broad Definition of FDI. *Annals of the Association of American Geographers*, 788-806.

Yackee, J. W. (2010). Do Bilateral Investment Treaties Promote Foreign Direct Investment? Some Hints from Alternative Evidence. *Virginia Journal of International Law*, 397-442.

Yan, Y. (2008). *Foreign Direct Investment and China's International Competitiveness.* Warsaw: Warsaw School of Economics.

Yannaca-Small, C. (2008). Definition of Investor and Investment in International Investment Agreements. *Survey*. OECD.

Young, E. (2011). *Doing Business in Iraq.* Baghdad: Ernst & Young Global Limited.

Zhu, B. (2008, June). Internationalization of Chinese MNEs and Dunning's Eclectic (OLI) Paradigm: A Case of Huawei Technologies Corporation's Internationalization Strategy. *Master Thesis*. Lund, Sweden: Lund University.

APPENDICES

Appendix 1.Input data Algeria

Series Name	Key drivers	Stimulant	Destimulant	Algeria 2005	2006	2007	2008	2009	2010
GDP growth (annual %)	E	x		5.9	1.7	3.4	2	1.6	3.6
GDP per capita (constant 2005 US$)	E	x		3038.7	3041.5	3092	3098.4	3091.1	3143.6
GDP per capita growth (annual %)	E	x		4.3	0.1	1.7	0.2	-0.2	1.7
Trade (% of GDP)	E	x		71.3	70.7	71.9	76.7	71.3	69.9
Tax payments (number)	E	x		41	41	29	29	29	29
Inflation, GDP deflator (annual %)	E		x	16.1	10.5	6.4	15.8	-11.2	16.1
Imports of goods and services (% of GDP)	E		x	24.1	21.9	24.9	28.7	36	31.4
Urban population (% of total)	E	x		66.7	67.8	68.8	69.9	71	72
Labour force, total	E	x		10362188	10603014	10860485	11081894	11341979	11641894
Secondary education, general pupils	S	x		3291971	3315701	3417684	3542924	4139007	4227264
Electricity production (kWh)	S	x		33915000000	35226000000	37196000000	40236000000	38501000000	45734000000
Political Stability(-2.5 to 2.5)	P	x		-0.93	-1.12	-1.13	-1.09	-1.22	-1.26
Rule of Law (-2.5 to 2.5)	P	x		-0.7	-0.64	-0.71	-0.71	-0.76	-0.75
Transparency	P	x		2.8	3.1	3	3.2	2.8	2.9
Time to export(days)	P		x	15	15	17	17	17	17
Time to import(days)	P		x	22	22	23	23	23	23
FDI US$ Million				1081	1795	1662	2594	2761	2291
FDI / WORLD %				0.109	0.12	0.08	0.14	0.23	0.16
GDP current US $				1.03E+11	1.17E+11	1.35E+11	1.71E+11	1.37E+11	1.61E+11
Population (Thousands of pupils)				33267.89	33749.33	34261.97	34811.06	35401.79	36036.16

E: Economic factor, S: Social factor, P: Political factor.

Source: World Data Bank. Joint Arab Economic Reports, UNCTAD, Transparency International Organization, Economic and Social Commission for Western Asia,

227

Appendix 2.Input data Bahrain

<table>
<thead>
<tr><th rowspan="2">Series Name</th><th rowspan="2">Key drivers</th><th rowspan="2">Stimulant</th><th rowspan="2">Destimulant</th><th colspan="6">Bahrain</th></tr>
<tr><th>2005</th><th>2006</th><th>2007</th><th>2008</th><th>2009</th><th>2010</th></tr>
</thead>
<tbody>
<tr><td>GDP growth (annual %)</td><td>E</td><td>x</td><td></td><td>6.8</td><td>6.5</td><td>8.3</td><td>6.2</td><td>2.5</td><td>4.3</td></tr>
<tr><td>GDP per capita (constant 2005 US$)</td><td>E</td><td>x</td><td></td><td>18156.4</td><td>17878.8</td><td>17835</td><td>17526.5</td><td>16833.9</td><td>16722.2</td></tr>
<tr><td>GDP per capita growth (annual %)</td><td>E</td><td>x</td><td></td><td>-0.4</td><td>-1.5</td><td>-0.2</td><td>-1.7</td><td>-4</td><td>-0.7</td></tr>
<tr><td>Trade (% of GDP)</td><td>E</td><td>x</td><td></td><td>148.3</td><td>147.1</td><td>137.8</td><td>145.9</td><td>118</td><td>120.5</td></tr>
<tr><td>Tax payments (number)</td><td>E</td><td>x</td><td></td><td>13</td><td>13</td><td>13</td><td>13</td><td>13</td><td>13</td></tr>
<tr><td>Inflation, GDP deflator (annual %)</td><td>E</td><td></td><td>x</td><td>13.7</td><td>8.8</td><td>8.4</td><td>11.4</td><td>-13</td><td>7.4</td></tr>
<tr><td>Imports of goods and services (% of GDP)</td><td>E</td><td></td><td>x</td><td>64.4</td><td>62.5</td><td>58.1</td><td>63.3</td><td>49.5</td><td>50.9</td></tr>
<tr><td>Urban population (% of total)</td><td>E</td><td>x</td><td></td><td>88.4</td><td>88.5</td><td>88.5</td><td>88.5</td><td>88.6</td><td>88.6</td></tr>
<tr><td>Labour force, total</td><td>E</td><td>x</td><td></td><td>424303</td><td>477508</td><td>540749</td><td>605930</td><td>664212</td><td>707016</td></tr>
<tr><td>Secondary education, general pupils</td><td>S</td><td>x</td><td></td><td>55907</td><td>58567</td><td>75889</td><td>65849</td><td>69974</td><td>73548</td></tr>
<tr><td>Electricity production (kWh)</td><td>S</td><td>x</td><td></td><td>8867000000</td><td>9745000000</td><td>10908000000</td><td>11933000000</td><td>12056000000</td><td>13230000000</td></tr>
<tr><td>Political Stability(-2.5 to 2.5)</td><td>P</td><td>x</td><td></td><td>-0.02</td><td>-0.39</td><td>-0.24</td><td>-0.24</td><td>-0.16</td><td>-0.51</td></tr>
<tr><td>Rule of Law (-2.5 to 2.5)</td><td>P</td><td>x</td><td></td><td>0.65</td><td>0.42</td><td>0.57</td><td>0.57</td><td>0.55</td><td>0.48</td></tr>
<tr><td>Transparency</td><td>P</td><td>x</td><td></td><td>5.8</td><td>5.7</td><td>5</td><td>5.4</td><td>5.1</td><td>4.9</td></tr>
<tr><td>Time to export(days)</td><td>P</td><td></td><td>x</td><td>14</td><td>14</td><td>14</td><td>14</td><td>14</td><td>14</td></tr>
<tr><td>Time to import(days)</td><td>P</td><td></td><td>x</td><td>15</td><td>15</td><td>15</td><td>15</td><td>15</td><td>15</td></tr>
<tr><td>FDI US$ Million</td><td></td><td></td><td></td><td>1049</td><td>2915</td><td>1756</td><td>1794</td><td>257</td><td>156</td></tr>
<tr><td>FDI / WORLD %</td><td></td><td></td><td></td><td>0.106</td><td>0.20</td><td>0.09</td><td>0.10</td><td>0.02</td><td>0.01</td></tr>
<tr><td>GDP current US $</td><td></td><td></td><td></td><td>1.6E+10</td><td>1.85E+10</td><td>2.17E+10</td><td>2.57E+10</td><td>2.29E+10</td><td>2.57E+10</td></tr>
<tr><td>Population (Thousands of pupils)</td><td></td><td></td><td></td><td>867.014</td><td>940.808</td><td>1026.568</td><td>1115.777</td><td>1196.774</td><td>1261.319</td></tr>
</tbody>
</table>

E: Economic factor; S: Social factor, P: Political factor.

Source: World Data Bank, Joint Arab Economic Reports, UNCTAD, Transparency International Organization, Economic, and Social Commission for Western Asia

Appendix 3.Input data Egypt

Series Name	Key drivers	Stimulant	Destimulant	Egypt					
				2005	2006	2007	2008	2009	2010
GDP growth (annual %)	E	x		4.5	6.8	7.1	7.2	4.7	5.1
GDP per capita (constant 2005 US$)	E	x		1249.5	1312.8	1382.4	1456.6	1499.3	1550.2
GDP per capita growth (annual %)	E	x		2.7	5.1	5.3	5.4	2.9	3.4
Trade (% of GDP)	E	x		63.0	61.5	65.1	71.7	56.6	47.5
Tax payments (number)	E	x		42	41	36	29	29	29
Inflation, GDP deflator (annual %)	E		x	6.2	7.4	12.6	12.2	11.2	10.1
Imports of goods and services (% of GDP)	E		x	32.6	31.6	34.8	38.6	31.6	26.1
Urban population (% of total)	E	x		43.0	43.1	43.2	43.2	43.3	43.4
Labour force, total	E	x		23105750	23118796	24149082	24773710	25348543	25986819
Secondary education, general pupils	S	x		8329822	9457000	8275579	8221336	6665801	6845748
Electricity production (kWh)	S	x		1.0869E+11	1.15407E+11	1.25129E+11	1.3104E+11	1.39E+11	1.46795E+11
Political Stability(-2.5 to 2.5)	P	x		-0.65	-0.87	-0.59	-0.52	-0.62	-0.91
Rule of Law (-2.5 to 2.5)	P	x		0.03	-0.2	-0.18	-0.09	-0.06	-0.12
Transparency	P	x		3.4	3.3	2.9	2.8	2.8	3.1
Time to export(days)	P		x	27	20	15	14	14	12
Time to import(days)	P		x	32	28	21	18	18	15
FDI US$ Million				5376	10043	11578	9495	6712	6386
FDI / WORLD %				0.543	0.68	0.58	0.52	0.55	0.45
GDP current US $				8.97E+10	1.07E+11	1.3E+11	1.63E+11	1.89E+11	2.19E+11
Population (Thousands of pupils)				74942.12	76274.29	77605.33	78976.12	80442.44	82040.99

E: Economic factor, S: Social factor, P: Political factor.

Source: World Data Bank, Joint Arab Economic Reports, UNCTAD, Transparency International Organization, Economic, and Social Commission for Western Asia

Appendix 4.Input data Iraq

Series Name	Key drivers	Stimulant	Destimulant	2005	2006	2007	2008	2009	2010
					Iraq				
GDP growth (annual %)	E	x		4.4	10.2	1.4	6.6	5.8	6.9
GDP per capita (constant 2005 US$)	E	x		1824.7	1960.8	1941.1	2020.9	2086.3	2172.7
GDP per capita growth (annual %)	E	x		1.7	7.5	-1	4.1	3.2	4.1
Trade (% of GDP)	E	x		115.7	89.7	74.1	81.1	78.7	71.8
Tax payments (number)	E	x		13	13	13	13	13	13
Inflation, GDP deflator (annual %)	E		x	32.3	18	15	32.2	-21.4	19.6
Imports of goods and services (% of GDP)	E		x	61.4	38.6	28.2	30.7	39.3	33.1
Urban population (% of total)	E	x		67.0	66.9	66.8	66.7	66.6	66.5
Labour force, total	E	x		6580414	6774003	6981557	7162271	7379172	7642667
Secondary education, general pupils	S	x		421665	463862	559905	546565	552859	641306
Electricity production (kWh)	S	x		3040000000	3382300000	3323700000	3683800000	4560700000	5016700000
Political Stability(-2.5 to 2.5)	P	x		-2.72	-2.83	-2.79	-2.48	-2.19	-2.26
Rule of Law (-2.5 to 2.5)	P	x		-1.77	-1.79	-1.92	-1.84	-1.77	-1.62
Transparency	P	x		2.2	1.9	1.5	1.3	1.5	1.5
Time to export(days)	P		x	102	102	102	102	102	80
Time to import(days)	P		x	101	101	101	101	101	83
FDI US$ Million				515	383	972	1856	1452	1426
FDI / WORLD %				0.052	0.03	0.05	0.10	0.13	0.10
GDP current US $				5E+10	6.51E+10	8.88E+10	1.32E+11	1.12E+11	1.43E+11
Population (Thousands of pupils)				27017.71	27716.98	28423.54	29163.33	29970.63	30868.16

E: Economic factor, S: Social factor, P: Political factor.

Source: World Data Bank, Joint Arab Economic Reports, UNCTAD, Transparency International Organization, Economic, and Social Commission for Western Asia

Appendix 5.Input data Jordan

Jordan

Series Name	Key drivers	Stimulant	Destimulant	2005	2006	2007	2008	2009	2010
GDP growth (annual %)	E	x		8.1	8.1	8.2	7.2	5.5	2.3
GDP per capita (constant 2005 US$)	E	x		2325.4	2457.5	2599.7	2727.5	2814.1	2817.5
GDP per capita growth (annual %)	E	x		5.7	5.7	5.8	4.9	3.2	0.1
Trade (% of GDP)	E	x		147.1	141.7	146	144	115	117.3
Tax payments (number)	E	x		26	26	26	26	26	26
Inflation, GDP deflator (annual %)	E		x	2.0	10.7	5.1	19.9	2.8	8.4
Imports of goods and services (% of GDP)	E		x	94.4	87.9	91.8	87.5	69.1	69
Urban population (% of total)	E	x		81.2	81.4	81.7	82	82.2	82.5
Labour force, total	E	x		1364267	1404213	1502969	1547009	1633844	1660162
Secondary education, general pupils	S	x		594733	616912	670836	672157	729847	685883
Electricity production (kWh)	S	x		9654000000	11120000000	13001000000	13838000000	14272000000	14777000000
Political Stability(-2.5 to 2.5)	P	x		-0.13	-0.77	-0.31	-0.36	-0.36	-0.31
Rule of Law (-2.5 to 2.5)	P	x		0.41	0.38	0.45	0.46	0.28	0.2
Transparency	P	x		5.7	5.3	4.7	5.1	5	4.7
Time to export(days)	P		x	28	19	19	19	17	14
Time to import(days)	P		x	28	22	22	22	19	18
FDI US$ Million				1984	3544	2622	2829	2429	1703
FDI / WORLD %				0.201	0.24	0.13	0.16	0.20	0.12
GDP current US $				1.26E+10	1.51E+10	1.71E+10	2.2E+10	2.38E+10	2.64E+10
Population (Thousands of pupils)				5332.982	5530.218	5759.424	6010.035	6266.865	6517.912

E: Economic factor, S: Social factor, P: Political factor.

Source: World Data Bank, Joint Arab Economic Reports, UNCTAD, Transparency International Organization, United Nations Population Division

Appendix 6.Input data Kuwait

Series Name	Key drivers	Stimulant	Destimulant	Kuwait 2005	2006	2007	2008	2009	2010
GDP growth (annual %)	E	x		10.1	7.5	6	2.5	-7.1	-2.4
GDP per capita (constant 2005 US$)	E	x		35185.9	35936.4	36040	34920.5	30765.8	28615.9
GDP per capita growth (annual %)	E	x		5.3	2.1	0.3	-3.1	-11.9	-7
Trade (% of GDP)	E	x		92.2	89.7	91.7	92.7	88.9	93.4
Tax payments (number)	E	x		12	12	12	12	12	12
Inflation, GDP deflator (annual %)	E		x	22.4	16.2	4.3	18.7	-17.2	15.5
Imports of goods and services (% of GDP)	E		x	28.3	24.2	28.3	25.9	29.4	29.2
Urban population (% of total)	E	x		98.2	98.2	98.2	98.2	98.2	98.2
Labour force, total	E	x		1159849	1217897	1283963	1354894	1436885	1512542
Secondary education, general pupils	S	x		234073	231236	242631	246100	250745	258098
Electricity production (kWh)	S	x		43734000000	47607000000	48753000000	51749000000	53216000000	57029000000
Political Stability(-2.5 to 2.5)	P	x		0.2	0.36	0.56	0.46	0.34	0.44
Rule of Law (-2.5 to 2.5)	P	x		0.6	0.58	0.65	0.62	0.61	0.6
Transparency	P	x		4.7	4.8	4.3	4.3	4.1	4.5
Time to export(days)	P		x	19	19	19	19	16	16
Time to import(days)	P		x	20	20	20	20	19	19
FDI US$ Million				234	122	112	-6	1114	81
FDI / WORLD %				0.024	0.01	0.01	0.00	0.09	0.03
GDP current US $				8.08E+10	1.02E+11	1.15E+11	1.47E+11	1.06E+11	1.2E+11
Population (Thousands of pupils)				2263.604	2389.498	2538.591	2705.29	2881.243	3059.473

E: Economic factor; S: Social factor, P: Political factor.

Source: World Data Bank, Joint Arab Economic Reports, UNCTAD, Transparency International Organization, Economic, and Social Commission for Western Asia

Appendix 7.Input data Lebanon

Series Name	Key drivers	Stimulant	Destimulant	Lebanon					
				2005	2006	2007	2008	2009	2010
GDP growth (annual %)	E	x		2.7	1.6	9.4	9.1	10.3	8
GDP per capita (constant 2005 US$)	E	x		5339.4	5301.4	5715.9	6167	6704.8	7083.9
GDP per capita growth (annual %)	E	x		-0.7	-0.7	7.8	7.9	8.7	5.7
Trade (% of GDP)	E	x		96.4	94.7	101.3	109.5	92.7	98.1
Tax payments (number)	E	x		19	19	19	19	19	19
Inflation, GDP deflator (annual %)	E		x	-1.1	0.8	3.1	7.5	10.5	0.2
Imports of goods and services (% of GDP)	E		x	58.6	58	63.1	69.9	58.6	61.9
Urban population (% of total)	E	x		86.6	86.7	86.8	86.9	87	87.1
Labour force, total	E	x		1325032	1375249	1412555	1445658	1486318	1546710
Secondary education, general pupils	S	x		329253	331268	332242	327716	328484	326513
Electricity production (kWh)	S	x		12433000000	11610000000	12072000000	13356000000	13771000000	15712000000
Political Stability(-2.5 to 2.5)	P	x		-1.02	-1.85	-2.13	-1.9	-1.58	-1.63
Rule of Law (-2.5 to 2.5)	P	x		-0.3	-0.63	-0.71	-0.68	-0.69	-0.69
Transparency	P	x		3.1	3.6	3	3	2.5	2.5
Time to export(days)	P		x	25	25	26	26	25	25
Time to import(days)	P		x	34	34	38	38	33	33
FDI US$ Million				3321	3132	3376	4333	4804	4955
FDI / WORLD %				0.336	0.21	0.17	0.24	0.39	0.30
GDP current US $				2.13E+10	2.18E+10	2.46E+10	2.88E+10	3.51E+10	3.8E+10
Population (Thousands of pupils)				3986.865	4057.041	4085.426	4109.389	4181.742	4337.156

E: Economic factor, S: Social factor, P: Political factor.

Source: World Data Bank, Joint Arab Economic Reports, UNCTAD, Transparency International Organization, United Nations Population Division

Appendix 8.Input data Morocco

Series Name	Key drivers	Stimulant	Destimulant	Morocco					
				2005	2006	2007	2008	2009	2010
GDP growth (annual %)	E	x		3.0	7.8	2.7	5.6	4.8	3.6
GDP per capita (constant 2005 US$)	E	x		1948.2	2079.6	2116	2212.6	2293.3	2348.6
GDP per capita growth (annual %)	E	x		2.0	6.7	1.7	4.6	3.6	2.4
Trade (% of GDP)	E	x		70.2	73.9	80.6	88.3	68.4	76.3
Tax payments (number)	E	x		28	28	28	28	28	28
Inflation, GDP deflator (annual %)	E		x	1.5	1.5	3.9	5.9	1.5	0.6
Imports of goods and services (% of GDP)	E		x	37.9	39.7	44.9	50.9	39.7	43.1
Urban population (% of total)	E	x		55.0	55.3	55.7	56	56.3	56.7
Labour force, total	E	x		10904602	10954557	11108545	11239022	11298026	11371616
Secondary education, general pupils	S	x		1834766	1942531	2051554	2114335	2189785	2246470
Electricity production (kWh)	S	x		19290000000	19864000000	19897000000	20560000000	21145000000	23509000000
Political Stability(-2.5 to 2.5)	P	x		-0.55	-0.47	-0.51	-0.6	-0.41	-0.38
Rule of Law (-2.5 to 2.5)	P	x		-0.12	-0.25	-0.26	-0.19	-0.19	-0.16
Transparency	P	x		3.2	3.2	3.5	3.5	3.3	3.4
Time to export(days)	P		x	17	17	13	13	13	13
Time to import(days)	P		x	30	30	19	18	17	17
FDI US$ Million				1653	2449	2805	2487	1952	1304
FDI / WORLD %				0.167	0.17	0.14	0.14	0.16	0.11
GDP current US $				5.95E+10	6.56E+10	7.52E+10	8.89E+10	9.09E+10	9.08E+10
Population (Thousands of pupils)				30385.48	30691.43	31011.32	31350.54	31714.96	32107.74

E: Economic factor, S: Social factor, P: Political factor.

Source: World Data Bank, Joint Arab Economic Reports, UNCTAD, Transparency International Organization, United Nations Population Division

234

Appendix 9.Input data Oman

Series Name	Key drivers	Stimulant	Destimulant	2005	2006	2007	2008	2009	2010
GDP growth (annual %)	E	x		4.0	5.5	6.8	12.8	1.1	5.6
GDP per capita (constant 2005 US$)	E	x		12252.6	12761.7	13550.8	15145.1	14911	14962
GDP per capita growth (annual %)	E	x		1.6	4.2	6.2	11.8	-1.5	0.3
Trade (% of GDP)	E	x		89.9	88.8	96.9	95.9	85.5	89.6
Tax payments (number)	E	x		14	14	14	14	14	14
Inflation, GDP deflator (annual %)	E		x	20.4	12.9	6.6	28.5	-21.4	15.4
Imports of goods and services (% of GDP)	E		x	31.2	32	40.2	37.3	34.8	32.6
Urban population (% of total)	E	x		71.9	72.2	72.4	72.7	72.9	73.2
Labour force, total	E	x		905047	938649	972084	1017388	1096874	1216740
Secondary education, general pupils	S	x		301568	308508	316019	317816	321670	319820
Electricity production (kWh)	S	x		12648000000	13287000000	14167000000	15829000000	17823000000	19819000000
Political Stability(-2.5 to 2.5)	P	x		0.92	0.82	0.91	0.92	0.8	0.59
Rule of Law (-2.5 to 2.5)	P	x		0.4	0.37	0.51	0.71	0.66	0.64
Transparency	P	x		6.3	5.4	4.7	5.5	5.5	5.3
Time to export(days)	P		x	14	14	14	14	14	10
Time to import(days)	P		x	15	15	15	15	15	9
FDI US$ Million				1538	1588	3431	2528	1471	2045
FDI / WORLD %				0.155	0.11	0.17	0.16	0.12	0.09
GDP current US $				3.09E+10	3.68E+10	4.19E+10	6.07E+10	4.82E+10	5.88E+10
Population (Thousands of pupils)				2506.891	2553.376	2593.75	2652.281	2762.073	2943.747

E: Economic factor, S: Social factor, P: Political factor.

Source: World Data Bank, Joint Arab Economic Reports, UNCTAD, Transparency International Organization, United Nations Population Division

Appendix 10.Input data Qatar

Series Name	Key drivers	Stimulant	Destimulant	Qatar					
				2005	2006	2007	2008	2009	2010
GDP growth (annual %)	E	x		7.5	26.2	18	17.7	12	16.7
GDP per capita (constant 2005 US$)	E	x		54228.8	58065.5	57519.8	57388.7	55831.1	58257
GDP per capita growth (annual %)	E	x		-5.7	7.1	-0.9	-0.2	-2.7	4.3
Trade (% of GDP)	E	x		94.7	98.6	96.1	89.4	80.5	83.7
Tax payments (number)	E	x		3	3	3	3	3	3
Inflation, GDP deflator (annual %)	E		x	30.5	8.4	11	22.9	-24.2	9.6
Imports of goods and services (% of GDP)	E		x	29.7	35.8	35.8	28.1	29	23.8
Urban population (% of total)	E	x		97.4	97.7	97.9	98.2	98.4	98.7
Labour force, total	E	x		501009	630119	794108	972980	1114916	1304192
Secondary education, general pupils	S	x		55186	58203	60451	65480	65952	68322
Electricity production (kWh)	S	x		14396000000	17080000000	19462000000	21616000000	24158000000	28144000000
Political Stability(-2.5 to 2.5)	P	x		0.99	0.91	0.94	1.1	1.21	1.12
Rule of Law (-2.5 to 2.5)	P	x		0.7	0.72	0.63	0.79	1.01	0.95
Transparency	P	x		5.9	6	6	6.5	7	7.7
Time to export(days)	P		x	21	21	21	21	21	21
Time to import(days)	P		x	20	20	20	20	20	20
FDI US$ Million				2500	3500	4700	3779	8125	5534
FDI / WORLD %				0.253	0.24	0.23	0.21	0.67	0.33
GDP current US $				4.45E+10	6.09E+10	7.97E+10	1.15E+11	9.78E+10	1.25E+11
Population (Thousands of pupils)				836.924	988.448	1178.955	1388.962	1591.151	1765.513

E: Economic factor, S: Social factor, P: Political factor.

Source: World Data Bank, Joint Arab Economic Reports, UNCTAD, Transparency International Organization, Economic, and Social Commission for Western Asia

Appendix 11.Input data Saudi

Series Name	Key drivers	Stimulant	Destimulant	Saudi 2005	2006	2007	2008	2009	2010
GDP growth (annual %)	E	x		7.3	5.6	6	8.4	1.8	7.4
GDP per capita (constant 2005 US$)	E	x		13303.3	13667.7	14182.8	15115.2	15144.6	15994.8
GDP per capita growth (annual %)	E	x		3.6	2.7	3.8	6.6	0.2	5.6
Trade (% of GDP)	E	x		82.0	89.9	94.9	96.1	84.9	82.8
Tax payments (number)	E	x		14	14	14	14	14	14
Inflation, GDP deflator (annual %)	E		x	18.3	8.6	4.2	15.3	-18.9	14.3
Imports of goods and services (% of GDP)	E		x	24.9	30.1	34.9	34	37.8	33.1
Urban population (% of total)	E	x		81.0	81.2	81.4	81.6	81.9	82.1
Labour force, total	E	x		8208531	8601112	8920244	9174577	9400411	9725111
Secondary education, general pupils	S	x		2523947	2675167	2746447	2788094	2881941	3036438
Electricity production (kWh)	S	x		1.76124E+11	1.81434E+11	1.90535E+11	2.042E+11	2.17082E+11	2.40067E+11
Political Stability(-2.5 to 2.5)	P	x		-0.25	-0.54	-0.5	-0.37	-0.51	-0.22
Rule of Law (-2.5 to 2.5)	P	x		0.1	0.11	0.19	0.19	0.16	0.26
Transparency	P	x		3.4	3.3	3.4	3.5	4.3	4.7
Time to export(days)	P		x	17	17	17	15	15	13
Time to import(days)	P		x	34	34	20	18	18	17
FDI US$ Million				12097	17140	22821	38151	32100	28105
FDI / WORLD %				1.222	1.24	1.21	2.17	3.00	2.08
GDP current US $				3.28E+11	3.77E+11	4.16E+11	5.2E+11	4.29E+11	5.27E+11
Population (Thousands of pupils)				24745.23	25419.994	26083.522	26742.842	27409.491	28090.647

E: Economic factor, S: Social factor, P: Political factor.

Source: World Data Bank, Joint Arab Economic Reports, UNCTAD, Transparency International organization,

Appendix 12.Input data Tunisia

Series Name	Key drivers	Stimulant	Destimulant	2005	2006	2007	2008	2009	2010
					Tunisia				
GDP growth (annual %)	E	x		3.8	5.7	6.2	4.7	3.6	3.6
GDP per capita (constant 2005 US$)	E	x		3219.0	3367.8	3543.3	3674	3766.1	3861.5
GDP per capita growth (annual %)	E	x		2.8	4.6	5.2	3.7	2.5	2.5
Trade (% of GDP)	E	x		90.3	93.9	104.1	115.4	94.4	105.7
Tax payments (number)	E	x		22	22	22	22	22	8
Inflation. GDP deflator (annual %)	E		x	3.8	3.4	2.6	5.8	2.5	3.7
Imports of goods and services (% of GDP)	E		x	45.3	47.9	53	59.2	48.5	55.3
Urban population (% of total)	E	x		65.1	65.3	65.5	65.7	65.9	66.1
Labour force, total	E	x		3431566	3509773	3584904	3659293	3732501	3801352
Secondary education, general pupils	S	x		1136657	1134177	1147889	1126764	1058911	1023993
Electricity production (kWh)	S	x		12661000000	13062000000	13740000000	14363000000	15252000000	16096000000
Political Stability(-2.5 to 2.5)	P	x		0.05	0.24	0.19	0.12	0.06	-0.04
Rule of Law (-2.5 to 2.5)	P	x		0.1	0.2	0.17	0.14	0.2	0.12
Transparency	P	x		4.9	4.6	4.2	4.4	4.2	4.3
Time to export(days)	P		x	16	16	15	15	13	13
Time to import(days)	P		x	29	29	22	23	21	17
FDI US$ Million				782	3308	1616	2758	1688	1513
FDI / WORLD %				0.079	0.22	0.08	0.15	0.14	0.11
GDP current US $				3.23E+10	3.44E+10	3.89E+10	4.49E+10	4.35E+10	4.41E+10
Population (Thousands of pupils)				10102.477	10196.441	10298.717	10408.091	10522.214	10639.194

E: Economic factor, S: Social factor, P: Political factor.

Source: World Data Bank, Joint Arab Economic Reports, UNCTAD, Transparency International Organization, Economic, and Social Commission for Western Asia

Appendix 13.Input data UAE

Series Name	Key drivers	Stimulant	Destimulant	2005	2006	2007	2008	2009	2010
				UAE					
GDP growth (annual %)	E	x		4.9	9.8	3.2	3.2	-4.8	1.7
GDP per capita (constant 2005 US$)	E	x		43533.9	40689	35309.6	31070.4	26053.4	24219.3
GDP per capita growth (annual %)	E	x		-7.5	-6.5	-13.2	-12	-16.1	-7
Trade (% of GDP)	E	x		119.6	119.5	136.8	148.5	152.7	150.3
Tax payments (number)	E	x		14	14	14	14	14	14
Inflation, GDP deflator (annual %)	E		x	16.5	12	12.5	18.5	-15.2	10.9
Imports of goods and services (% of GDP)	E		x	52.0	50.8	64.4	69.6	73.4	71.9
Urban population (% of total)	E	x		82.3	82.6	83	83.3	83.7	84
Labour force, total	E	x		2541209	3066204	3735627	4461176	5136379	5686382
Secondary education, general pupils	S	x		283621	296972	309476	324482	322470	335012
Electricity production (kWh)	S	x		60698000000	66768000000	76106000000	86260000000	90573000000	97728000000
Political Stability(-2.5 to 2.5)	P	x		0.85	0.91	0.97	0.7	0.91	0.79
Rule of Law (-2.5 to 2.5)	P	x		0.48	0.37	0.36	0.49	0.46	0.37
Transparency	P	x		6.2	6.2	5.7	5.9	6.5	6.3
Time to export(days)	P		x	9	9	9	9	8	7
Time to import(days)	P		x	9	9	9	9	9	7
FDI US$ Million				10900	12806	14187	13724	4003	3948
FDI / WORLD %				1.101	0.86	0.71	0.76	0.33	0.39
GDP current US $				1.81E+11	2.22E+11	2.58E+11	3.15E+11	2.55E+11	2.87E+11
Population (Thousands of pupils)				4481.976	5171.255	6010.1	6900.142	7705.423	8329.453

E: Economic factor, S: Social factor, P: Political factor.

Source: World Data Bank, Joint Arab Economic Reports, UNCTAD, Transparency International Organization, United Nations Population Division

Appendix 14.Input data Poland

Series Name	Key drivers	Stimulant	Destimulant	Poland					
				2005	2006	2007	2008	2009	2010
GDP growth (annual %)	E	x		3.6	6.2	6.8	5.1	1.8	3.9
GDP per capita (constant 2005 US$)	E	x		7963.0	8464.3	9043.5	9505.8	9669.6	10035.9
GDP per capita growth (annual %)	E	x		3.7	6.3	6.8	5.1	1.7	3.8
Trade (% of GDP)	E	x		74.9	82.5	84.4	83.8	78.8	85.7
Tax payments (number)	E	x		40	40	40	40	40	29
Inflation, GDP deflator (annual %)	E		x	2.6	1.5	4	3.1	3.6	1.4
Imports of goods and services (% of GDP)	E		x	37.8	42.2	43.6	43.9	39.4	43.4
Urban population (% of total)	E	x		61.5	61.4	61.3	61.1	61	60.9
Labour force, total	E	x		17450631	17334574	17332847	17586185	17868450	18141020
Secondary education, general pupils	S	x		2631314	2537580	2421626	2278925	2141971	2027552
Electricity production (kWh)	S	x		1.55359E+11	1.60764E+11	1.58761E+11	1.5471E+11	1.51121E+11	1.57089E+11
Political Stability(-2.5 to 2.5)	P	x		0.34	0.33	0.64	0.86	0.9	0.99
Rule of Law (-2.5 to 2.5)	P	x		0.42	0.35	0.37	0.51	0.6	0.66
Transparency	P	x		3.4	3.7	4.2	4.6	5	5.3
Time to export(days)	P		x	17	17	17	17	17	17
Time to import(days)	P		x	17	17	17	17	17	17
FDI US$ Million				10293	19603	23561	14839	12932	13876
FDI / WORLD %				1.040	1.32	1.18	0.82	1.06	0.99
GDP current US $				3.04E+11	3.42E+11	4.25E+11	5.29E+11	4.31E+11	4.7E+11
Population (Thousands of pupils)				38463.51	38478.76	38500.36	38525.75	38551.49	38574.68

E: Economic factor, S: Social factor, P: Political factor.

Source: World Data Bank. Joint Arab Economic Reports, UNCTAD, Transparency International organization,

Appendix15. Vector measure of Arab countries and Poland for the year 2005

for the year 2005	Result for the year 2005
Kuwait 100	
Poland 94.06	
Jordan 92.23	
Egypt 88.13	
Bahrain 87.61	
Saudi 85.93	
UAE 84.44	Correlation 0.33
Qatar 82.82	
Oman 73.80	
Algeria 70.94	
Tunisia 68.34	
Morocco 57.34	
Lebanon 47.66	
Iraq 0	

Source: author's elaboration.

Appendix16. Vector measure of Arab countries and Poland for the year 2006

for the year 2006	Result for the year 2006
Poland 100	
Qatar 98.73	
Egypt 83.18	
Saudi 70.08	
Kuwait 68.72	
UAE 66.29	Correlation 0.51
Tunisia 64.44	
Morocco 64.03	
Oman 62.28	
Bahrain 58.82	
Jordan 57.81	
Algeria 52.27	
Lebanon 37.59	
Iraq 0	

Source: author's elaboration.

Appendix17. Vector measure of Arab countries and Poland for the year 2007

for the year 2007	Result for year 2007
Poland 100	
Qatar 86.72	
Saudi 82.29	
Kuwait 80.77	
Egypt 75.26	
Oman 69.29	
Jordan 69.10	Correlation 0.47
Tunisia 68.08	
Bahrain 66.13	
Algeria 59.15	
UAE 57.71	
Morocco 57.55	
Lebanon 53.52	
Iraq 0	

Source: author's elaboration.

Appendix18. Vector measure of Arab countries and Poland for the year 2008

for the year 2008	Result for year 2008
Poland 100	
Qatar 85.17	
Saudi 79.23	
Egypt 76.55	
Oman 67.59	
Kuwait 64.78	
UAE 63.25	Correlation 0.42
Bahrain 61.95	
Tunisia 57.52	
Morocco 55.78	
Jordan 54.53	
Algeria 51.06	
Lebanon 39.78	
Iraq 0	

Source: author's elaboration.

Appendix19. Vector measure of Arab countries and Poland for the year 2009

Qatar	100	Result for year 2009
Poland	89.25	
Saudi	77.64	
Oman	60.80	
UAE	58.83	
Egypt	58.16	Correlation 0.51
Kuwait	52.85	
Bahrain	47.92	
Algeria	42.47	
Jordan	38.62	
Morocco	35.85	
Tunisia	33.24	
Lebanon	8.44	
Iraq	0	

Source: author's elaboration.

Appendix20. Vector measure of Arab countries and Poland for the year 2010

Poland	100	Result for year 2010
Qatar	96.16	
Saudi	79.30	
Egypt	73.20	
UAE	62.75	
Morocco	61.43	Correlation 0.53
Bahrain	54.14	
Oman	53.71	
Jordan	50.64	
Kuwait	50.31	
Algeria	46.15	
Tunisia	45.22	
Lebanon	43.12	
Iraq	0	

Source: author's elaboration.

Appendix21. Vector measure of Arab countries and Poland average 2005-2010

Poland	100	Result for average 2005-2010
Qatar	87.23	
Saudi	79.27	
Egypt	75.46	
Kuwait	67.77	
UAE	65.53	
Oman	64.70	Correlation 0.50
Bahrain	63.03	
Morocco	62.08	
Tunisia	61.37	
Jordan	56.27	
Algeria	56.09	
Lebanon	43.37	
Iraq	0	

Source: author's elaboration.

Appendix22.Statistics Descriptive of Raw Data and Boxplot to The year 2005

Year 2005 data characteristics

Variables	Mean	Standard Deviation	Minimum	Median	Maximum
1 GDP growth	5.4714	2.1910	2.7000	4.7000	10.1000
2 GDP p/c	14.5406	17.3124	1.2495	6.6512	54.2288
3 GDP p/c growth	1.3643	3.8594	-7.5000	2.3500	5.7000
4 Trade	96.8286	26.8527	63.0000	91.2500	148.3000
5 Tax payment	21.5000	12.2710	3.0000	16.5000	42.0000
6 Inflation	13.2286	10.9638	-1.1000	14.9000	32.3000
7 Import	44.4714	19.8379	24.1000	37.8500	94.4000
8 Urban population	74.6643	15.9977	43.0000	76.4500	98.2000
9 Labour force	6.3046	7.0348	0.4243	2.9864	23.1058
10 Secondary education	1.5732	2.2257	0.0552	0.5082	8.3298
11 Electricity	24.9596	28.0727	4.4335	12.4225	88.0620
12 Political stability	-0.2086	0.9690	-2.7200	-0.0750	0.9900
13 Rule of law	0.0714	0.6612	-1.7700	0.2500	0.7000
14 Transparency	4.3571	1.4303	2.2000	4.0500	6.3000
15 Time to export	24.3571	22.9702	9.0000	17.0000	102.0000
16 Time to import	29.0000	22.1741	9.0000	25.0000	101.0000

Source: author's elaboration.

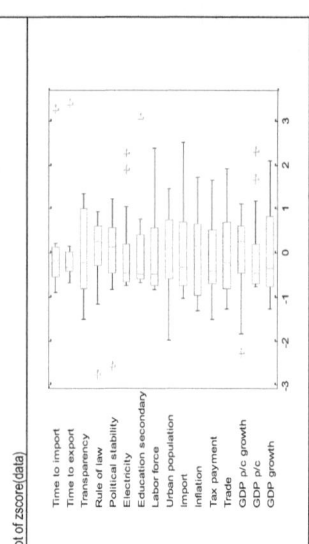

Boxplot of zscore(data)

Source: author's elaboration.

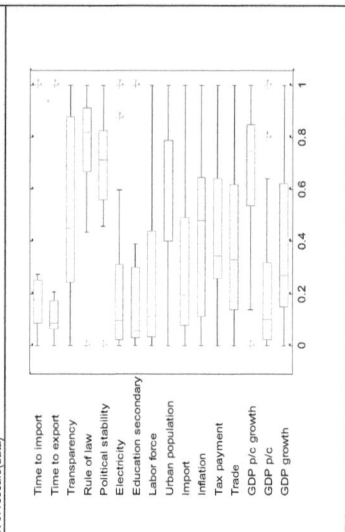

Boxplot of rescale(data)

Source: author's elaboration.

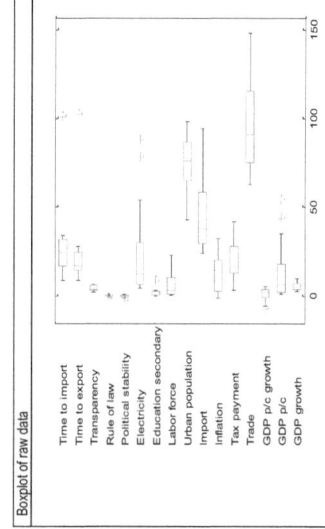

Boxplot of raw data

Source: author's elaboration.

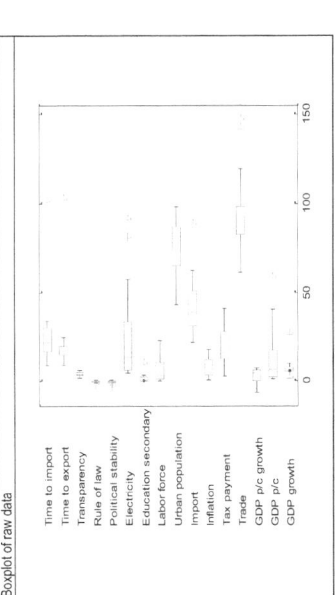

244

Appendix23.Statistics Descriptive of Raw Data and Boxplot to the year 2006

The year 2006 data characteristics

Variables	Mean	Standard Deviation	Minimum	Median	Maximum
1 GDP growth	7.8000	5.8437	1.6000	6.6500	26.2000
2 GDP p/c	14.7846	17.6810	1.3128	6.8828	58.0655
3 GDP p/c growth	3.1000	4.0259	-6.5000	4.4000	7.5000
4 Trade	95.8714	24.7044	61.5000	89.8000	147.1000
5 Tax payment	21.4286	12.1447	3.0000	16.5000	41.0000
6 Inflation	8.6214	5.3666	0.8000	8.7000	18.0000
7 Import	43.0857	17.5516	21.9000	39.1500	87.9000
8 Urban population	74.8786	15.9799	43.1000	76.7000	98.2000
9 Labour force	6.4290	7.0010	0.0582	3.2880	23.1188
10 Secondary education	1.6734	2.4935	0.0582	0.5404	9.4570
11 Electricity	26.3142	29.0232	4.8725	13.4217	90.7170
12 Political stability	-0.3764	1.0863	-2.8300	-0.4300	0.9100
13 Rule of law	-0.0007	0.6643	-1.7900	0.2750	0.7200
14 Transparency	4.2929	1.3088	1.9000	4.1500	6.2000
15 Time to export	23.2143	22.9855	9.0000	17.0000	102.0000
16 Time to import	28.2857	22.2311	9.0000	22.0000	101.0000

Source: author's elaboration.

Boxplot of raw data

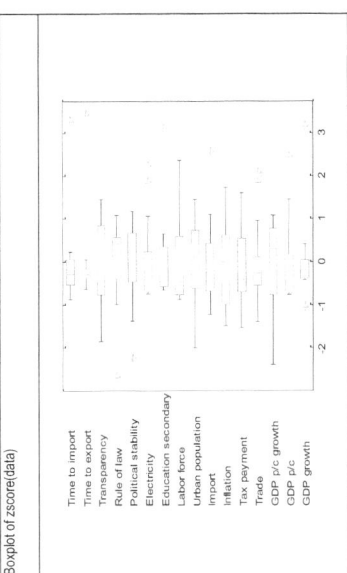

Source: author's elaboration.

Boxplot of zscore(data)

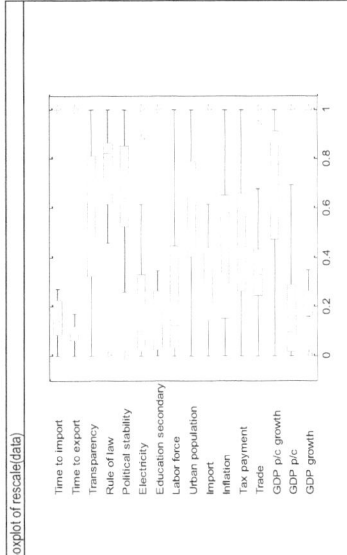

Source: author's elaboration.

Boxplot of rescale(data)

Source: author's elaboration.

Appendix24.Statistics Descriptive of Raw Data and Boxplot to the year 2007

The year 2007 data characteristics

Variables	Mean	Standard Deviation	Minimum	Median	Maximum
1 GDP growth	6.6786	4.0041	1.4000	6.5000	18.0000
2 GDP p/c	14.5623	16.9653	1.3824	7.3797	57.5198
3 GDP p/c growth	2.0929	5.3304	-13.2000	2.7500	7.8000
4 Trade	98.6929	25.2853	65.1000	95.5000	146.0000
5 Tax payment	20.2143	10.3788	3.0000	16.5000	40.0000
6 Inflation	7.1214	4.0743	2.6000	5.7500	15.0000
7 Import	46.1429	18.3814	24.9000	41.9000	91.8000
8 Urban population	75.0857	15.9518	43.2000	76.9000	98.2000
9 Labour force	6.6557	7.1665	0.5407	3.6603	24.1491
10 Secondary education	1.6163	2.2130	0.0605	0.6154	8.2756
11 Electricity	27.6059	29.9822	5.4540	13.2835	95.2675
12 Political stability	-0.2850	1.1397	-2.7900	-0.2750	0.9700
13 Rule of law	0.0086	0.7196	-1.9200	0.2750	0.6500
14 Transparency	4.0071	1.2124	1.5000	4.2000	6.0000
15 Time to export	22.7143	23.1697	9.0000	17.0000	102.0000
16 Time to import	25.8571	22.5384	9.0000	20.0000	101.0000

Source: author's elaboration.

Boxplot of zscore(data)

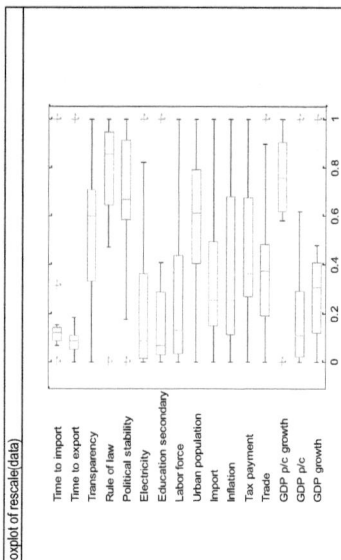

Source: author's elaboration.

Boxplot of rescale(data)

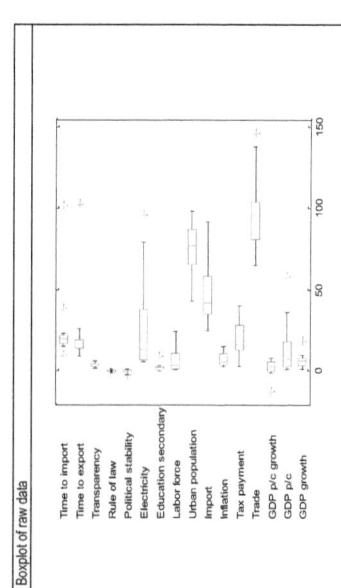

Source: author's elaboration.

Boxplot of raw data

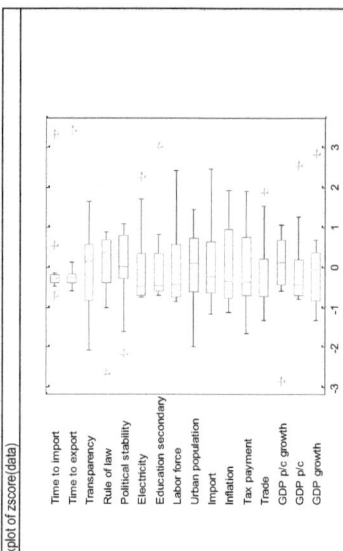

Source: author's elaboration.

Appendix25.Statistics Descriptive of Raw Data and Boxplot to the year 2008

The year 2008 data characteristics

Variables	Mean	Standard Deviation	Minimum	Median	Maximum
1 GDP growth	7.0214	4.1688	2.0000	6.4000	17.7000
2 GDP p/c	14.4307	16.4034	1.4566	7.8364	57.3887
3 GDP p/c growth	2.6643	5.7730	-12.0000	4.3500	11.8000
4 Trade	102.7857	26.1825	71.7000	94.3000	148.5000
5 Tax payment	19.7143	9.7067	3.0000	16.5000	40.0000
6 Inflation	15.5500	8.6516	3.1000	15.5500	32.2000
7 Import	47.6857	19.3049	25.9000	41.2500	87.5000
8 Urban population	75.2857	15.9634	43.2000	77.1500	98.2000
9 Labour force	6.8630	7.2862	0.6059	0.6094	24.7737
10 Secondary education	1.6170	2.2080	0.0655	0.6094	8.2213
11 Electricity	29.1617	31.0506	5.9665	14.6135	102.1000
12 Political stability	-0.2429	1.0594	-2.4800	-0.3000	1.1000
13 Rule of law	0.0693	0.7303	-1.8400	0.3250	0.7900
14 Transparency	4.2143	1.4174	1.3000	4.3500	6.5000
15 Time to export	22.5000	23.2404	9.0000	16.0000	102.0000
16 Time to import	25.5000	22.6605	9.0000	19.0000	101.0000

Source: author's elaboration.

Boxplot of raw data

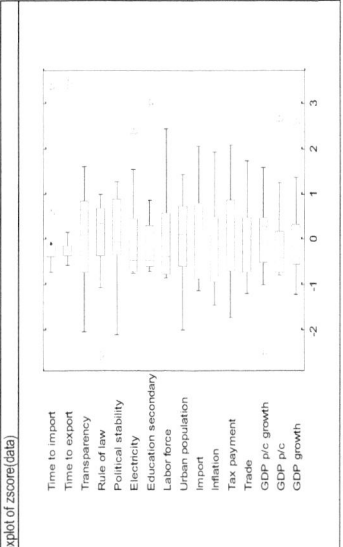

Source: author's elaboration.

Boxplot of zscore(data)

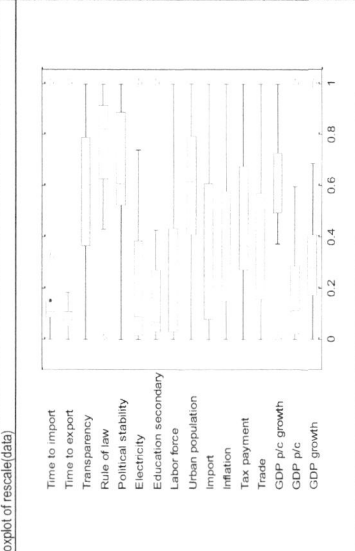

Source: author's elaboration.

Boxplot of rescale(data)

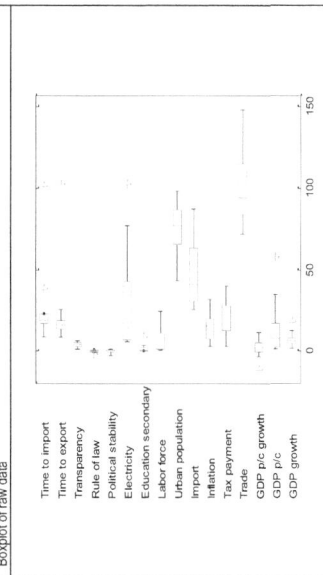

Source: author's elaboration.

Appendix26.Statistics Descriptive of Raw Data and Boxplot to the year 2009

The year 2009 data characteristics

Variables	Mean	Standard Deviation	Minimum	Median	Maximum
1 GDP growth	3.1143	5.0095	-7.1000	3.0500	12.0000
2 GDP p/c	13.6760	15.2946	1.4993	8.1872	55.8311
3 GDP p/c growth	-0.7429	6.4771	-16.1000	0.9500	8.7000
4 Trade	90.4571	24.3163	56.6000	85.2000	152.7000
5 Tax payment	19.7143	9.7067	3.0000	16.5000	40.0000
6 Inflation	-7.8857	12.6324	-24.2000	-12.1000	11.2000
7 Import	44.0071	14.1388	29.0000	39.3500	73.4000
8 Urban population	75.5000	15.9585	43.3000	77.4000	98.4000
9 Labour force	7.0695	7.3979	0.6642	4.4344	25.3485
10 Secondary education	1.5514	1.9196	0.0660	0.6414	6.6658
11 Electricity	30.4849	32.2127	6.0280	15.6648	108.5410
12 Political stability	-0.2021	1.0015	-2.1900	-0.2600	1.2100
13 Rule of law	0.0757	0.7334	-1.7700	0.2400	1.0100
14 Transparency	4.2571	1.5639	1.5000	4.2500	7.0000
15 Time to export	21.8571	23.4024	8.0000	15.5000	102.0000
16 Time to import	24.6429	22.5955	9.0000	18.5000	101.0000

Source: author's elaboration.

Boxplot of raw data

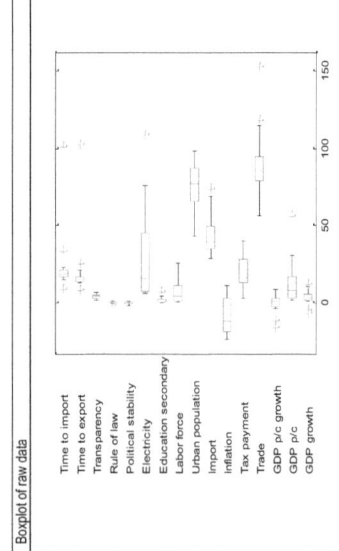

Source: author's elaboration.

Boxplot of zscore(data)

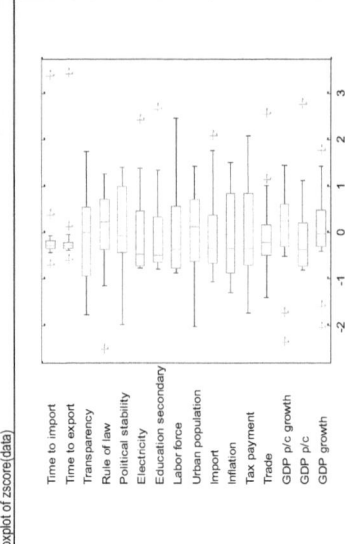

Source: author's elaboration.

Boxplot of rescale(data)

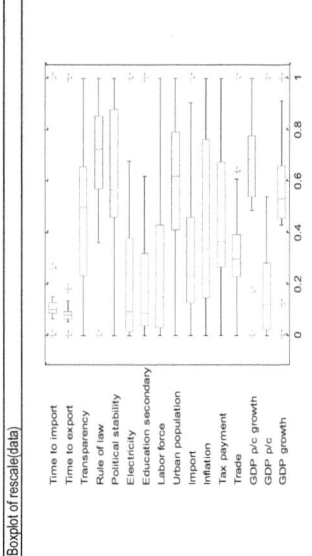

Source: author's elaboration.

Appendix27.Statistics Descriptive of Raw Data and Boxplot to the year 2010

The year 2010 data characteristics

Variables	Mean	Standard Deviation	Minimum	Median	Maximum
1 GDP growth	5.0214	4.2620	-2.4000	4.1000	16.7000
2 GDP p/c	13.6989	15.5110	1.5502	8.5599	58.2570
3 GDP p/c growth	1.3714	4.0412	-7.0000	2.4500	5.7000
4 Trade	92.3286	25.4177	47.5000	87.6500	150.3000
5 Tax payment	17.9286	8.7131	3.0000	14.0000	29.0000
6 Inflation	9.5143	6.2777	0.2000	9.8500	19.6000
7 Import	43.2000	16.0891	23.8000	38.1000	71.9000
8 Urban population	75.7143	15.9513	43.4000	77.6500	98.7000
9 Labour force	7.2817	7.5336	0.7070	4.7439	25.9968
10 Secondary education	1.5797	1.9710	0.0683	0.6636	6.8457
11 Electricity	33.0677	34.7163	6.6150	18.4695	120.0335
12 Political stability	-0.2564	1.0081	-2.2600	-0.2650	1.1200
13 Rule of law	0.0671	0.6926	-1.6200	0.2300	0.9500
14 Transparency	4.3643	1.6056	1.5000	4.6000	7.7000
15 Time to export	19.4286	17.9902	7.0000	14.0000	80.0000
16 Time to import	22.1429	18.5300	7.0000	17.0000	83.0000

Source: author's elaboration

Boxplot of raw data

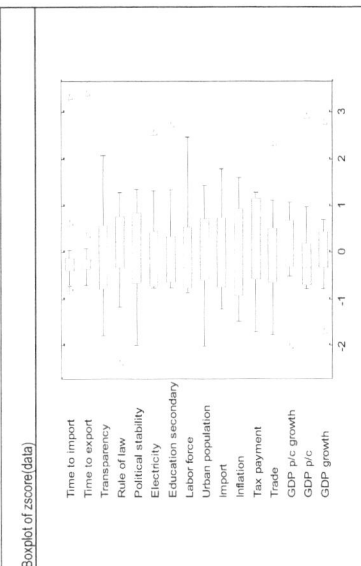

Source: author's elaboration

Boxplot of zscore(data)

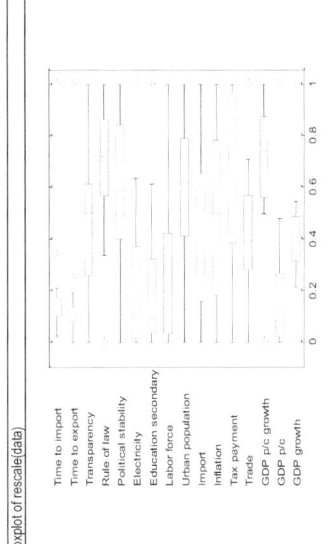

Source: author's elaboration

Boxplot of rescale(data)

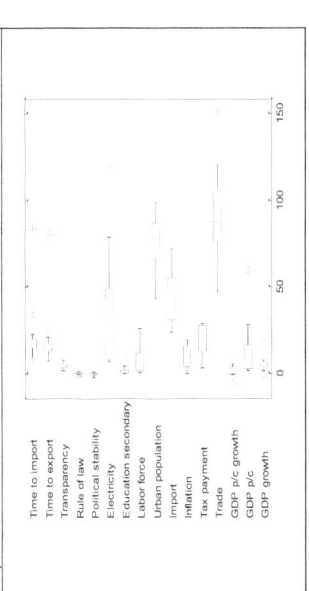

Source: author's elaboration

Appendix28. A composite measure of Arab countries and Poland using vector measures for the year 2005

Country	Composite Vector measure	Key Economic determinant	Key Social determinant	Key Political determinant
Egypt	100	66.07	100	58.79
Poland	99.40	76.10	64.55	72.28
Kuwait	98.05	100	11.62	82.11
Saudi	92.66	69.78	69.64	62.71
Jordan	87.54	83.56	4.85	83.61
Bahrain	78.89	64.29	0	91.09
Algeria	74.78	72.49	35.05	49.54
UAE	74.09	35.66	16.96	100
Qatar	71.38	43.90	1.59	97.00
Tunisia	60.54	36.90	10.38	77.21
Oman	59.91	20.08	3.20	98.86
Morocco	53.67	37.04	18.30	58.16
Lebanon	42.30	32.86	3.38	51.23
Iraq	0	0	9.37	0

Correlation 0.41

Source: author's elaboration.

Appendix29. A composite measure of Arab countries and Poland using vector measures for the year 2006

Country	Composite Vector measure	Key Economic determinant	Key Social determinant	Key Political determinant
Poland	100	100	65.08	74.38
Qatar	86.78	89.94	2.30	99.04
Egypt	85.34	70.57	100	56.09
Saudi	65.47	46.53	72.56	60.32
Morocco	59.57	67.13	16.56	57.37
Kuwait	52.20	34.85	13.12	84.73
Tunisia	50.00	38.84	8.68	77.53
Algeria	46.68	42.67	31.15	50.12
UAE	40.92	0	19.61	100
Jordan	40.15	22.9	4.39	78.93
Oman	39.84	13.00	2.88	91.77
Bahrain	37.78	14.96	0	86.48
Lebanon	28.57	28.29	2.52	46.63
Iraq	0	10.16	10.44	0

Correlation 0.58

Source: author's elaboration.

Appendix30. A composite measure of Arab countries and Poland using vector measures for the year 2007

Country	Composite Vector measure	Key Economic determinant	Key Social determinant	Key Political determinant
Poland	100	100	64.81	80.92
Saudi	86.75	75.00	77.34	64.57
Egypt	85.06	59.74	100	56.01
Qatar	76.57	77.67	2.56	100
Kuwait	73.02	78.25	13.19	83.82
Oman	61.24	52.95	2.90	88.66
Jordan	61.20	62.17	5.30	79.00
Tunisia	61.01	62.09	9.26	75.56
Bahrain	57.77	52.66	0	84.02
Algeria	57.40	63.33	34.38	47.33
UAE	55.64	11.55	22.32	96.44
Morocco	53.26	51.97	18.26	60.91
Lebanon	45.66	74.35	2.36	38.96
Iraq	0	0	10.80	0

Correlation 0.61

Source: author's elaboration.

Appendix31. A composite measure of Arab countries and Poland using vector measures for the year 2008

Country	Composite Vector measure	Key Economic determinant	Key Social determinant	Key Political determinant
Poland	100	100	64.56	82.43
Egypt	81.65	64.56	100	53.58
Saudi	81.59	66.30	85.06	62.28
Qatar	73.60	68.73	3.27	100
Kuwait	55.85	44.06	14.81	77.92
Oman	54.60	36.61	3.16	91.53
Morocco	51.30	51.54	17.90	57.12
Bahrain	50.83	40.70	0	80.71
UAE	50.39	12.12	27.07	91.44
Algeria	49.75	47.43	35.01	45.79
Tunisia	48.58	38.68	8.58	71.60
Jordan	43.46	26.37	5.07	75.79
Lebanon	37.15	50.63	2.39	36.80
Iraq	0	0	11.95	0

Correlation 0.52

Source: author's elaboration.

Appendix33.A composite measure of Arab countries and Poland using vector measures for the year 2010

Country	Composite Vector measure	Key Economic determinant	Key Social determinant	Key Political determinant
Poland	100	100	60.58	83.70
Qatar	86.28	95.51	4.44	100
Saudi	81.71	54.83	94.48	65.69
Egypt	80.90	66.37	100	47.28
Morocco	59.74	71.15	22.27	53.12
UAE	49.66	15.73	27.76	86.00
Algeria	47.74	45.40	46.44	35.63
Bahrain	44.41	42.42	0	66.36
Lebanon	44.05	74.11	2.97	29.15
Jordan	41.04	33.38	5.86	64.09
Oman	38.67	13.86	4.15	81.08
Kuwait	37.55	10.95	14.82	73.66
Tunisia	34.34	17.27	9.25	63.83
Iraq	0	0	16.13	0

Correlation 0.62

Source: author's elaboration.

Appendix32.A composite measure of Arab countries and Poland using vector measures for the year 2009

Country	Composite Vector measure	Key Economic determinant	Key Social determinant	Key Political determinant
Qatar	100	100	3.85	100
Poland	93.03	66.85	63.28	81.01
Saudi	88.60	60.58	91.12	59.23
Egypt	64.68	30.15	100	46.80
Algeria	51.16	57.28	45.02	34.03
Oman	45.89	33.90	4.11	83.97
Kuwait	42.45	33.49	14.84	70.21
UAE	36.66	0	27.49	89.79
Bahrain	33.98	29.75	0	71.45
Morocco	28.33	24.68	21.94	50.69
Jordan	22.02	12.42	6.63	66.02
Tunisia	14.07	0.09	9.90	64.25
Iraq	7.22	41.30	15.11	0
Lebanon	0	14.30	2.87	28.68

Correlation 0.63

Source: author's elaboration.

Appendix34.A composite measure of Arab countries and Poland using vector measures averaged data for the period 2005-2010

Country	Composite Vector measure	Key Economic determinant	Key Social determinant	Key Political determinant
Poland	100	100	64.24	78.80
Egypt	81.06	62.14	100	52.31
Saudi	80.88	65.31	82.09	62.43
Qatar	71.52	68.34	3.04	100
Morocco	58.00	65.05	18.96	55.48
Algeria	56.52	60.51	37.30	42.57
Kuwait	55.90	48.28	13.87	78.05
Tunisia	50.15	45.08	9.25	71.25
Bahrain	48.53	41.92	0	79.25
UAE	47.12	14.91	23.74	93.88
Oman	46.89	29.95	3.39	89.05
Jordan	42.19	30.65	5.27	74.06
Lebanon	40.33	54.59	2.74	37.28
Iraq	0	0	12.35	0

Correlation 0.62

Source: author's elaboration.

Appendix35. Importance variables for the period from 2005 to 2010

Series Name	Key drivers	Importance variables						Average 2005-2010
		2005	2006	2007	2008	2009	2010	
GDP growth (annual %)	E	0.06	0.07	0.06	0.06	0.07	0.06	0.07
GDP per capita (constant 2005 US$)	E	0.10	0.03	0.08	0.06	0.06	0.05	0.03
GDP per capita growth (annual %)	E	0.06	0.12	0.08	0.07	0.07	0.06	0.07
Trade (% of GDP)	E	0.09	0.05	0.06	0.08	0.05	0.07	0.06
Tax payments (number)	E	0.07	0.10	0.10	0.10	0.12	0.11	0.11
Inflation, GDP deflator (annual %)	E	-0.10	-0.13	-0.12	-0.10	-0.14	-0.12	-0.13
Imports of goods and services (% of GDP)	E	-0.09	-0.09	-0.09	-0.11	-0.08	-0.09	-0.12
Urban population (% of total)	E	0.08	0.11	0.09	0.09	0.10	0.08	0.10
Labour force, total	E	0.08	0.11	0.09	0.09	0.11	0.08	0.10
Secondary education, general pupils	S	0.49	0.56	0.52	0.54	0.51	0.50	0.53
Electricity production (kWh)	S	0.58	0.54	0.48	0.42	0.42	0.42	0.47
Political Stability(-2.5 to 2.5)	P	0.18	0.22	0.25	0.24	0.26	0.27	0.23
Rule of Law (-2.5 to 2.5)	P	0.16	0.18	0.24	0.20	0.20	0.20	0.18
Transparency	P	0.31	0.31	0.32	0.30	0.27	0.25	0.29
Time to export(days)	P	-0.07	-0.04	-0.05	-0.04	-0.02	-0.04	-0.04
Time to import(days)	P	-0.12	-0.11	-0.05	-0.05	-0.03	-0.05	-0.05

Source: author's elaboration. 0.06 0.07 0.06 0.06 0.07 0.06 0.07

253

Appendix36. Importance key driver for the period 2005 to 2010

Key Drivers	Years						
	2005	2006	2007	2008	2009	2010	Average 2005-2010
Key Economic determinant	0.31	0.34	0.30	0.33	0.28	0.28	0.34
Key Social determinant	0.23	0.18	0.35	0.29	0.22	0.20	0.26
Key Political Determinant	0.28	0.23	0.37	0.32	0.23	0.21	0.25

Source: author's elaboration.

Appendix37.Composite Vector measure and key determinant groups in the year 2005 (the year 2005 as a reference) for the Arab countries and Poland

Year	2005			
Country	Composite Vector measure	Key Economic determinant	Key Social determinant	Key Political determinant
Algeria	0.56	0.63	0.97	-0.19
Bahrain	0.64	0.58	-0.09	0.99
Egypt	1.08	0.59	2.92	0.07
Iraq	-0.97	0.15	0.19	-1.60
Jordan	0.82	0.70	0.05	0.78
Kuwait	1.04	0.81	0.26	0.73
Lebanon	-0.10	0.37	0.01	-0.14
Morocco	0.13	0.40	0.46	0.05
Oman	0.26	0.28	0.004	1.21
Qatar	0.49	0.44	-0.04	1.16
Saudi	0.93	0.61	2.01	0.18
Tunis	0.27	0.39	0.22	0.60
UAE	0.55	0.39	0.42	1.24
Poland	1.06	0.65	1.85	0.46

Correlation 0.42

Source: author's elaboration.

Appendix38.Composite Vector measure and key determinant groups in the year 2006 (the year 2005 as a reference) for the Arab countries and Poland

Year	2006			
Country	Composite Vector measure	Key Economic determinant	Key Social determinant	Key Political determinant
Algeria	0.25	0.42	0.89	-0.1
Bahrain	0.49	0.46	-0.08	0.92
Egypt	1.25	0.57	2.99	0.04
Iraq	-0.92	0.31	0.22	-1.63
Jordan	0.37	0.42	0.06	0.71
Kuwait	0.60	0.48	0.28	0.83
Lebanon	-0.19	0.36	0.002	-0.2
Morocco	0.43	0.57	0.46	0.07
Oman	0.33	0.30	0.01	1.03
Qatar	1.53	0.99	-0.01	1.23
Saudi	0.87	0.50	1.97	0.15
Tunis	0.41	0.44	0.20	0.64
UAE	0.77	0.40	0.46	1.29
Poland	1.39	0.76	1.77	0.53

Correlation 0.58

Source: author's elaboration.

Appendix39.Composite Vector measure and key determinant groups in the year 2007 (the year 2005 as a reference) for the Arab countries and Poland

Year	2007			
Country	Composite Vector measure	Key Economic determinant	Key Social determinant	Key Political determinant
Algeria	0.34	0.48	0.98	-0.12
Bahrain	0.44	0.53	-0.10	0.86
Egypt	1.15	0.45	2.97	0.07
Iraq	-1.35	0.01	0.20	-1.7
Jordan	0.48	0.56	0.07	0.7
Kuwait	0.73	0.66	0.25	0.78
Lebanon	0.04	0.62	-0.03	-0.38
Morocco	0.17	0.38	0.48	0.24
Oman	0.42	0.46	-0.01	0.95
Qatar	0.97	0.75	-0.04	1.27
Saudi	1.16	0.63	2.06	0.29
Tunis	0.42	0.52	0.20	0.6
UAE	0.35	0.19	0.49	1.23
Poland	1.42	0.76	1.71	0.73

Correlation 0.59

Source: author's elaboration.

Appendix40.Composite Vector measure and key determinant groups in the year 2008 (the year 2005 as a reference) for the Arab countries and Poland

Year	2008			
Country	Composite Vector measure	Key Economic determinant	Key Social determinant	Key Political determinant
Algeria	0.25	0.4	1.02	-0.1
Bahrain	0.46	0.52	-0.11	0.85
Egypt	1.34	0.56	2.96	0.07
Iraq	-1.09	0.19	0.21	-1.67
Jordan	0.27	0.43	0.06	0.68
Kuwait	0.34	0.43	0.25	0.69
Lebanon	0.14	0.59	-0.03	-0.38
Morocco	0.39	0.50	0.49	0.19
Oman	0.54	0.5	-0.02	1.09
Qatar	1.12	0.74	-0.04	1.31
Saudi	1.27	0.63	2.12	0.31
Tunis	0.32	0.46	0.18	0.54
UAE	0.38	0.30	0.54	1.14
Poland	1.53	0.76	1.59	0.81

Correlation 0.53

Source: author's elaboration.

Appendix41.Composite Vector measure and key determinant groups in the year 2009 (the year 2005 as a reference) for the Arab countries and Poland

Year	2009			
Country	Composite Vector measure	Key Economic determinant	Key Social determinant	Key Political determinant
Algeria	0.57	0.53	1.27	-0.23
Bahrain	0.37	0.52	-0.16	0.75
Egypt	1.08	0.43	2.79	0.06
Iraq	-0.28	0.55	0.24	-1.55
Jordan	0.25	0.42	0.06	0.60
Kuwait	0.29	0.41	0.21	0.62
Lebanon	-0.09	0.48	-0.07	-0.41
Morocco	0.26	0.42	0.54	0.18
Oman	0.45	0.48	-0.04	1.02
Qatar	1.26	0.91	-0.07	1.42
Saudi	1.29	0.6	2.25	0.42
Tunis	0.13	0.35	0.16	0.50
UAE	0.5	0.33	0.52	1.25
Poland	1.14	0.58	1.52	0.90

Correlation 0.68

Source: author's elaboration.

Appendix42.Composite Vector measure and key determinant groups in the year 2010 (the year 2005 as a reference) for the Arab countries and Poland

Year	2010			
Country	Composite Vector measure	Key Economic determinant	Key Social determinant	Key Political determinant
Algeria	0.42	0.44	1.29	-0.24
Bahrain	0.33	0.51	-0.15	0.62
Egypt	1.10	0.54	2.77	0.07
Iraq	-0.49	0.28	0.27	-1.52
Jordan	0.21	0.39	0.04	0.53
Kuwait	0.13	0.24	0.21	0.70
Lebanon	0.24	0.68	-0.06	-0.47
Morocco	0.48	0.56	0.55	0.19
Oman	0.28	0.35	-0.04	0.98
Qatar	1.22	0.97	-0.05	1.49
Saudi	1.19	0.60	2.31	0.57
Tunis	0.19	0.35	0.14	0.49
UAE	0.51	0.35	0.52	1.17
Poland	1.21	0.73	1.43	0.97

Correlation 0.67

Source: author's elaboration.

YOUR KNOWLEDGE HAS VALUE

- We will publish your bachelor's and master's thesis, essays and papers

- Your own eBook and book - sold worldwide in all relevant shops

- Earn money with each sale

Upload your text at www.GRIN.com and publish for free